THE
BRIEF HOLT
HANDBOOK

Third Edition

THE
BRIEF HOLT
HANDBOOK

Third Edition

LAURIE G. KIRSZNER
University of the Sciences in Philadelphia

STEPHEN R. MANDELL
Drexel University

HEINLE & HEINLE

THOMSON LEARNING

Australia Canada Mexico Singapore Spain United Kingdom United States

HEINLE & HEINLE

———✶——— ™

THOMSON LEARNING

The Brief Holt Handbook/Third Edition
Kirszner • Mandell

Publisher: Earl McPeek
Acquisitions Editor: Julie McBurney
Market Strategist: John Meyers
Developmental Editor: Camille Adkins
Project Editor: Katherine Dennis
Art Director: Vicki Whistler
Production Manager: Linda McMillan

For permission to use material fromthis text or product contact us:

Tel: 1-800-730-2214
Fax: 1-800-730-2215
Web: www.thomsonrights.com

Printed in the United States of America   **ISBN: 0-15-506737-0**

4 5 6 7 8 9 10   06 05 04 03 02

Library of Congress Catalog Card Number:
99-067764

For more information contact Heinle & Heinle, 25 Thomson Place, Boston, MA 02210 USA, or you can visit our Internet site at http://www.heinle.com

PREFACE

We would like to introduce you to the third edition of *The Brief Holt Handbook,* a compact reference guide for college students. This handbook offers concise yet comprehensive coverage of the writing process, critical thinking and argumentation, research and documentation (including MLA, APA, CMS, and CBE styles), document design, common sentence errors, grammar and style, word choice, punctuation and mechanics, English for speakers of other languages, and many other topics that you might expect to find only in a much larger handbook. Despite its compact size, *The Brief Holt Handbook* is more than just a quick reference; it can also serve as a two-semester classroom text and as a guide to writing that can be used throughout college and beyond.

What makes *The Brief Holt Handbook* **so easy to use?**

When preparing the third edition of *The Brief Holt Handbook*, we concentrated on making it clear, useful, inviting, and easy to navigate. The book's many innovative design features, listed below, have helped us to achieve these goals.

- A color-coded concise guide to the book appears on the inside front cover. Each section of the book—writing/research, grammar/style, and punctuation/mechanics—has its own design color—red, blue, and taupe, respectively. Tabbed dividers in corresponding colors set off the parts of the text and help students to locate the section they need. The section on MLA style is marked with a white tab.
- Close-up boxes that focus on special programs are identified by a magnifying glass icon.
- Checklists designed to reinforce key concepts are distinguished by a check mark icon.
- Boxed lists and charts set off other information that students are likely to turn to on a regular basis.
- Directories that list models for MLA, APA, CMS, and CBE documentation styles make a complex task easier by listing the situations students are likely to encounter most often as they document their sources.
- Computer boxes throughout the book, identified by a special icon, highlight information that students will use as they write and revise.
- Marginal "hyperlink" cross-references (which are keyed to blue, underlined terms in the text) direct readers to related discussions in other parts of the book.

- Frequently asked questions (FAQs) related to each chapter are listed on the back of each tab. Each FAQ is cross-referenced to a page where the answer to the question is marked with a question mark icon. A complete list of these frequently asked questions appears in its own tabbed section at the back of the book, after the index.
- An open, uncluttered design, the hallmark of *The Brief Holt Handbook*, enables students to find information quickly and easily.

What's new in the third edition of *The Brief Holt Handbook*?

In the third edition of *The Brief Holt Handbook*, we resisted change for the sake of change. Instead, we kept what students and instructors told us worked well, and we fine-tuned what we thought could work better. In addition, we added the material that students will need to function in the high-tech wired classrooms and workplaces of the twenty-first century.

- A new chapter order enhances the "writing first" orientation of the book and emphasizes the interrelatedness of the writing and research chapters.
- New hand-edited examples enable students to see revision and editing in action.
- In chapters 6 and 7, new material has been added on using the library's electronic resources and on using the Internet to address the impact of the new technology on the changing nature of research.
- The treatment of documenting electronic sources has been significantly expanded and updated—especially in Chapter 9, "MLA Documentation Style." In addition, a new MLA style research paper, "The Great Digital Divide," illustrates the use of both print and electronic source materials.
- A new discussion of creating a Web page has been added to Chapter 14, "Document Design and Manuscript Format." This chapter also contains guidelines for manuscript format from the latest edition of the *MLA Handbook for Writers of Research Papers*.
- Electronic addresses (URLs) for relevant Web sites have been added to every chapter, enabling students to use the Internet to find additional information about the topics discussed in *The Brief Holt Handbook*.
- Frequently asked questions (FAQs), which enable students to find answers to their most pressing problems, appear on the back of each tab. These FAQs address the problems students encounter most often, and because they are phrased in students' own words, they enable students to find answers without knowing technical or grammatical terminology.

- A CD-ROM version of the third edition of *The Brief Holt Handbook* is available either with the book or packaged separately. Even faster and easier to use than before, this CD-ROM enables students to access information through a system of menus, a searchable index, and hyperlinks.

Ancillaries

The following materials are available for use with *The Brief Holt Handbook*:

        Instructor's Resource Guide
        Supplementary Exercises
        Guide to the Internet
        CD-ROM
        ExaMaster + Test Bank—Macintosh, Windows, and
           Print versions.

Contact your Harcourt representative for information about these supplements.

Acknowledgments

We begin at the beginning, by thanking Julie McBurney, Acquisitions Editor, for her commitment to this book. We also thank Camille Adkins, Senior Developmental Editor, for keeping track of a thousand and one details (and continuing to take our phone calls). We thank Katherine Dennis in project editorial and Linda McMillan in production management for accomplishments above and beyond, and we also thank our talented book designer, Vicki Whistler.

Next, we want to acknowledge the debt we owe to the deft pencil and creative insights of Mark Gallaher, who helped us to see and re-see the first edition of this book as it developed. Also, we thank Carol Clark Powell of the University of Texas at El Paso, Patricia D. Arnott of the University of Delaware, Clyde Moneyhun of Youngstown State University and Tom Hartman of Liard Hart & White for their expert advice.

We are grateful to the following colleagues who offered their advice in the form of reviews:

Rick Becker, Illinois Central
Susan Becker, Illinois Central
Dan Butcher, Southeastern Louisiana University
Henry Castillo, Temple Junior College
Laurie Chesley, Grand Valley State University
Scott Douglass, Chattanooga State Technical Community College
Maurice Duperre, Midlands Technical College
Judith Funston, SUNY Potsdam
Barbara Gaffney, University of New Orleans
Joan Gagnon, Honolulu Community College

José Grave de Peralta, University of Miami
Eleanor Hansen, Stockton State College
Brooke Hessler, Texas Christian University
Dona Hickey, University of Richmond
Maureen Hoag, Wichita State University
Susan Hunter, Kennesaw State University
Susan Jackson, Spartanburg Technical College
Peggy Jolly, University of Alabama at Birmingham
Brian Kennedy, Cedarville College
Pamela Kennedy-Cross, Stockton State College
Anne Maxham-Kastrinos, Washington State University
J. L. McClure, Kirkwood Community College
Peter Mortensen, University of Kentucky
Kathleen Parrish, Niagra County Community College
Judy Pearce, Montgomery College
Robbie Pinter, Belmont University
John Pennington, St. Norbert College
Marcia Peoples Halio, University of Delaware
Robert Perry, Lock Haven University
Kathryn Raign, University of North Texas
Paul Rogalus, Plymouth State College
Laura Ross, Seminole Community College
Gary Simmers, Southern College of Technology
Anne Slater, Frederick Community College
Beverly Slaughter, Brevard Community College
Stephen Szilagyi, University of Alabama in Huntsville
Bonnie Tensen, Seminole Community College
Bob Whipple, Crieghton University
Connie White, Salisbury State University

We would also like to thank our families—Mark, Adam, and Rebecca Kirszner and Demi, David and Sarah Mandell—for being there when we needed them. And, finally, we each thank the person on the other side of the ampersand for making our collaboration work one more time.

CONTENTS

Contents

Contents

Contents

Contents

Contents

Contents

Writing Essays and Paragraphs

ESSAYS & PARAGRAPHS

PART 1

CHAPTER 1

WRITING ESSAYS

1a   Understanding the Writing Process

Writing is a constant process of decision making, of selecting, deleting, and rearranging material.

THE WRITING PROCESS

Planning: Consider your purpose, audience, and assignment; explore your topic.

Shaping: Decide how to organize your material.

Writing: Draft your essay.

Revising: "Re-see" what you have written; write additional drafts.

Editing: Check grammar, spelling, punctuation, and mechanics.

Proofreading: Check for typographical errors.

The neatly defined stages listed above do not communicate either the complexity or the flexibility of the writing process. These stages actually overlap: as you seek ideas, you begin to shape your material; as you shape your material, you begin to write; as you write a first draft, you reorganize your ideas; as you revise, you continue to discover more material. Moreover, these stages are repeated again and again throughout the writing process. During your college years and in the years that follow, you will develop your own version of the writing process and use it whenever you write.

Getting Started (Princeton U.)
   http://webware.princeton.edu/Writing/wc4a.htm
Coping with Writing Anxiety (Purdue)
   http://owl.english.purdue.edu/Files/61.html

1b Planning

Planning your essay—thinking about what you want to say and how you want to say it—begins well before you actually record your thoughts in any organized way.

(1) Determining Your Purpose

In general, we write to *express emotions*, to *inform*, or to *persuade*.

Writing to Express Emotions   In diaries and journals, writers explore ideas and feelings to make sense of their experiences; in autobiographical memoirs and in personal letters, they communicate their emotions and reactions to others.

At the age of five, six, well past the time when most other children no longer easily notice the difference between sounds uttered at home and words spoken in public, I had a different experience. I lived in a world magically compounded of sounds. I remained a child longer than most; I lingered too long, poised at the edge of language—often frightened by the sounds of *los gringos,* delighted by the sounds of Spanish at home. I shared with my family a language that was startlingly different from that used in the great city around us.

(Richard Rodriguez, *Aria: A Memoir of a Bilingual Childhood*)

Writing to Inform   In newspaper and magazine articles and in encyclopedia entries, writers report information, communicating to readers what they observe; in reference texts, instruction manuals, textbooks, and the like, they provide definitions and explain concepts or processes, trying to help readers see relationships and understand ideas.

Most tarantulas live in the tropics, but several species occur in the temperate zone and a few are common in the southern U.S. Some varieties are large and have powerful fangs with which they can inflict a deep wound. These formidable-looking spiders do not, however, attack man; you can hold one in your hand, if you are gentle, without being bitten. Their bite is dangerous only to insects and small mammals such as mice; for man it is no worse than a hornet's sting.

(Alexander Petrunkevitch, "The Spider and the Wasp")

Writing to Persuade   In proposals, editorials, and position papers, writers try to convince readers to accept their position on an issue.

Testing and contact tracing may lead to a person's being deprived of a job, health insurance, housing, and privacy, many civil libertarians fear. These are valid and grave concerns. But we can find ways to protect civil rights without sacrificing public health. A major AIDS-prevention campaign ought to be accompanied by intensive public education about the ways the illness is *not* transmitted, by additional safeguards on data banks and by greater penalties for those who abuse HIV victims. It may be harsh to say, but the fact that an individual may suffer as a result of doing what is right does not make doing so less of an imperative.

(Amitai Etzioni, "HIV Sufferers Have a Responsibility")

Whenever you write, you may have one of these three general purposes—or, you may have other, more specific aims or a combination of purposes.

✔ CHECKLIST: DETERMINING YOUR PURPOSE

Is your purpose:

✔ to express emotions?   ✔ to define?
✔ to inform?   ✔ to satirize?
✔ to persuade?   ✔ to speculate?
✔ to explain?   ✔ to warn?
✔ to evaluate?   ✔ to reassure?
✔ to discover?   ✔ to amuse or entertain?
✔ to analyze?   ✔ to take a stand?
✔ to debunk?   ✔ to identify problems?
✔ to criticize?   ✔ to suggest solutions?
✔ to draw comparisons?   ✔ to define causes?
✔ to make an analogy?   ✔ to predict effects?

---

(2) Identifying Your Audience

At different times, in different roles, you address different kinds of **audiences.** As you move through the stages of the writing process, you try to assess your readers' interests, educational level, biases, and expectations. This assessment determines not only the information you include but also your emphasis, the arrangement of your material, and the style or tone you adopt.

As a student, you most often write for an audience of one: the instructor who assigns the paper. Instructors expect correct information, specific support for general statements, standard grammar and correct spelling, logical presentation of ideas, and some stylistic fluency. If you are writing in your instructor's academic field, you can omit long overviews and basic definitions. Outside his or her area of expertise, however, an instructor will need the definitions, examples, and analogies that will make your ideas clear.

Keep in mind that because different academic disciplines have their own document design formats, documentation styles, methods of reporting data, technical vocabularies, and stylistic conventions, instructors in different disciplines have somewhat different expectations.

✔ CHECKLIST: IDENTIFYING YOUR AUDIENCE

- ✔ Who will read your paper?
- ✔ What are your audience's needs? expectations? biases? interests?
- ✔ Does your audience need you to supply definitions? overviews? examples? analogies?
- ✔ What does your audience expect in terms of style and tone? format? documentation style? methods of collecting and reporting data? use of formulas and symbols or specialized vocabulary?

---

(3) Analyzing Your Assignment

Before you begin any writing task, you must know the exact requirements of your assignment. Ask questions, and be sure you understand the answers.

✔ CHECKLIST: ANALYZING YOUR ASSIGNMENT

- ✔ Has your instructor assigned a specific topic or a general subject area, or are you free to choose your own topic?
- ✔ What is the word, paragraph, or page limit?
- ✔ How much time do you have to complete your assignment?
- ✔ Will you get feedback from other students or from your instructor? Will anyone review your drafts?
- ✔ Does the assignment require research?
- ✔ If the assignment requires a specific format, do you know what its conventions are?

---

(4) Choosing a Topic

Although you are sometimes able to choose your own topic, more often you will be given a general assignment, which you must narrow to a **topic** that suits your purpose and audience.

NARROWING AN ASSIGNMENT

Course	Assignment	Topic
American History	Analyze the effects of a social program on one segment of American society.	How did the G.I. Bill of Rights affect American servicewomen?
Composition	Describe a place that is very important to you.	The Acoma Pueblo: My grandfather's home
Psychology	Write a three- to five-page paper assessing one method of treating depression.	Animal-assisted therapy for severely depressed patients

---

(5) Finding Something to Say

Once you have a topic, you can begin to develop ideas for your paper, using one (or several) of the following strategies.

Reading and Observing As you read textbooks, magazines, and newspapers or browse the **Internet**, be on the lookout for ideas that relate to your topic, and make a point of talking informally with friends or family about it. Films, television programs, interviews, telephone calls, letters, and questionnaires can also provide material. But be sure your instructor permits such research—and remember to document ideas that are not your own. If you do not, you will be committing **plagiarism**.

See Ch. 7

See 8b

Keeping a Journal Journals, unlike diaries, do more than simply record personal experiences and reactions. In a **journal** you explore ideas as well as record events and emotions; you think on paper, asking questions and drawing conclusions. You might, for example, explore your position on a political issue, try to solve an ethical problem, or trace the development of your thinking about an academic assignment.

7

Freewriting   When you **freewrite,** you let yourself go and write *nonstop* about anything that comes to mind, moving as quickly as you can. Give yourself a set period of time—say, five minutes—and do not stop to worry about punctuation, spelling, or grammar, or about where your mind is wandering. This strategy encourages your mind to make free associations; thus, it can help you discover ideas that you aren't even aware you have. When your time is up, look over what you have written and underline, bracket, or star the most promising ideas. You can then use each of these ideas as the center of a focused freewriting exercise.

When you do **focused freewriting,** you zero in on your topic. Here too, however, you write without stopping to reconsider or reread, so you have no time to be self-conscious about style or form or to worry about the relevance of your ideas. At its best, freewriting can suggest new details, a new approach to your topic, or even a more interesting topic.

Brainstorming   One of the most useful ways to accumulate ideas is brainstorming. This strategy encourages you to recall pieces of information and to see connections among them.

When you **brainstorm,** you list all the points you can think of that seem pertinent to your topic, writing down ideas—comments, questions, single words—as quickly as you can, without pausing to consider their relevance or trying to understand their significance. Your goal is to let one idea suggest another, so do nothing to slow down your momentum. Sample brainstorming notes appear on page 9.

NOTE: You can also do **collaborative brainstorming**—that is, you can brainstorm with your classmates in small groups or enlist some friends to help you work through your ideas.

   GENERATING IDEAS

If you like, you can keep a computer journal. You can also use your computer for freewriting and brainstorming.

When you freewrite, try turning down the screen, leaving it blank to eliminate distractions and encourage spontaneity.

When you brainstorm, type your notes randomly. Later, after you print them out, you can add further notes and graphic elements (arrows, circles, and so on) to indicate parallels and connections.

SAMPLE BRAINSTORMING NOTES

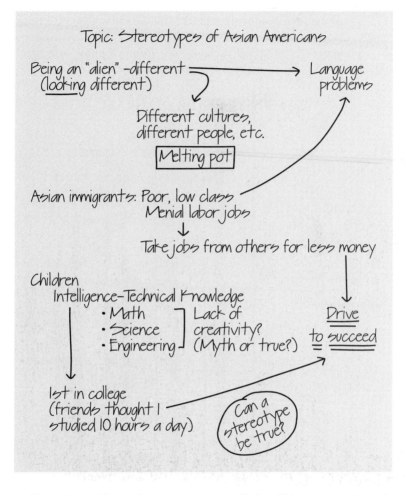

Clustering   **Clustering**—sometimes called *webbing* or *mapping*—is similar to brainstorming. However, clustering allows you to explore your topic in a somewhat more systematic (and more visual) manner.

Begin making a cluster diagram by writing your topic in the center of a sheet of paper. Then surround your topic with related ideas as they

Freewriting (Mercer County (NJ) Comm. College)
http://www.mccc.edu/TVC/freewriting.html

occur to you, moving outward from the general topic in the center and writing down increasingly specific ideas and details as you move toward the edges of the page. Eventually, following the path of one idea at a time, create a diagram (often lopsided rather than symmetrical) that arranges ideas on spokes or branches radiating out from a central core (your topic). A sample cluster diagram appears below.

SAMPLE CLUSTER DIAGRAM

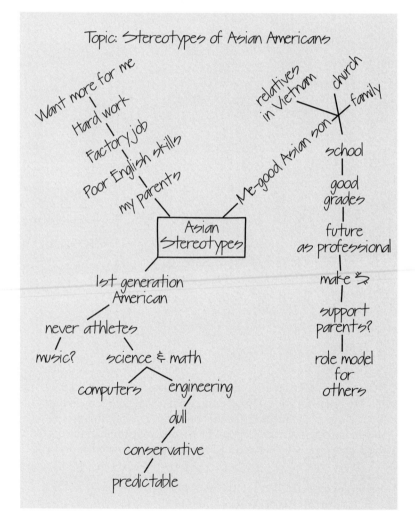

Topic: Stereotypes of Asian Americans

Want more for me
│
Hard work
│
Factory job
│
Poor English skills
│
my parents

relatives in Vietnam — church — family
│
Me-good Asian son
│
school
│
good grades
│
future as professional

Asian Stereotypes

1st generation American

never athletes

music?   science & math

computers   engineering
│
dull
│
conservative
│
predictable

make $
│
support parents?
│
role model for others

Asking Journalistic Questions   A more structured way of finding something to say about your topic is to ask questions. Your answers to these questions will enable you to explore your topic in an orderly and systematic fashion. Journalists often use the questions *Who?*, *What?*, *Why?*, *Where?*, *When?*, and *How?* to assure themselves that they have explored all angles of a story. You can use these questions to see whether you have considered all aspects of your topic.

Asking In-Depth Questions   If you have time, you can also ask a series of more focused questions about your topic. These questions can give you a great deal of information, and they may also suggest ways you can eventually shape your ideas into paragraphs and essays.

IN-DEPTH QUESTIONS

What happened?
When did it happen?
Where did it happen?
} Suggest <u>narration</u> (your first day of school; Emily Dickinson's life)

What does it look like?
What does it sound like, smell like, taste like, or feel like?
} Suggest <u>description</u> (of the Louvre; of a lab specimen)

What are some typical cases or examples of it?
} Suggests <u>exemplification</u> (three infant day-care settings; four popular fad diets)

How did it happen?
What makes it work?
How is it made?
} Suggest <u>process</u> (how to apply for financial aid; how a bill becomes a law)

Why did it happen?
What caused it?
What does it cause?
What are its effects?
} Suggest <u>cause and effect</u> (events leading to the Korean War; results of Prohibition)

How is it like other things?
How is it different from other things?
} Suggest <u>comparison and contrast</u> (of 1950s and 1960s music; of two paintings)

What are its parts or types?
Can they be separated or grouped?
Do they fall into a logical order?
Can they be categorized?
} Suggest <u>division and classification</u> (components of the catalytic converter; techniques of occupational therapy; kinds of dietary supplements)

continued on the following page

---

continued from the previous page

What is it?	Suggest <u>definition</u> (What is
How does it resemble and	Marxism? What is
differ from other members	photosynthesis? What is
of its class?	romanticism?)

❓ 1c   Shaping

(1) Grouping Ideas: Making a Topic Tree

As you begin to see the direction your ideas are taking, start to sift through your notes and choose those ideas and details that you can use to build the most effective essay. At this point, you may find it useful to make a **topic tree,** a diagram that enables you to arrange material logically and to see relationships among ideas.

✔ CHECKLIST: MAKING A TOPIC TREE

- ✔ Review all your notes carefully.
- ✔ Decide on the three or four general categories of information that best suit your material.
- ✔ Write or type these categories across the top of a piece of paper.
- ✔ Review your notes again to select ideas and details that fall within each category.
- ✔ List each idea under a relevant heading, moving from general information to increasingly specific details as you move down the page.
- ✔ Draw lines to indicate relationships between ideas in each category.

As you accumulate additional material and as you review the material you have, you will add, delete, and rearrange the items on the branches of your topic tree. Your completed tree will help you develop a tentative thesis and organize supporting information in your essay.

(2) Understanding Thesis and Support

The essays you write in college will have a thesis-and-support structure. A **thesis-and-support essay** includes a **thesis statement** (which expresses the **thesis,** or main idea, of the essay) and the specific information that explains and develops that thesis. Your essay will eventually consist of several

SAMPLE TOPIC TREE

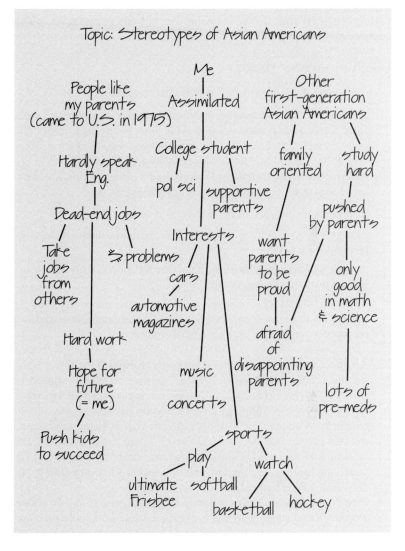

Developing a Thesis (Princeton)
    http://webware.princeton.edu/Writing/wc4c/htm
Strategies for Writing Thesis Statements (U. of Wisc.)
    http://www.wisc.edu/writing/Handbook/thesis.html#Strategies

paragraphs—an **<u>introductory paragraph</u>**, which introduces your thesis; a **<u>concluding paragraph</u>**, which gives your essay a sense of completion, perhaps restating your thesis; and a number of **body paragraphs,** which support your essay's thesis.

(3) Stating Your Thesis

An effective thesis statement has four characteristics.

1. *An effective thesis statement clearly communicates your essay's main idea.* It tells your readers not only what your essay's topic is, but also how you will approach that topic and what you will say about it. Thus, your thesis statement reflects your essay's **purpose**.
2. *An effective thesis statement is more than a general subject, a statement of fact, or an announcement of your intent.*

SUBJECT: Intelligence tests

STATEMENT OF FACT: Intelligence tests are used extensively in some elementary schools.

ANNOUNCEMENT: The paragraphs that follow will show that intelligence tests may be inaccurate.

THESIS STATEMENT: Although intelligence tests are widely used for placement in many elementary schools, they are not always the best measure of a student's academic performance.

3. *An effective thesis statement is carefully worded.* Your thesis statement—usually expressed in a single, concise sentence—should be direct and straightforward, including no vague, abstract language, overly complex terminology, or unnecessary details that might confuse or mislead readers. Moreover, effective thesis statements should not include phrases like "As I will show," "I plan to demonstrate," and "It seems to me," which weaken your credibility by suggesting that your conclusions are based on opinion rather than on reading, observation, and experience.
4. *Finally, an effective thesis statement suggests your essay's direction, emphasis, and scope.* Your thesis statement should not make promises that your essay will not fulfill. It should suggest how your ideas are related, in what order your major points will be introduced, and where you will place your emphasis, as the following thesis statement does.

EFFECTIVE THESIS STATEMENT: Widely ridiculed as escape reading, romance novels are becoming increasingly important as a proving ground for many first-time writers and, more significantly, as a showcase for strong heroines.

This thesis statement tells readers that the essay to follow will focus on two major new roles of the romance novel: providing markets for new writers and (more important) presenting strong female characters; it also suggests that the role of the romance as escapist fiction will be treated briefly. This effective thesis statement even maps out the possible order in which the various ideas will be discussed.

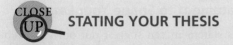

STATING YOUR THESIS

Do not use vague phrases—*centers on, deals with, involves, revolves around, has a lot to do with, is primarily concerned with,* and so on. Be direct and forceful.

The real problem in our schools ~~does~~ not ~~revolve around~~ the absence of nationwide goals and standards; the problem is ~~primarily concerned with~~ the absence of resources with which to implement them.

✔ CHECKLIST: STATING YOUR THESIS

- ✔ Does your thesis statement clearly communicate your essay's main idea? Does it suggest the approach you will take toward your material? Does it reflect your essay's purpose?
- ✔ Is your thesis statement more than a subject, a statement of fact, or an announcement of your intent?
- ✔ Is your thesis statement carefully worded?
- ✔ Does your thesis statement suggest your essay's direction, emphasis, and scope?

(4) Revising Your Thesis Statement

The thesis statement that you develop as you plan your essay is only tentative. As you write and rewrite, you may modify your essay's direction, emphasis, and scope several times; if you do so, you must reword your thesis statement as well. Notice how the following thesis statement changed as the writer moved through successive drafts:

TENTATIVE THESIS STATEMENT *(rough draft):* Professional sports can easily be corrupted by organized crime.

REVISED THESIS STATEMENT *(final paper):* Although proponents of legalized gambling argue that organized crime cannot make inroads into professional sports, the way in which underworld figures compromised the 1919 World Series suggests the opposite.

(5) Using a Thesis Statement to Shape Your Essay

The wording of a thesis statement can suggest not only a possible order and emphasis for an essay's ideas, but also a specific **pattern of development**: narration, description, exemplification, process, cause and effect, comparison and contrast, division and classification, or definition. Remember, though, that a pattern of development is never imposed on your essay; it emerges naturally during the course of the writing process. (Patterns of development can also shape the individual body paragraphs of your essay.)

USING A THESIS STATEMENT TO SHAPE YOUR ESSAY

Thesis Statement	*Pattern of Development*
As the months went by and I grew more and more involved with the developmentally delayed children at the Learning Center, I came to see how important it is to treat every child as an individual.	Narration
Looking around the room where I had spent my childhood, I realized that every object I saw told me I was now an adult.	Description
The risk-taking behavior that characterized the 1990s can be illustrated by the increasing interest and involvement in such high-risk sports as mountain biking, ice climbing, skydiving, and bungee jumping.	Exemplification
Armed forces basic training programs take recruits through a series of tasks designed to build camaraderie as well as skills and confidence.	Process

continued on the following page

The exceptionally high birthrate of the post–World War II years had many significant social and economic consequences.	Cause and Effect
Although people who live in cities and people who live in small towns have some obvious basic similarities, their views on issues like crime, waste disposal, farm subsidies, and educational vouchers tend to be very different.	Comparison and Contrast
The section of the proposal that recommends establishing satellite health centers is quite promising; unfortunately, however, the sections that call for the creation of alternative educational programs, job training, and low-income housing are seriously flawed.	Division and Classification
Until quite recently, most people assumed rape was an act perpetrated by a stranger, but today's wider definition encompasses acquaintance rape as well.	Definition

(6) Preparing an Outline

An **outline** is a blueprint for an essay. A **formal outline** indicates both the order of the ideas you will explore and the relationship of those ideas to one another. An **informal outline** is less detailed. Still, it arranges your essay's main points and supporting ideas in an orderly way to guide you as you write.

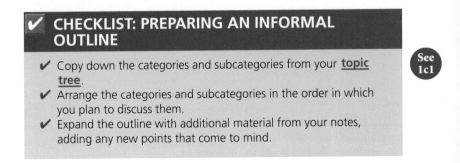

✔ CHECKLIST: PREPARING AN INFORMAL OUTLINE

✔ Copy down the categories and subcategories from your **topic tree**.
✔ Arrange the categories and subcategories in the order in which you plan to discuss them.
✔ Expand the outline with additional material from your notes, adding any new points that come to mind.

See
1c1

SAMPLE INFORMAL OUTLINE

Asian American Stereotypes

<u>Thesis Statement:</u> As an Asian American, I am frequently a victim of ethnic stereotyping, and this has been a serious problem for me.

Stereotypes of Asian immigrants

–Poor English

–Can't use skills and education here

–Low-paid jobs

    –Sacrifice for children

    –Take from U.S. citizens

Stereotypes of children of Asian immigrants

–Hard workers

–Study hard

    –Pushed by parents

–Focus on math and science

    –Premed

Stereotypes applied to me

–Science major

–Forced to study all day

    –No social life

Outlining (Purdue)
http://owl.english.purdue.edu/Files/63.html

CONSTRUCTING A FORMAL OUTLINE

For a short paper, an informal outline is usually sufficient. For a long or complex essay, however, you will need to construct a formal outline like the one that accompanies the student research paper in Chapter 9.

- Outline format should be followed strictly.
  I. First major point of your paper
     A. First subpoint
     B. Next subpoint
        1. First supporting example
        2. Next supporting example
           a. First specific detail
           b. Next specific detail
  II. Second major point
- Each heading should have at least two subheadings.
- Outline should include the paper's thesis statement.
- Outline should cover only the body of the essay.
- Headings should be concise and specific.
- Headings of the same rank should be grammatically parallel.

NOTE: A formal outline can be a *topic* outline or a *sentence* outline. In a **topic outline,** each entry is a word or short phrase; in a **sentence outline,** each entry is a complete sentence.

CONSTRUCTING A FORMAL OUTLINE

If you use your computer to construct a formal outline, set your tabs so that you can easily format the various levels of the outline.

1d   Writing and Revising

Inexperienced writers often do little more than change a word here and there, correct grammatical or mechanical errors, or make their papers neater. Experienced writers, however, expect **revision** to involve a major reworking of their papers, so they are willing to rethink a thesis statement or even to completely rewrite and rearrange an entire essay. (You can see how this revision process operates in the three drafts of the student essay about Asian American stereotypes that appear in this chapter.)

(1) Writing a Rough Draft

Because its purpose is really just to get your emerging ideas down on paper so that you can react to them, a rough draft usually includes false starts, irrelevant information, and seemingly unrelated details. Try not to see this absence of focus and order as a problem. You will generally rewrite your essay several times, so expect to add or delete words, to reword sentences, to rethink ideas, to reorder paragraphs—and even to take an unexpected detour that may lead you to a new perspective on your topic.

To facilitate such extensive revision, leave plenty of room on the page so that you can add material or rewrite. If you type, triple-space; if you write, write on every other line. Also, be sure to use only one side of a sheet of paper so that you can cut and paste freely without destroying material on the other side of the page. To simplify your revision process, try using symbols—arrows, circles, boxes, numbers, and so on—that will signal various operations to you.

The rough draft that follows includes a student's handwritten revisions on his typed draft.

ROUGH DRAFT WITH HANDWRITTEN REVISIONS

The unique characteristic of American culture is its genuine desire to understand & embrace the wide range of traditions and values of its people.

The United States prides itself on being the "melting pot" of the world, —*a nation where diverse cultures intermingle to form a unique and enlightened society.* However, in reality, the abundance of different cultures in America often causes misunderstandings and even conflicts within the society. These misunderstandings and conflicts result from the society's lack of knowledge about other cultures. ~~As~~ *Still, as* an Asian American, I am frequently a victim of ethnic stereotyping, *people keep trying to make me something I'm not, and this is a* ~~and this has been a~~ serious problem for me.

continued on the following page

It has been within the last twenty years or so that the United States has seen a large rise in the number of Asian immigrants. First-generation immigrants are seen as an underclass of poor ~~people~~ who struggle in low paying jobs so that their children will have a better future. Many accuse immigrants of accepting ~~less~~ *lower* pay for their work than ~~the established~~ *other American citizens are* ~~majority is~~ willing to accept, thus putting the established majority out of work. While it is true that most newly arrived Asians do seek low paying, low-skill jobs, they are just following the same ~~trend~~ *road* that other immigrant groups followed when they first arrived in the ~~U.S.~~ *United States.* Because the first generation of Asian Americans, *my parents included* have poorly developed skills in ~~English~~ *English,* ~~their backs.~~ *The Irish who escaped the potato famine came to the U.S. without many advanced skills. To this day, many Latinos come to the US in search of a better life with little more than the shirts on they are forced into jobs which do not require ~~these skills~~.* Many Asians received degrees from institutions in their native countries or received advanced training of some kind but cannot use those skills in the United States. *Therefore, they have no choice but to accept whatever low-paying job they can get—not to steal jobs from others, but to survive.*

Along with the view of the first-generation Asian Americans as low skilled workers comes the notion that Asian-American children are ~~seen as~~ hard workers who are pushed by their families to succeed. Asian children are seen as intelligent, but only in *terms of* scientific and technical knowledge. The media likes to point ~~to the facts~~ *out* that most Asians succeed only in ~~the~~ math, science, and engineering ~~fields~~ and that ~~there is an inordinate~~ *a great* number of Asian college students who identify themselves as "premed." *What the media seems to forget is that other immigrant groups also seem to prize success above all else.*

In my personal experience, in college, many of my friends assume that I am either a science or an engineering major and that my parents force me to study five to ten hours a day. They believe that I sacrifice all my free time and social life in pursuit of a high grade point average. *My friends are quite surprised when I tell them that I take drawing classes and that I am majoring in political science not as a stepping stone into law school, but as a study of man & society.* ~~In fact, I am a political science major.~~ I also like to go to basketball games, listen to music, and read automotive magazines, just ~~like other~~

continued on the following page

continued from the previous page

college students I know. My parents do encourage me to do well in school because they see that education is a stepping stone to social class mobility; however, I am lucky because my parents do not push me in one direction or another as many of my Asian friends' parents do. Many of my friends do not realize that just two or three generations ago, their parents and grandparents were going through the same process of social adjustment that all immigrants endure.

^It is important to remember that *most people don't* ~~not all Asians~~ fit^ *these cultural stereotypes.* *For example, not all Asians fit* into the overachieving, success-oriented stereotype. When any child comes from an economically disadvantaged background, many times they must sacrifice their academic pursuits in order to support their families. Also, as Asians, particularly the children, become more integrated into the society, the traditional Asian values of hard work & familial obligations will certainly clash with the American pursuits of recreation & individualism. The resolution of that conflict will add yet another facet to the complexity of America's society.

This practice of assuming people of similar ethnic backgrounds share certain traits is certainly not limited to Asian Americans. African-American students complain people expect them to be athletes, to like rap music, to be on scholarship, to be from single-parent families even to be gang members. Athletes say people expect them to be dumb jocks, to drink a lot, and to mistreat their girlfriends. Latinos say people assume their parents are immigrants and that they speak Spanish better than English. Business majors say people think they're politically conservative and not creative. Engineering students are expected to be dull & wear pocket protectors. Women are supposed to be weak in math & science. Overweight people are expected to be class clowns. In fact, my friends (of all ethnic groups) buy their clothes where I do, & we listen to the same music & laugh at the same jokes. But outsiders don't know this. They have different expectations for each of us, & these expectations are based on culture, not ability.

REVISING

Because it is much more difficult to see errors on the computer screen than on hard copy, it is a good idea to print out every draft

continued on the following page

so that you can revise on paper rather than on the screen, making revisions by hand on your typed draft and then returning to the computer to type these changes into your document. If you do revise directly on the computer screen, be very careful not to delete any information that you may need later; instead, move such material to the end of your document so that you can assess its relevance later on. (If you have a hard copy, you will have a record of these deletions.) As you type your draft, include notes to yourself in parentheses or brackets, perhaps highlighting your comments and questions in boldface or italic type.

(2) Using Specific Revision Strategies

Everyone revises differently, and every writing task demands a slightly different process of revision. Four strategies in particular can help you revise at any stage of the writing process.

Using a Formal Outline   Making a **formal outline** of a draft helps you check the structure of your paper and reveals whether points are irrelevant, poorly placed, or missing. This strategy is especially helpful early in revision, when you are reworking the larger structural elements of your essay.

See 1c6

Doing Collaborative Revision   Instead of trying to imagine an audience, you can address a real audience, doing **collaborative revision** by asking a friend, classmate, or family member to read your draft and comment on it. Collaborative revision can also be more formal. Your instructor may conduct the class as a workshop, assigning students to work in groups to critique other students' essays or having students exchange essays and write evaluations. The checklists on pages 24–26 can be useful for collaborative revision as well as for revision that you do on your own.

Using Instructors' Comments   Instructors frequently make marginal comments on your papers to suggest changes in content or structure. Such comments may ask you to add supporting information or to arrange paragraphs differently within the essay, or they may recommend stylistic changes, such as using more varied sentences. Marginal comments may also question your logic, suggest a more explicit thesis statement, ask for clearer transitions, or propose a new direction for a

23

discussion. Although you may disagree with some of these suggestions, consider your instructor's comments seriously.

Also take note of any correction symbols that correspond to those on the inside back covers of this handbook. With these symbols, your instructor may direct you to explanations and illustrations of particular stylistic, grammatical, or mechanical problems.

Instructors also comment on your papers in one-on-one conferences.

✔ CHECKLIST: GETTING THE MOST OUT OF A CONFERENCE

- ✔ **Make an appointment.** If you are unable to keep your appointment, be sure to call or e-mail your instructor to reschedule.
- ✔ **Review your work carefully.** Before the conference, reread your notes and drafts and go over all your instructor's comments and suggestions. Make all the changes you can on your draft.
- ✔ **Bring a list of questions.** Preparing a list in advance will enable you to get the most out of the conference in the allotted time.
- ✔ **Bring your paper-in-progress.** If you have several drafts, you may want to bring them all, but be sure you bring any draft that has your instructor's comments on it.
- ✔ **Take notes.** As you discuss your paper, write down any suggestions that you think will be helpful so that you won't forget them when you revise.
- ✔ **Participate actively.** A successful conference is not a monologue; it should be an open exchange of ideas.

Using Checklists   The following four checklists parallel the revision process, moving in stages from the most global or general to the most specific concerns. As your familiarity with the writing process increases and you are better able to assess the strengths and weaknesses of your writing, you may want to add questions to these checklists. You can also use your instructor's comments to tailor the checklists to your own needs.

✔ CHECKLIST: REVISING THE WHOLE ESSAY

- ✔ Are thesis and support logically related, with each body paragraph supporting your thesis statement? **(See 1c2)**

continued on the following page

✔ Is your thesis statement clearly and specifically worded?
(See 1c3)

✔ Have you discussed everything promised in your thesis statement? **(See 1c3)**

✔ Have you presented your ideas in a logical sequence? Can you think of a different arrangement that might be more appropriate for your purpose? **(See 1c6)**

✔ Do clear transitions between paragraphs allow your readers to follow your essay's structure? **(See 2b2)**

✔ CHECKLIST: REVISING PARAGRAPHS

✔ Does each body paragraph have one main idea? **(See 2a)**

✔ Are topic sentences clearly worded and logically related to the thesis? **(See 2a1)**

✔ Are your body paragraphs developed fully enough to support your points? **(See 2c)**

✔ Does your introductory paragraph arouse interest and prepare readers for what is to come? **(See 2e1)**

✔ Does each body paragraph have a clear organizing principle? **(See 2b1)**

✔ Are the relationships of sentences within paragraphs clear? **(See 2b2–4)**

✔ Are your paragraphs arranged according to familiar patterns of development? **(See 2d)**

✔ Does your concluding paragraph sum up your main points? **(See 2e2)**

✔ CHECKLIST: REVISING SENTENCES

✔ Have you strengthened sentences with repetition, balance, and parallelism? **(See 25c and 25d)**

✔ Have you avoided overloading your sentences with too many clauses? **(See 26c)**

continued on the following page

continued from the previous page

✔ Have you used correct sentence structure? **(See Chs. 16 and 17)**

✔ Have you placed modifiers clearly and logically? **(See Ch. 20)**

✔ Have you avoided potentially confusing shifts in tense, voice, mood, person, or number? **(See 19a–d)**

✔ Are your sentences constructed logically? **(See 19f–h)**

✔ Have you used emphatic word order? **(See 25a)**

✔ Have you used sentence structure to signal the relative importance of clauses in a sentence and their logical relationship to one another? **(See 25b)**

✔ Have you eliminated nonessential words and unnecessary repetition? **(See 26a–b)**

✔ Have you varied your sentence structure? **(See 24a)**

✔ Have you combined sentences where ideas are closely related? **(See 24b1)**

✔ CHECKLIST: REVISING WORDS

✔ Is your level of diction appropriate for your audience and your purpose? **(See 28a)**

✔ Have you selected words that accurately reflect your intentions? **(See 28b1)**

✔ Have you chosen words that are specific, concrete, and unambiguous? **(See 28b3–4)**

✔ Have you enriched your writing with figurative language? **(See 28d)**

✔ Have you eliminated jargon, neologisms, pretentious diction, clichés, ineffective figures of speech, and offensive language from your writing? **(See 28c and 28e)**

The following draft incorporates the rough draft's handwritten revisions and includes comments made by an instructor to guide the student's future revisions.

SECOND DRAFT WITH INSTRUCTOR'S COMMENTS

The Danger of Stereotypes

The United States prides itself on being the "melting pot" of the world--a nation where diverse cultures intermingle to form a unique and enlightened society. However, in reality, the abundance of different cultures in America often causes misunderstandings and even conflicts within the society. These misunderstandings result from the society's lack of knowledge about other cultures. The unique characteristic of American culture is its genuine desire to understand and embrace the wide range
Can you sharpen the thesis so it takes a stand? Why is stereotyping a problem?
of traditions and values of its people. Still, as an Asian American, I am a victim of ethnic stereotyping: people keep trying to make me something I'm not, and this is a serious problem for me.
Wordy — see 26a

It has been within the last twenty years or so that the United States has seen a large rise in the number of Asian immigrants. First-generation immigrants are seen as an underclass of poor people who struggle in low-paying jobs so that their children will have a better future. Many are angry at immigrants, accusing them of accepting lower pay for their work than other American citizens are willing to accept, thus putting the established majority out of work.
Good background. But you might condense ⁏⁵ 2 & 3 a bit. You're wandering from your topic.

While it is true that most newly arrived Asians do seek low-paid, low-skill jobs, they are just following the same road that other immigrant groups followed when they first arrived in the United States. The Irish who escaped the potato famines came to the United States without many advanced skills. To this day, many Latinos come to the United States
cliché (See 28c4). Also — you may be guilty of stereotyping here.
in search of a better life with little more than the shirts on their backs. Because the first generation of Asian Americans, my parents included,

continued on the following page

continued from the previous page

have poorly developed skills in English, they are forced into jobs which do not require English. Many Asians received degrees from institutions in their native countries or received advanced training of some kind but cannot use *those* skills in the United States. Therefore, they have no choice but to accept whatever low-paying job they can get--not to steal jobs from others, but to survive.

pronoun ref.—see 22c2

Along with the view of the first-generation Asian Americans as low-skilled workers comes the notion that Asian American children are hard workers who are pushed by their families to succeed. Asian children are seen as intelligent, but only in terms of scientific and technical knowledge. The media likes to point to the facts that most Asians succeed only in math, science, and engineering and that a great number of Asian college students identify themselves as "premed." What the media seems to forget is that other immigrant groups also seem to prize success above all else.

agreement — see 7a6
(Media-plural; medium-singular)

Wordy — see 26a
In my personal experience, in college, many of my friends assume that I am either a science or an engineering major and that my parents force me to study five to ten hours a day. They believe that I sacrifice all my free time and social life in pursuit of a high grade point average. My friends are really surprised when I tell them that I take drawing classes and that I am majoring in political science--not as a stepping-stone into law school, but as a study of *man* and society.

sexist language
See 28e2

This practice of assuming people of similar ethnic backgrounds share certain traits is certainly not limited to Asian Americans. African American students complain people expect them to be athletes, to like rap music, to be on scholarship, to be from single-parent families--even to be gang

Are you sure you need all this? Your focus in this paper is on ethnic (specifically Asian) stereotypes, remember?

continued on the following page

members. Athletes say people expect them to be dumb jocks, to drink a lot, and to mistreat their girlfriends. Latinos say people assume their parents are immigrants and think they speak Spanish better than English. Business majors say people think they're politically conservative and not creative. Engineering students are expected to be dull and wear pocket protectors. Women are supposed to be weak in math and science. Overweight people are expected to be class clowns. In fact, my friends (of all ethnic groups) buy their clothes where I do, and we listen to the same music and laugh at the same jokes. But outsiders don't know this. They have different expectations for each of us, and these expectations are based on culture, not ability.

good point — but wordy (see 13a)

It is important to remember that most people do not fit these cultural stereotypes. For example, not all Asians fit into the overachieving, success-oriented stereotype. When any child comes from an economically *agreement* disadvantaged background, many times they must sacrifice their academic *see 18b* pursuits in order to support their families. Also, as Asians, particularly the children, become more integrated into the society, the traditional Asian values of hard work and familial obligations will certainly clash with the American pursuits of recreation and individualism. The resolution of that conflict will add yet another facet to the complexity of America's society.

Are you sure this is what you want to leave your readers with? It doesn't really address your essay's main point.

I like what you've done here, but something important is still missing. You really do need more examples from your own experience. Also, think about this question before our conference on Tuesday: exactly why are the stereotypes you enumerate so harmful, so damaging? This idea needs to be developed in some detail (it's really the heart of your paper), and it should certainly be addressed in your thesis statement and conclusion as well.

1e   Editing and Proofreading

After you have revised your rough draft to your satisfaction, two additional steps remain: *editing* and *proofreading* your paper.

When you **edit,** you concentrate on grammar and spelling, punctuation and mechanics. You will have done some of this work as you revised previous drafts of your paper, but now your *focus* is on editing. Approach your work as a critical reader would, reading each sentence carefully.

USING SPELL CHECKERS AND GRAMMAR CHECKERS

Spell checkers and grammar checkers can make the process of editing and proofreading your papers a lot easier. Remember, though, that both have limitations. Neither a spell checker nor a grammar checker is a substitute for careful editing and proofreading.

- **Spell checkers** A spell checker simply identifies strings of letters it does not recognize; it does *not* distinguish between homophones or spot every typographical error. For example, it does not recognize *there* in "They forgot there books" as incorrect, nor does it spot a typo that produces a correctly spelled word, such as *word* for *work* or *thing* for *think*.
- **Grammar checkers** Grammar checkers are not always accurate. For example, they may identify a long sentence as a run-on when it is in fact grammatically correct, and they generally advise against using passive voice—even in contexts where it is appropriate. Moreover, grammar checkers do not always supply answers; often, they ask questions—for example, whether *which* should be *that* or *which* preceded by a comma—that you must answer, based on what you know or what you can find out. In short, grammar checkers can guide your editing, but you yourself must always be the one who decides when a sentence is or is not correct.

Proofreading (Bowling Green)
   http://www.bgsu.edu/departments/writing-lab/goproofreading.html

After you have completed your editing, print or type a final draft and **proofread,** rereading every word carefully to make sure you did not make any errors as you typed. Also make sure the final copy of your paper conforms to your instructor's format requirements.

CLOSE UP CHOOSING A TITLE ❓

When you are ready to decide on a title for your essay, keep these criteria in mind.

- A title should be descriptive, giving an accurate sense of your essay's focus. Whenever possible, include one or more of the key words and phrases that are central to your paper.
- A title's wording can echo the wording of your assignment, reminding you (and your instructor) that you have not lost sight of it.
- Ideally, a title should arouse interest, perhaps by using a provocative question or a suitable quotation (or, if appropriate, by introducing a note of controversy).

ASSIGNMENT: Write about a problem faced on college campuses today.

TOPIC: Free speech on campus

POSSIBLE TITLES:
Free Speech: A Problem for Today's Colleges (descriptive; echoes wording of assignment and includes key words of essay)

How Free Should Free Speech on Campus Be? (provocative question)

The Right to "Shout 'Fire' in a Crowded Theater" (quotation)

Hate Speech: A Dangerous Abuse of Free Speech on Campus (controversial position)

Introductions, Conclusions and Titles (George Mason U.)
http://www.gmu.edu/departments/writingcenter/handouts/introcon.html

EDITING AND PROOFREADING

- As you edit, try looking at only a small portion of text at a time. If your software allows you to split the screen, create another window so small that you can see only one or two lines of text at a time.

- Use the *search* or *find* command to look for words or phrases in usage errors that you commonly make—for instance, confusing *it's* with *its, lay* with *lie, effect* with *affect, their* with *there,* or *too* with *to.* You can also uncover **sexist language** by searching for words like *he, his, him,* or *man.*
- Finally, keep in mind that neatness does not equal correctness. The computer's ability to produce neat-looking text can disguise flaws that might otherwise be readily apparent. Take special care to ensure that spelling and typographical errors do not slip by.

See
28e2

The annotated student paper that follows is a final draft of the essay you first saw on pages 20–22. It incorporates the suggestions made by the instructor on the second draft (pages 27–29).

Dao 1

?

Nguyen Dao

Professor Cross

English 101

10 October 2000

My Problem: Escaping the Stereotype

of the "Model Minority"

The United States prides itself on being a nation where

diverse cultures intermingle to form a unique and enlightened

society. However, in reality, the existence of so many different

cultures in America often causes misunderstandings within the

society. These misunderstandings result from most people's

lack of knowledge about other cultures. The unique character-

istic of American culture is its genuine desire to understand

and embrace the wide range of traditions and values of its

people. Still, as an Asian American, I am frequently confronted

with other people's ideas about who I am and how I should

behave. Such stereotypes are not just limiting to me, but also

dangerous to the nation because they challenge the image of

the United States as a place where people can be whatever

they want to be.

Within the last twenty years, the United States has expe-

rienced a sharp rise in the number of Asian immigrants, and

these immigrants, and their children, are stereotyped. First-

generation immigrants are seen as an underclass of poor peo-

ple who struggle in low-paying jobs, working long hours so

Sidebar annotations:

Introductory paragraph presents basic background

Thesis statement

First body paragraph: Common stereotypes applied to Asian Americans

Dao 2

that their children will have a better future. Along with the view of the first-generation Asian Americans as driven, low-skilled workers comes the notion that all Asian-American chil-dren are hard workers who are pushed by their families to succeed. Asian children are seen as intelligent, but only in terms of scientific and technical knowledge. The media like to point out that most Asians succeed only in math, science, and engineering and that a disproportionately large number of Asian college students identify themselves as premed. What the media seem to forget is that many other immigrant groups also value success. In a larger sense, America has always been seen as the land of opportunity, where everyone is in search of the American dream.

Second body paragraph: Stereotypes applied to student himself

Many of my college friends assume that I am some kind of robot. They think I must be either a science or an engineering major and that my parents force me to study many hours each day. They believe that I sacrifice all my free time and social life in pursuit of a high grade point average. Naturally, these assump-tions are incorrect. My friends are really surprised when I tell them that I take drawing classes and that I am majoring in polit-ical science--not as a stepping-stone into law school, but as a foundation for a liberal arts education. They are also surprised to find that I am not particularly quiet or shy, that I do not play a musical instrument, and that I do not live in Chinatown. (I don't know why this surprises people; I'm not even Chinese.)

Dao 3

I try to see these stereotypes as harmless, but they aren't. Even neutral or positive stereotypes can have negative consequences. For example, teachers have always had unreasonably high expectations for me, and these expectations have created pressure for academic success. And even though teachers expect me to do well, they only expect me to excel in certain areas. So, they have encouraged me to take AP math and science classes, try out for band, sign up for an advanced computer seminar, and join the chess club. No one has ever suggested that I (or any other Asian American I know) pursue athletics, creative writing, or debating. I spent my high school years trying to be what other people wanted me to be, and I got to be pretty good at it.

Third body paragraph: Negative effects of stereotypes on student

I realize now, however, that I have been limited and that similar stereotypes also limit the options other groups have. The law says we can choose our activities and choose our careers, but things do not always work out that way. Often, because of long-held stereotypes, we are gently steered (by peers, teachers, bosses, parents, and even by ourselves) in a certain direction, toward some options and away from others. We may have come a long way from the time when African Americans were expected to be domestics or blue-collar workers, Latinos to be migrant farmers or gardeners, and Asians to be restaurant workers. But at the college, high school, and even elementary school level, students are expected to follow

Fourth body paragraph: Negative effects of stereotypes on society

Dao 4

certain predetermined paths, and too often these expectations
are based on culture, not interests or abilities.

Conclusion   Most people do not fit these cultural stereotypes. For example, not all Asians fit into the overachieving, success-
oriented mold. When children come from an economically
disadvantaged background, as the children of some recent
Asian immigrants do, they must work hard and study hard.
But this situation is only temporary. Even as Asian children become more assimilated into American society, they retain the
traditional Asian values of hard work and family obligations--
but they also acquire the American drive for individualism. I
know from my own experience that the stereotypes applied to
Asians are not accurate. In the same way, people of other
ethnic groups know that the cultural stereotypes applied to
them are not valid. My problem is not just _my_ problem because ethnic and cultural stereotypes are never harmless.
Whenever someone is stereotyped, that person has fewer
choices. And freedom to choose our futures, to be whoever
we want to be, is what the United States is supposed to be all
about.

CHAPTER 2

WRITING PARAGRAPHS

A **paragraph** is a group of related sentences, which may be complete in itself or part of a longer piece of writing.

✔ CHECKLIST: WHEN TO PARAGRAPH

- ✔ Begin a new paragraph whenever you move from one major point to another.
- ✔ Begin a new paragraph whenever you move your readers from one time period or location to another.
- ✔ Begin a new paragraph every time you begin discussing a new step in a process.
- ✔ Begin a new paragraph when you want to emphasize an important idea.
- ✔ Begin a new paragraph every time a new person speaks.
- ✔ Begin a new paragraph to signal the end of your introduction and the beginning of your conclusion.

2a   Writing Unified Paragraphs

A paragraph is **unified** when it develops a single idea. Each paragraph should have a **topic sentence** that states the main idea of the paragraph.

(1) Using Topic Sentences

Usually, a topic sentence comes at the beginning of a paragraph, where it tells readers what to expect.

Paragraphs (from Harvard U.)
   http://www.fas.harvard.edu/~wricntr/para.html
Paragraph Unity (U. Vic)
   http://webserver.maclab.comp.uvic.ca/writersguide/Pages/ParUnity.html
Writing Topic Sentences (U. Ottawa)
   http://aix1.uottawa.ca/academic/arts/writcent/hypergrammar/partopic.html

<u>I was a listening child, careful to hear the very different sounds of Spanish and English.</u> Wide-eyed with hearing, I'd listen to sounds more than words. First, there were English (*gringo*) sounds. So many words were still unknown that when the butcher or the lady at the drugstore said something to me, exotic polysyllabic sounds would bloom in the midst of their sentences. Often the speech of people in public seemed to me very loud, booming with confidence. The man behind the counter would literally ask, "What can I do for you?" But by being so firm and so clear, the sound of his voice said that he was a *gringo;* he belonged in public society.

(Richard Rodriguez, *Aria: A Memoir of a Bilingual Childhood*)

Occasionally, the topic sentence may appear at the end of a paragraph, particularly when a writer needs to lead readers gradually to a controversial or surprising conclusion.

These sprays, dusts and aerosols are now applied almost universally to farms, gardens, forests, and homes—nonselective chemicals that have the power to kill every insect, the "good" and the "bad," to still the song of the birds and the leaping of fish in the streams, to coat the leaves with a deadly film, and to linger on in soil—all this though the intended target may be only a few weeds or insects. Can anyone believe it is possible to lay down such a barrage of poisons on the surface without making it unfit for life? <u>They should not be called "insecticides," but "biocides."</u>

(Rachel Carson, "The Obligation to Endure")

(2) Testing for Unity

Each sentence in a paragraph should support the main idea stated in the topic sentence. In the following paragraph, the italicized sentences do not support the main idea:

NOT UNIFIED: <u>One of the first problems students have is learning to use a computer.</u> All students were required to buy a computer before school started. Throughout the first semester we took a special course to teach us to use a computer. *My notebook computer has a large memory and can do word processing and spreadsheets. It has an eighty-character screen and a hard drive. My parents were happy that I had a computer, but they were concerned about the price. Tuition was high, and when they added in the price of the computer, it was almost out of reach. To offset expenses, I got a part-time job in the school library.* By the end of the first week of the course, I was convinced that I would never be able to work with my computer.

(Student Writer)

To unify this paragraph, the writer deleted the sentences about his parents' financial situation and the computer's characteristics, keeping only those details related to the main idea.

UNIFIED: <u>One of the first problems I had as a college student was learning to use my computer.</u> All first-year students were required to buy a computer before school started. Throughout the first semester, we took a special course to teach us to use the computer. In theory this system sounded fine, but in my case it was a disaster. In the first place, the closest I had ever come to a computer was the handheld calculator I used in math class. In the second place, I could not type. And to make matters worse, many of the people in my computer orientation course already knew how to operate a computer. By the end of the first week I was convinced that I would never be able to work with my computer.

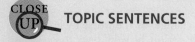 **TOPIC SENTENCES**

In some situations you may not need a topic sentence. For example, sometimes a topic sentence stated in one paragraph covers a subsequent paragraph as well. Also, in some narrative or descriptive paragraphs an explicit topic sentence may seem forced or artificial.

2b Writing Coherent Paragraphs

A paragraph is **coherent** if all its sentences are logically related to one another. You can achieve coherence by arranging details according to an organizing principle and by using transitional words and phrases, parallel constructions, and repeated key words and phrases.

(1) Arranging Details

Even if all a paragraph's sentences are about the same subject, the paragraph lacks coherence if the sentences are not arranged according to a general organizing principle—that is, in *spatial, chronological,* or *logical order.*

Spatial order establishes the perspective from which readers view details. For example, an object or scene can be viewed from top to bottom or from near to far. Spatial order is central to **descriptive paragraphs**.

See 2d2

Chronological order presents details in time sequence, using transitional words and phrases that establish the sequence of events—*at first,*

See
2d1;
2d4

yesterday, later, and so on. Chronological order is central to **narrative paragraphs** and **process paragraphs**.

Logical order presents details or ideas in terms of their logical relationships to one another. The ideas in a paragraph may move from *general* to *specific,* as in the conventional topic-sentence-at-the-beginning paragraph, or the ideas may progress from *specific* to *general,* as they do when the topic sentence appears at the end. A writer may also choose to begin with the *least important* idea and move to the *most important.*

(2) Using Transitional Words and Phrases

Transitional words and phrases clarify the relationships among sentences by establishing the spatial, chronological, and logical connections within a paragraph. In the following paragraph, transitional words and phrases such as *after, finally, once again,* and *in the end* indicate the order in which events occurred:

> Napoleon certainly made a change for the worse by leaving his small kingdom of Elba. <u>After Waterloo,</u> he went back to Paris, and he abdicated for a second time. <u>A hundred days after</u> his return from Elba, he fled to Rochefort in hope of escaping to America. <u>Finally,</u> he gave himself up to the English captain of the ship *Bellerophon.* <u>Once again,</u> he suggested that the Prince Regent grant him asylum, and <u>once again,</u> he was refused. <u>In the end,</u> all he saw of England was the Devon coast and Plymouth Sound as he passed on to the remote island of St. Helena. <u>After six years of exile,</u> he died on May 5, 1821, at the age of fifty-two.
>
> (Norman Mackenzie, *The Escape from Elba*)

?

USING TRANSITIONAL WORDS AND PHRASES

To Signal Sequence or Addition

again	furthermore
also	in addition
besides	one . . . another
first . . . second . . . third	too

continued on the following page

Writing Transitions
   http://www.unc.edu/depts/wcweb/handouts/transitions.html

To Signal Time

afterward	later
as soon as	meanwhile
at first	next
at the same time	now
before	soon
earlier	subsequently
finally	then
in the meantime	until

To Signal Comparison

also	likewise
by the same token	similarly
in comparison	

To Signal Contrast

although	nevertheless
but	nonetheless
despite	on the contrary
even though	on the one hand . . . on the
however	other hand
in contrast	still
instead	whereas
meanwhile	yet

To Signal Examples

for example	specifically
for instance	thus
namely	

To Signal Narrowing of Focus

after all	in particular
indeed	specifically
in fact	that is
in other words	

continued on the following page

continued from the previous page

To Signal Conclusions or Summaries

as a result	in summary
consequently	therefore
in conclusion	thus
in other words	to conclude

To Signal Concession

admittedly	naturally
certainly	of course
granted	

To Signal Causes or Effects

accordingly	since
as a result	so
because	then
consequently	therefore
hence	

(3) Using Parallel Structure

See
27a

Parallelism—the use of matching words, phrases, clauses, or sentence structures to express similar ideas—can help increase coherence in a paragraph.

Note in the following paragraph how parallel clauses (sentences that begin with "He was _____") link Thomas Jefferson's accomplishments:

> Thomas Jefferson was born in 1743 and died at Monticello, Virginia, on July 4, 1826. During his eighty-four years he accomplished a number of things. Although best known for his draft of the Declaration of Independence, Jefferson was a man of many talents who had a wide intellectual range. He was a patriot who was one of the revolutionary founders of the United States. He was a reformer who, when he was governor of Virginia, drafted the Statute for Religious Freedom. He was an innovator who drafted an ordinance for governing the West and devised the first decimal monetary system. He was a president who abolished internal taxes, reduced the national debt, and made the Louisiana Purchase. And, finally, he was an architect who designed Monticello and the University of Virginia.
>
> (Student Writer)

(4) Repeating Key Words and Phrases

Repeating **key words and phrases**—those essential to meaning—throughout a paragraph connects the sentences to one another and to the paragraph's main idea.

The following paragraph repeats the key word *mercury* to help readers focus on the subject:

> Mercury poisoning is a problem that has long been recognized. "Mad as a hatter" refers to the condition prevalent among nineteenth-century workers who were exposed to mercury during the manufacturing of felt hats. Workers in many other industries, such as mining, chemicals, and dentistry, were similarly affected. In the 1950s and 1960s there were cases of mercury poisoning in Minamata, Japan. Research showed that there were high levels of mercury pollution in streams and lakes surrounding the village. In the United States this problem came to light in 1969 when a New Mexico family got sick from eating food tainted with mercury. Since then pesticides containing mercury have been withdrawn from the market, and chemical wastes can no longer be dumped into the ocean.
>
> (Student Writer)

Notice that to avoid monotony the writer sometimes refers indirectly to the subject with phrases such as *similarly affected* and *this problem.*

CLOSE UP   COHERENCE BETWEEN PARAGRAPHS

The methods you use to establish coherence within paragraphs may also be used to link paragraphs in an essay. In addition, you can use a transitional paragraph as a bridge between two paragraphs.

2c Writing Well-Developed Paragraphs

A paragraph is **well developed** when it contains all the information—examples, statistics, expert opinion, and so on—that readers need to understand and accept the main idea.

At first glance the following paragraph may seem well developed:

> From Thanksgiving until Christmas, children are bombarded with ads for violent toys and games. Toy manufacturers persist in thinking that only toys that appeal to children's aggressiveness will sell. Despite claims that they (unlike action toys) have educational value, video games have increased the level of violence. The real question is why parents continue to buy these violent toys for their children.
>
> (Student Writer)

Upon closer observation, however, it becomes clear that the paragraph does not contain enough support to convince readers that children are "bombarded with ads for violent toys and games."

The following revision includes specific examples that support the topic sentence:

Topic sentence

Specific examples

Specific examples

From Thanksgiving until Christmas, children are bombarded with ads for violent toys and games. Toy manufacturers persist in thinking that only toys that appeal to children's aggressiveness will sell. One television commercial praises the merits of a commando team that attacks and captures a miniature enemy base. Toy soldiers wear realistic uniforms and carry automatic rifles, pistols, knives, grenades, and ammunition. Another commercial shows laughing children shooting one another with plastic rocket fighters and tank-like vehicles. Despite claims that they (unlike action toys) have educational value, video games have increased the level of violence. The most popular video games involve children in strikingly realistic combat situations. One game lets children search out and destroy enemy fighters in outer space. Other best-selling games graphically simulate hand-to-hand combat on city streets. The real question is why parents continue to buy these violent toys and games for their children.

CLOSE UP WELL-DEVELOPED PARAGRAPHS

Keep in mind that length does not determine whether a paragraph is well developed. The amount and kind of support you need depends on your audience, your purpose, and your paragraph's main idea.

continued on the following page

- *Identify your audience.* Will readers be familiar with your subject? Given the needs of your audience, is your paragraph well developed?
- *Identify your purpose.* Should the paragraph give readers a general overview of your topic, or should it present detailed information? Given your purpose, is your paragraph well developed?
- *Identify your paragraph's main idea.* Do you need to explain it more fully? Do you need another example, a statistic, an anecdote, or expert opinion? Given the complexity and scope of your main idea, is your paragraph well developed?

2d   Patterns for Paragraph Development

The pattern of a paragraph—*narration, description,* and so on—like the pattern of an entire essay, reflects the way a writer arranges ideas to express ideas most effectively.

(1) Narration

Narrative paragraphs tell a story. Transitional words and phrases move readers from one time period to another.

My academic career almost ended as soon as it began when, three weeks after I arrived at college, I decided to pledge a fraternity. By midterms I was wearing a straw hat and saying "Yes, sir" to every fraternity brother I met. When classes were over, I ran errands for the fraternity members, and after dinner I socialized and worked on projects with the other people in my pledge class. In between these activities, I tried to study. Somehow I managed to write papers, take tests, and attend lectures. By the end of the semester, though, my grades had slipped, and I was exhausted. It was then that I realized that I wanted to be popular, but not at the expense of my grades and my future career. At the beginning of my second semester, I dropped out of the fraternity and got a job in the biology lab. Looking back, I realize that it was then that I actually began to grow up.

(Student Writer)

(2) Description

Descriptive paragraphs convey how something looks, sounds, smells, tastes, or feels. Transitional words and phrases clarify spatial relationships.

When you are inside the jungle, away from the river, the trees vault out of sight. It is hard to remember to look up the long trunks and see the fans, strips, fronds, and sprays of glossy leaves. Inside the jungle you are more likely to notice the snarl of climbers and creepers round the trees' boles, the flowering bromeliads and epiphytes in every bough's crook, and the fantastic silk-cotton tree trunks thirty or forty feet across, trunks buttressed in flanges of wood whose curves can make three high walls of a room—a shady, loamy-aired room where you would gladly live, or die. Butterflies, iridescent blue, striped, or clear-winged, thread the jungle paths at eye level. And at your feet is a swath of ants bearing triangular bits of green leaf. The ants with their leaves look like a wide fleet of sailing dinghies—but they don't quit. In either direction they wobble over the jungle floor as far as the eye can see. I followed them off the path as far as I dared, and never saw an end to ants or to those luffing chips of green they bore.

(Annie Dillard, "In the Jungle")

(3) Exemplification

Exemplification paragraphs use specific illustrations to clarify a general statement. Some exemplification paragraphs, like the following, use several examples to support the topic sentence (others may develop a single extended example).

Illiterates cannot travel freely. When they attempt to do so, they encounter risks that few of us can dream of. They cannot read traffic signs and, while they often learn to recognize and to decipher symbols, they cannot manage street names which they haven't seen before. The same is true for bus and subway stops. While ingenuity can sometimes help a man or a woman to discern directions from familiar landmarks, buildings, cemeteries, churches, and the like, most illiterates are virtually immobilized. They seldom wander past the streets and neighborhoods they know. Geographical paralysis becomes a bitter metaphor for their entire existence. They are immobilized in almost every sense we can imagine. They can't move up. They can't move out. They cannot see beyond. Illiterates may take an oral test for drivers' permits in most sections of America. It is a questionable concession. Where will they go? How will they get there? How will they get home? Could it be that some of us might like it better if they stayed where they belong?

(Jonathan Kozol, Illiterate America)

(4) Process

Process paragraphs describe how something works, presenting a series of steps in chronological order. The topic sentence identifies the process, and the rest of the paragraph presents the steps involved.

> Members of the court have disclosed, however, the general way the conference is conducted. It begins at ten A.M. and usually runs on until later afternoon. At the start each justice, when he enters the room, shakes hands with all others there (thirty-six handshakes altogether). The custom, dating back generations, is evidently designed to begin the meeting at a friendly level, no matter how heated the intellectual differences may be. The conference takes up, first, the applications for review—a few appeals, many more petitions for certiorari. Those on the Appellate Docket, the regular paid cases, are considered first, then the pauper's applications on the Miscellaneous Docket. (If any of these are granted, they are then transferred to the Appellate Docket.) After this the justices consider, and vote on, all the cases argued during the preceding Monday through Thursday. These are tentative votes, which may be and quite often are changed as the opinion is written and the problem thought through more deeply. There may be further discussion at later conferences before the opinion is handed down.

(Anthony Lewis, Gideon's Trumpet)

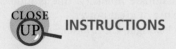 **INSTRUCTIONS**

When a process paragraph presents instructions to enable readers to actually perform the process, it is written in the present tense and in the **imperative mood**: "*Remove* the cover . . . and *check* the valve."

See 21c

(5) Cause and Effect

Cause-and-effect paragraphs explore why events occur and what happens as a result of them.

The main reason that a young baby sucks his thumb seems to be that he hasn't had enough sucking at the breast or bottle to satisfy his sucking needs. Dr. David Levy pointed out that babies who are fed every 3 hours don't suck their thumbs as much as babies fed every 4 hours, and that babies who have cut down on nursing time from 20 minutes to 10 minutes . . . are more likely to suck their thumbs than babies who still have to work for 20 minutes. Dr. Levy fed a litter of puppies with a medicine dropper so that they had no chance to suck during their feedings. They acted just the same as babies who don't get enough chance to suck at feeding time. They sucked their own and each other's paws and skin so hard that the fur came off.

(Benjamin Spock, *Baby and Child Care*)

(6) Comparison and Contrast

Comparison-and-contrast paragraphs examine the similarities and differences between two subjects. Comparison emphasizes similarities, whereas contrast emphasizes differences.

Comparison and contrast can be organized in one of two ways. One strategy is to compare the subjects **point by point:** the paragraph alternates points about one subject with comparable points about the other subject.

There are two Americas. One is the America of Lincoln and Adlai Stevenson; the other is the America of Teddy Roosevelt and the modern superpatriots. One is generous and humane, the other narrowly egotistical; one is self-critical, the other self-righteous; one is sensible, the other romantic; one is good-humored, the other solemn; one is inquiring, the other pontificating; one is moderate, the other filled with passionate intensity; one is judicious and the other arrogant in the use of great power.

(J. William Fulbright, *The Arrogance of Power*)

Other paragraphs, **subject-by-subject** comparisons, treat one subject completely and then move on to the other subject. In the following paragraph, notice how the writer shifts from one subject to the other with the transitional word *however:*

First, it is important to note that men and women regard conversation quite differently. For women it is a passion, a sport, an activity even more important to life than eating because it doesn't involve weight gain. The first sign of closeness among women is when they find themselves engaging in endless, secretless rounds of conversation with one another. And as soon as a woman begins to relax and feel comfortable in a relationship with a man, she tries to have that type of conversation with him as well. However, the first sign that a man is feeling close to a woman is when he admits that he'd rather she please quiet down so he can hear the TV. A man who feels truly intimate with a woman often reserves for her and her alone the precious gift of one-word answers. Everyone knows that the surest way to spot a successful long-term relationship is to look around a restaurant for the table where no one is talking. Ah . . . now *that's* real love.

(Merrill Markoe, "Men, Women, and Conversation")

An **analogy** is a special kind of comparison that explains an unfamiliar concept or object by likening it to a familiar one. Here an author uses the behavior of people to explain the behavior of ants:

Ants are so much like human beings as to be an embarrassment. They farm fungi, raise aphids as livestock, launch armies into wars, use chemical sprays to alarm and confuse enemies, capture slaves. The families of weaver ants engage in child labor, holding their larvae like shuttles to spin out the thread that sews the leaves together for their fungus gardens. They exchange information ceaselessly. They do everything but watch television.

(Lewis Thomas, "On Societies As Organisms")

(7) Division and Classification

Division paragraphs take a single item and break it into its components.

The blood can be divided into four distinct components: plasma, red cells, white cells, and platelets. Plasma is 90 percent water and holds a great number of substances in suspension. It contains proteins, sugars, fat, and inorganic salts. Plasma also contains urea and other by-products from the breaking down of proteins, hormones, enzymes, and dissolved gases. In addition, plasma contains the red blood cells that give it color, the white cells, and the platelets. The red cells are most numerous; they get oxygen from the lungs and release it in the tissues. The less numerous white cells are part of the body's defense against invading organisms. The platelets, which occur in almost the same number as white cells, are responsible for clotting.

(Student Writer)

Classification paragraphs take many separate items and group them into categories according to qualities or characteristics they share.

Charles Babbage, an English mathematician, reflecting in 1830 on what he saw as the decline of science at the time, distinguished among three major kinds of scientific fraud. He called the first "forging," by which he meant complete fabrication—the recording of observations that were never made. The second category he called "trimming"; this consists of manipulating the data to make them look better, or, as Babbage wrote, "in clipping of little bits here and there from those observations which differ most in *excess* from the mean and in sticking them on to those which are too small." His third category was data selection, which he called "cooking"—the choosing of those data that fitted the researcher's hypothesis and the discarding of those that did not. To this day, the serious discussion of scientific fraud has not improved on Babbage's typology.

(Morton Hunt, *New York Times Magazine*)

(8) Definition

A **formal definition** includes the term defined, the class to which it belongs, and the details that distinguish it from other members of its class.

(term)   (class to which it belongs)
Carbon is a nonmetallic element

(distinguishing details)
sometimes occurring as diamond.

Definition paragraphs develop the formal definition with other patterns, defining *happiness,* for instance, by telling a story (narration), or defining a diesel engine by telling how it works (process).

The following paragraph begins with a straightforward definition of *gadget* and then cites an example:

A gadget is nearly always novel in design or concept and it often has no proper name. For example, the semaphore which signals the arrival of the mail in our rural mailbox certainly has no proper name. It is a contrivance consisting of a piece of shingle. Call it what you like, it saves us frequent frustrating trips to the mailbox in winter when you have to dress up and wade through snow to get there. That's a gadget!

(*Smithsonian*)

✔ CHECKLIST: DEVELOPING PARAGRAPHS

Narration   Do you present enough explanation to enable readers to understand the events you discuss? Do you support your main idea with descriptive details?

Description   Do you supply enough detail about what things look like, sound like, smell like, taste like, and feel like? Will your readers be able to visualize the person, object, or setting that your paragraph describes?

Exemplification   Do you present enough individual examples to support your paragraph's main idea? If you use a single extended example, is it developed in enough detail to enable readers to understand how it supports the paragraph's main idea?

Process   Do you present enough steps to enable readers to understand how the process is performed? Is the sequence of steps clear? If you are writing instructions, do you include enough explanation—including reminders and warnings—to enable readers to perform the process?

Cause and Effect   Do you identify enough causes (subtle as well as obvious, minor as well as major) to enable readers to understand why something occurred? Do you identify enough effects to show the significance of the causes and the impact they had?

Comparison and Contrast   Do you supply a sufficient number of details to illustrate and characterize each of the subjects in the comparison? Do you present a similar number of details for each subject? Do you discuss the same or similar details for each subject?

Division and Classification   Do you present enough information to enable readers to identify each category and distinguish one from another?

Definition   Do you present enough support (examples, analogies, descriptive details, and so on) to enable readers to understand the term you are defining and to distinguish it from others in its class?

2e   Writing Introductory and Concluding Paragraphs

(1) Introductory Paragraphs

An **introductory paragraph** introduces the subject, narrows it down, and then states the essay's thesis.

Christine was just a girl in one of my classes. I never knew much about her except that she was strange. She didn't talk much. Her hair was dyed black and purple, and she wore heavy black boots and a black turtleneck sweater, even in the summer. She was attractive—in spite of the ring she wore through her left eyebrow—but she never seemed to care what the rest of us thought about her. Like the rest of my classmates, I didn't really want to get close to her. <u>It was only when we were assigned to do our chemistry project</u> <u>together that I began to understand why Christine dressed the way</u> <u>she did.</u>

Thesis statement

(Student Writer)

To arouse an audience's interest, writers may vary this direct approach and begin with an interesting *quotation,* a compelling *question,* an unusual *comparison,* or a *controversial statement.*

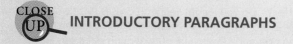

CLOSE UP   INTRODUCTORY PARAGRAPHS

Avoid introductions that do no more than announce your subject ("In my paper, I will talk about Lady Macbeth") or that undercut your credibility ("I don't know much about alternative energy sources, but I would like to present my opinion about the subject").

✔ CHECKLIST: INTRODUCTORY PARAGRAPHS

✔ Does your introduction include your essay's thesis statement?
✔ Does it lead naturally into the body of your essay?
✔ Does it arouse your readers' interest?
✔ Does it avoid statements that simply announce your subject or that undercut your credibility?

(2) Concluding Paragraphs

A **concluding paragraph** typically begins with specifics—for example, a review of your essay's main points—and then moves to more gen-

Introductions, Conclusions and Titles (George Mason U.)
http://www-english.tamu.edu/wcenter/revising/html

eral statements. Whenever possible, it should end with a sentence readers will remember.

> As an Arab American, I feel I have the best of two worlds. I'm proud to be part of the melting pot, proud to contribute to the tremendous diversity of cultures, customs and traditions that makes this country unique. But Arab-bashing—public acceptance of hatred and bigotry—is something no American can be proud of.
>
> (Ellen Mansoor Collier, "I Am Not a Terrorist")

Conclusions may also offer a *prediction,* a *recommendation,* a forceful *opinion,* or a pertinent *quotation.*

CLOSE UP   CONCLUDING PARAGRAPHS

Avoid conclusions that introduce new points or go off in new directions. Because your conclusion is your last word, a weak or uninteresting one detracts from an otherwise strong essay. Do not just repeat your introduction in different words or apologize or in any way cast doubt on your concluding points ("I may not be an expert" or "At least this is my opinion").

✔ CHECKLIST: CONCLUDING PARAGRAPHS

✔ Does your conclusion remind readers of the primary focus of your essay?
✔ Does it review your essay's main points?
✔ Does it end memorably?
✔ Does it do more than repeat the introduction?
✔ Does it avoid apologies?

PART 2

Critical Thinking and Argumentation

CRITICAL THINKING & ARGUMENT

? FREQUENTLY ASKED QUESTIONS

CRITICAL THINKING
& ARGUMENT

PART 2

CHAPTER 3

THINKING CRITICALLY

? Reading **arguments**—essays that take a stand on a debatable topic—requires special **critical thinking** skills. As you read, you must think very carefully about the ideas you encounter and consider the merits of opposing points of view. In addition, you must remain open-minded, realizing that a text may challenge your own beliefs and expose your biases.   **See Ch .4**

In order to evaluate the effectiveness of an argument, you must understand the difference between *fact* and *opinion.*

3a Distinguishing Fact from Opinion

? A **fact** is a verifiable statement that something is true or that something occurred. An **opinion** is a conclusion or belief that can never be substantiated beyond any doubt and is, therefore, debatable.

FACT: Measles is a potentially deadly disease.

OPINION: All children should be vaccinated against measles.

An opinion may be *supported* or *unsupported.*

UNSUPPORTED OPINION: All children in Pennsylvania should be vaccinated against measles.

SUPPORTED OPINION: Despite the fact that an effective measles vaccine is widely available, several unvaccinated Pennsylvania children have died of measles each year since 1992. States that have instituted

Critical Thinking (UMSL)
   http://www.umsl.edu/~klein/Critical_Thinking.html
Critical Thinking (Humboldt)
   http://www.humboldt.edu/~act/

vaccination programs have had no deaths in the same time period. For this reason, all children in Pennsylvania should be vaccinated against measles.

As these examples show, supported opinion is more convincing than unsupported opinion. Remember, however, that supporting evidence can only make a statement more convincing; it cannot turn an opinion into a fact.

3b   Evaluating Supporting Evidence

See
4b1

The more reliable the supporting **evidence**—examples, statistics, or expert testimony—the more willing readers will be to accept a statement. No matter what kind of evidence writers use, however, it must be *accurate, sufficient, representative,* and *relevant.*

Evidence is likely to be **accurate** if it comes from a trustworthy source. Such a source quotes *exactly* and does not present remarks out of context. It also presents examples, statistics, and expert testimony fairly, drawing them from other reliable sources.

For evidence to be **sufficient,** a writer must present an adequate amount of evidence. It is not enough, for instance, for a writer to cite just one example in an attempt to demonstrate that most poor women receive adequate prenatal care. Similarly, the opinions of a single expert, no matter how reputable, are not enough to support this idea.

Writers should also select evidence that is **representative** of a fair range of sources and viewpoints; they should not choose evidence that supports their arguments and ignore evidence that does not. In other words, they should not permit their biases to govern their choice of evidence. For example, a writer who is arguing that Asian immigrants have had great success in achieving professional status in the United States must draw from the experience of a range of Asian immigrant groups—Vietnamese, Chinese, Japanese, Indian, and Korean, for example—and a representative sample of professions—law, medicine, teaching, and so forth. No matter how accurate the information or how numerous the examples, a writer cannot draw a general conclusion about Asians by citing examples that apply only to Chinese.

Finally, evidence must be **relevant**—that is, it must apply to the case being discussed. For example, you cannot support the position that the

United States should send medical aid to developing nations by citing examples that apply just to our own nation's health-care system.

3c Understanding Inductive and Deductive Reasoning

Arguments must be based on **logical reasoning.** The two most common methods of reasoning, *induction* and *deduction,* often occur together in a single argument.

(1) Using Inductive Reasoning

Inductive reasoning moves from specific facts, observations, or experiences to a general conclusion. Writers use inductive reasoning when they address a skeptical audience that requires a lot of evidence before it will accept a conclusion. You can see how inductive reasoning operates by studying the following list of statements, which focuses on the relationship between SAT scores and admissions at one liberal arts college.

- The SAT is an admission requirement for all applicants.
- High school grades and rank in class are also examined.
- Nonacademic factors such as sports, activities, and interests are taken into account as well.
- Special attention is given to the applications of athletes, minorities, and children of alumni.
- Fewer than 52 percent of applicants for a recent class with SAT verbal scores between 600 and 700 were accepted.
- Fewer than 39 percent of applicants with similar math scores were accepted.
- Approximately 18 percent of applicants with SAT verbal scores between 450 and 520 and about 19 percent of applicants with similar SAT math scores were admitted.

After reading the statements above, you can use inductive reasoning to conclude that although important, SAT scores are not the single factor that determines whether a student is admitted.

Logic in Argumentation (Purdue)
  http://owl.english.purdue.edu/Files/123.html

CLOSE UP   **INDUCTIVE REASONING**

No matter how much evidence is presented, an inductive conclusion is never certain, only probable. An inductive conclusion is an **inference,** a statement about the unknown based on what is known. The more observations you make, the narrower the gap between your observations and your conclusion.

(2) Using Deductive Reasoning

Deductive reasoning moves from a generalization believed to be true or self-evident to a more specific conclusion. Writers use deductive reasoning when they address an audience that is more likely to be influenced by logic than by evidence. The process of deduction has traditionally been illustrated with a **syllogism,** a three-part set of statements or propositions that includes a **major premise,** a **minor premise,** and a **conclusion.**

MAJOR PREMISE: All books from that store are new.

MINOR PREMISE: These books are from that store.

CONCLUSION: Therefore, these books are new.

The major premise of a syllogism makes a general statement that the writer believes to be true. The minor premise presents a specific example of the belief that is stated in the major premise. If the reasoning is sound, the conclusion should follow from these two premises. (Note that no terms are introduced in the conclusion that have not already appeared in the major and minor premises.) The strength of a deductive argument is that if readers accept the premises, they usually grant the conclusion.

3d   Recognizing Logical Fallacies

Fallacies are flawed arguments. A writer who inadvertently uses logical fallacies is not thinking clearly or logically; a writer who intentionally uses them is trying to deceive readers. Learn to recognize fallacies—to challenge them when you read and to avoid them when you write.

GUIDE TO LOGICAL FALLACIES

- **Hasty Generalization** Drawing a conclusion based on too little evidence

  The person I voted for is not doing a good job in Congress. Therefore, voting is a waste of time. (One disappointing experience does not warrant the statement that you will never vote again.)

- **Sweeping Generalization** Making a generalization that cannot be supported, no matter how much evidence is supplied

  Everyone should exercise. (Some people, for example those with severe heart conditions, might not benefit from exercise.)

- **Equivocation** Shifting the meaning of a key word during an argument

  It is not in the public interest for the public to lose interest. (Although clever, the shift in the meaning of the term *public interest* clouds the issue.)

- **Circular Reasoning** Writing the same thing again in different words, instead of supplying evidence

  First-year students are not qualified to take senior seminars because those courses are for seniors. (Where is the evidence to support this claim?)

- **Non Sequitur (Does Not Follow)** Arriving at a conclusion that does not follow logically from what comes before

  Kim Williams is a good lawyer, so she will make a good senator. (Just because Kim Williams is a good lawyer, it does not follow that she will make a good senator.)

continued on the following page

Logical Fallacies (or Errors in Thinking)
   http://www.intrepidsoftware.com/fallacy/toc.htm
Avoiding Common Errors in Logic and Reasoning (Princeton U.)
   http://webware.princeton.edu/Writing/logic-re.htm

continued from the previous page

- **Either/Or Fallacy** Treating a complex issue as if it has only two sides

  Either we institute universal health care, or the health of all people will decline. (Good health does not necessarily depend on universal health care.)

- **Post Hoc** Establishing an unjustified link between cause and effect

  The United States sold wheat to Russia. This must have caused the price of wheat to rise. (Other factors, unrelated to the sale, could have caused the price to rise.)

- **Begging the Question** Stating a debatable premise as if it were true

  Animal experimentation, which is sadistic and unnecessary, must be stopped immediately. (Are *all* animal experiments sadistic and unnecessary?)

- **False Analogy** Assuming that because things are similar in some ways they are similar in other ways

  When forced to live in crowded conditions, people act like rats. They turn on each other and act violently. (Both people and rats might dislike living in crowded conditions, but unlike rats, most people do not necessarily resort to violence in this situation.)

- **Red Herring** Changing the subject to distract readers from the issue

  This company may charge high prices, but it gives a lot to charity each year. (What does charging high prices have to do with giving to charity?)

- **Argument to Ignorance** Saying that something is true because it cannot be proved false, or vice versa

continued on the following page

How can you tell me to send my child to a school where there is a child who has AIDS? After all, doctors can't say for sure that my child won't catch AIDS, can they? (Just because a doctor cannot prove the speaker's claim to be false, it does not follow that the claim is true.)

- **Bandwagon** Trying to establish that something is true because everyone believes it is true

  Everyone knows that eating candy makes a child hyperactive. (Where is the evidence to support this claim?)

- **Argument to the Person** (*Ad Hominem*) Attacking the person and not the issue

  Of course the Congressman supports increases in the defense budget. He worked for a defense contractor before he was elected to Congress. (By attacking his opponent, the speaker attempts to avoid the issue.)

- **Argument to the People** Appealing to people's prejudices

  Because foreigners are attempting to overrun our shores, we should cut back on immigration. (By exploiting prejudice, the speaker attempts to avoid the issue.)

✔ CHECKLIST: THINKING CRITICALLY

- ✔ What point is the writer making? What is stated? What is suggested?
- ✔ Do you agree with the writer's ideas?
- ✔ Are the writer's points supported primarily by fact or by opinion? Does the writer present opinion as fact?
- ✔ Does the writer offer supporting evidence for his or her statements?
- ✔ What kind of evidence is provided? How convincing is it?
- ✔ Is the evidence accurate? Sufficient? Representative? Relevant?

continued on the following page

continued from the previous page

✔ Does the writer display any bias? If so, is the bias revealed through language, tone, or choice of evidence?

✔ Does the writer present a balanced picture of the issue?

✔ Are any alternative viewpoints overlooked?

✔ Does the writer omit pertinent examples?

✔ Do your reactions reveal biases in your own thinking?

✔ Does the writer challenge your own values, beliefs, and assumptions?

✔ Does the writer use valid reasoning?

✔ Does the writer use logical fallacies?

✔ Does the writer oversimplify complex ideas?

✔ Does the writer make reasonable inferences?

✔ Does the writer represent the ideas of others accurately? Fairly?

✔ Does the writer distort the ideas of others or present them out of context?

CHAPTER 4

WRITING ARGUMENTATIVE ESSAYS

For most people, the true test of their critical thinking skills comes when they write an **argument,** which takes a position on an issue and uses logic and evidence to convince readers. The goal of an argument is to change the way readers think—and, sometimes, to cause them to take action.

4a Planning an Argumentative Essay

(1) Choosing a Topic

Because an argumentative essay attempts to change the way people think, it must focus on a **debatable topic,** one about which reasonable people disagree. Factual statements—those about which people do not disagree—are therefore not suitable for argument.

FACT: Many countries hold political prisoners.

DEBATABLE TOPIC: The United States should not trade with countries that hold political prisoners.

Some topics—such as "The Need for Gun Control" or "The Effectiveness of the Death Penalty"—have been written about so much that you will probably not be able to say anything interesting about them. Such topics usually inspire uninteresting essays that add little or nothing to a reader's understanding of an issue. Instead of relying on a tired topic, choose one that enables you to contribute something to the debate.

Be sure your topic is narrow enough so that you can write about it within the page limit you have been given. Remember, though, that you will have to develop your own ideas and present supporting evidence while also

Writing an Argument Paper (Muskingum College)
http://muskingum.edu/~cal/database/writing.html#Argument
Writing Argumentative Essays
http://www2.rscc.cc.tn.us/~jordan_jj/OWL/Argumentation.html

pointing out the strengths and weaknesses of opposing arguments. If your topic is too broad, you will not be able to cover it in enough detail.

(2) Developing a Thesis

After you have chosen a topic, your next step is to state your position in an **argumentative thesis,** one that takes a strong stand. One way to make sure your <u>thesis statement</u> actually does take a stand is to formulate an **antithesis,** a statement that takes an arguable position opposite from yours.

See 1c2

THESIS: Term limits would improve government by bringing fresh faces into office every few years.

ANTITHESIS: Term limits would harm government because elected officials would always be inexperienced.

NOTE: Be careful to use precise language in your thesis statement, avoiding vague and judgmental words such as *wrong, bad, good, right,* and *immoral.*

CLOSE UP DEVELOPING AN ARGUMENTATIVE THESIS

You can determine if your thesis is argumentative by asking the following questions:

- Is your thesis one with which reasonable people would disagree?
- Can you think of arguments against your thesis?
- Can your thesis be supported by evidence?
- Does your thesis make clear to readers what position you are taking?

(3) Considering Your Audience

See 1b2

As you plan your essay, keep a specific <u>audience</u> in mind. Are your readers unbiased observers or people deeply concerned about the issue? Can they be cast in a specific role—concerned parents, victims of discrimination, irate consumers—or are they so diverse that they cannot be categorized? Are they likely to be sympathetic or hostile to your position? Although you may never be able to convince hostile readers that your conclusion is valid, you may be able to get these readers to concede the strength of your argument.

(4) Refuting the Opposition

As you develop your argument, you must also refute opposing arguments by showing that opposing views are untrue, unfair, illogical, unimportant, or irrelevant. In the following paragraph a student refutes an argument against her position that Sea World should not keep whales in captivity.

> Of course some will say Sea World only wants to capture a few whales, as George Will points out in his commentary in *Newsweek*. However, Will downplays the fact that Sea World wants to capture a hundred whales, not just "a few." And after releasing ninety whales, Sea World intends to keep ten for "further work." At hearings in Seattle last week, several noted marine biologists went on record as condemning Sea World's research program.

NOTE: When you acknowledge an opposing view, do not distort or oversimplify it. This tactic, called creating a **straw man,** can seriously undermine your credibility.

REFUTING THE OPPOSITION

Construct a table with your computer, making two columns. Label the first column *Arguments Against* and the second column *Refutations.* In the first column, list all the arguments you can think of against your position. In the second column, list refutations for these arguments. When you are finished, cross out the weakest opposing arguments and consider the ones that are left. In your essay, concede the strength of any particularly compelling arguments against your position; then, use arguments of your own to refute them.

4b   Using Evidence and Establishing Credibility

(1)   Using Evidence

Most arguments are built on **assertions**—claims you make about a debatable topic—backed by **evidence**—supporting information, in the form of examples, statistics, or expert opinion. Only statements that are *self-evident* ("All human beings are mortal"), true by *definition* (2 + 2 = 4), or *factual* ("The Atlantic Ocean separates England and the United States") need no proof. All other kinds of assertions require supporting evidence.

See Chs. 9–10
NOTE: If you use words or ideas that are not your own, be sure to use proper **documentation**.

(2) Establishing Credibility and Being Fair

In order to convince readers, you must prove you have **credibility**— in other words, that you are someone they should listen to. Readers will also judge your argument on the basis of its fairness.

✔ CHECKLIST: ESTABLISHING CREDIBILITY

FIND COMMON GROUND
- ✔ Identify the various sides of the issue.
- ✔ Identify the points on which you and your readers agree.
- ✔ Work these areas of agreement into your argument.

DEMONSTRATE KNOWLEDGE
- ✔ Include relevant personal experiences.
- ✔ Include relevant special knowledge of your subject.
- ✔ Include the results of any relevant research you have done.

MAINTAIN A REASONABLE TONE
- ✔ Avoid talking down to or insulting your readers.
- ✔ Use moderate language, and qualify your statements.

✔ CHECKLIST: BEING FAIR

- ✔ Do not distort evidence.
- ✔ Do not misrepresent opponents' views by exaggerating them and then attacking this extreme position.
- ✔ Do not change the meaning of a statement by focusing on certain words and ignoring others.
- ✔ Do not select only information that supports your case and ignore information that does not.
- ✔ Do not use inflammatory language calculated to appeal to the emotions or prejudices of readers.

Finally, readers will not accept your argument unless it is logical. Revise carefully to be sure you have avoided **logical fallacies**.

See 3d

4c   Organizing an Argumentative Essay

In its simplest form, an argument consists of a thesis statement and supporting evidence. However, argumentative essays frequently contain additional elements calculated to win audience approval and to overcome potential opposition.

ELEMENTS OF AN ARGUMENTATIVE ESSAY

Introduction

The **introduction** of your argumentative essay orients your readers to your subject. Here you can show how your subject concerns your audience, establish common ground with your readers, or explain how your subject has been misunderstood.

See 2e1

Background

In this section, you may present a brief summary of past events, an overview of others' opinions on the issue, definitions of key terms, or a review of basic facts.

Thesis Statement

Your **thesis statement** can appear anywhere in your argumentative essay. In many cases, you state your thesis in your introduction. However, in highly controversial arguments—those to which your audience might react negatively—you may postpone stating your thesis until later in your essay, when you have prepared readers to accept it.

See 1c2

Arguments in Support of Your Thesis

Here you present your points and the evidence to support them. Most often, you begin with your weakest argument and work up to your strongest. If all your arguments are equally strong, you might

continued on the following page

---

continued from the previous page

begin with ideas with which your readers are familiar (and therefore likely to accept) and then move on to relatively unfamiliar ideas.

Refutation of Opposing Arguments

If the opposing arguments are relatively weak, refute them after you have made your case. However, if the opposing arguments are strong, you may want to concede their strengths and then refute them before you present your own points.

Conclusion

Most often, the **conclusion** restates the major arguments in support of your thesis. Your conclusion can also summarize key points, restate your thesis, reinforce the weaknesses of opposing arguments, or underscore the logic of your position. Many writers like to end their arguments with a strong last line, such as a quotation or a statement that sums up the argument.

CLOSE UP — USING TRANSITIONS WITH ARGUMENTATIVE ESSAYS

Argumentative essays should include transitional words and phrases to indicate which paragraphs are arguments in support of the thesis (*because, for example, given*); which are refutations of opposing positions (*although, certainly, granted, of course*); and which are conclusions (*in conclusion, therefore, in summary*). These transitional words and phrases send important signals that help readers follow the progression of the argument.

4d Writing an Argumentative Essay

The following essay includes many of the elements discussed above. The student writer was asked to write an argumentative essay, drawing her supporting evidence from her own knowledge of the subject as well as from other sources.

Samantha Masterton   Masterton 1

Professor Wade

English 102

15 March 2000

The Returning Student:

Older Is Definitely Better

Introduction After graduating from high school, young people must decide what they want to do with the rest of their lives. Many graduates (often without much thought) decide to continue their education uninterrupted, and they go on to college. This group of teenagers makes up what many see as the typical first-year college student. Recently, however, this stereotype has been challenged by an influx of older students into American colleges and universities. Not only do these students make a valuable contribution to the schools they attend, but they also present an alternative to young people who go to college simply because it is the thing to do. A few years off between high school and college can give many--perhaps most-- students the life experience they need to appreciate the value Thesis statement of higher education.

Background The college experience of an eighteen-year-old is quite different from that of an older student. The typical teenager is often concerned with things other than cracking books--going to parties, dating, and testing personal limits, for example. Although the maturation process from teenager to adult is something we must all go through, college is not necessarily the appropriate place for this to occur. My experience as an adult enrolled in a university has convinced me that many students would benefit from delaying entry into college. I almost never see older students cutting lectures or not studying. Most have saved for tuition and want to get their money's worth, just as I do. Many are also balancing the demands of home and work to attend classes, so they know how important it is to do well.

Argument in support of thesis

Generally, young people just out of high school have not been challenged by real-world situations that include meeting deadlines and setting priorities. Younger college students often find themselves hopelessly behind or scrambling at the last minute simply because they have not learned how to budget their time. Although success in college depends on the ability to set realistic goals and organize time and materials, college itself does little to help students develop these skills. On the contrary, the workplace--where reward and punishment are usually immediate and tangible--is the best place to learn such lessons. Working teaches the basics that college takes for granted: the value of punctuality and attendance, the importance of respect for superiors and colleagues, and the need for establishing priorities and meeting deadlines.

Argument in support of thesis

The adult student who has gained experience in the workplace has advantages over the teenaged freshman. In general, the older student enrolls in college with a definite course of study in mind. As Laura Mansnerus observes in her article "A Milieu Apart," for the older student, "college is no longer a stage of life but a place to do work" (17). For the adult student, then, college becomes an extension of work rather than a place to discover what work will be. This greater sense of purpose is not lost on college instructors. Dr. Laurin Porter, assistant professor of English at the University of Texas at Arlington, echoes the sentiments of many of her colleagues when she says, "Returning older students, by and large, seem more focused, more sure of their goals, and more highly motivated."

Given their age and greater experience, older students bring more into the classroom than younger students do. Eighteen-year-olds have been driving for only a year or two, have just gotten the right to vote, and usually have not lived on their own. In contrast, the older student has generally had a variety of real-life experiences. Most have worked for several years; many have started families. Their years in the "real world" have helped them to become more focused and more responsible than they were when they graduated from high school. As a result, they are better prepared for college. Thus, they not only bring more into the classroom, but also take more out of it.

Argument in support of thesis

Of course, postponing college for a few years is not for everyone. There are certainly some teenagers who have a

Refutation of opposing argument

Masterton 4

definite sense of purpose and a maturity well beyond their
years, and these individuals might benefit from an early college experience so that they can get a head start on their careers. Charles Woodward, a law librarian, went to college
directly after high school, and for him the experience was positive. "I was serious about learning, and I loved my subject,"
he said. "I felt fortunate that I knew what I wanted from college and from life." For the most part, though, students are
not like Woodward; they graduate from high school without
any clear sense of purpose. For this reason, it makes sense for
most students to stay away from college until they are mature
enough to benefit from the experience.

Refutation of opposing argument   Granted, some older students do have difficulties when
they return to college. Because these students have been out
of school so long, they may have trouble studying and adapt-
ing to the routines of academic life. Some older students may
even feel ill at ease because they are in class with students
who are many years younger than they are and because they
are too busy to participate in extracurricular activities. As I
have seen, though, these problems soon disappear. After a
few weeks, older students get into the swing of things and
adapt to college. They make friends, get used to studying, and
even begin to participate in campus life.

Conclusion   All things considered, higher education is wasted on the
young, who are either too immature or too unfocused to take

Masterton 5

advantage of it. Taking a few years off between high school and college would give younger students the breathing room they need to make the most of a college education. According to a 1991 study, 45 percent of the students enrolled in American colleges in 1987 were twenty-five years of age or older (Aslanian 57) and these numbers, according to Dr. Porter, have since grown. These older students have taken time off to serve in the military, to get a job, or to raise a family. Many have traveled, engaged in informal study, and taken the time to grow up. By the time they get to college they have defined their goals and made a commitment to achieve them. It is clear that postponing college for a few years can result in a better educational experience for both students and teachers. As Dr. Porter says, when the older student brings more life experience into the classroom, "everyone benefits."

Quotation in conclusion sums up argument

Masterton 6

Works Cited

Aslanian, Carol B. "The Changing Face of American

Campuses." USA Today Magazine May 1991: 57–59.

Mansnerus, Laura. "A Milieu Apart." New York Times 4 Aug.

1991, late ed.: A7.

Porter, Laurin. E-Mail to the author. 23 Feb. 2000.

Woodward, Charles B. Personal interview. 25 Feb. 2000.

Works Cited list begins new page

✔ CHECKLIST: WRITING ARGUMENTATIVE ESSAYS

- ✔ Is your topic debatable?
- ✔ Does your essay develop an argumentative thesis?
- ✔ Have you considered the opinions, attitudes, and values of your audience?
- ✔ Have you identified and refuted opposing arguments?
- ✔ Are your arguments logically constructed?
- ✔ Have you supported your assertions with evidence?
- ✔ Have you documented all material that is not your own?
- ✔ Have you established your credibility?
- ✔ Have you been fair?
- ✔ Have you avoided logical fallacies?
- ✔ Have you provided your readers with enough background information?
- ✔ Have you presented your points clearly and organized them logically?
- ✔ Have you written an interesting introduction and a strong conclusion?

PART 3

The Research Process

RESEARCH

❓ FREQUENTLY ASKED QUESTIONS

RESEARCH

PART 3

CHAPTER 5

THE RESEARCH PROCESS

Research is the systematic study and investigation of a topic outside your own experience and knowledge. When you do research, you move from what you know about a topic to what you do not know.

Doing research means more than just reading about other people's ideas; when you undertake a research project, you become involved in a process that requires you to **think critically**, evaluating and interpreting the ideas explored in your sources and formulating ideas of your own that will control your paper's focus. Research is rewarding, but it is also demanding and time consuming. It requires discipline, strategic planning, careful time management, and a constant willingness to rethink ideas and reshape discussions. It is precisely because the research process encourages you to develop these skills that instructors assign research papers.

See Ch. 3

THE RESEARCH PROCESS

Activity	Date Due	Date Completed
Choose a Topic 5a	_____	_____
Map Out a Search Strategy 5b	_____	_____
Do Exploratory Research and Formulate a Research Question 5c	_____	_____
Assemble a Working Bibliography 5d	_____	_____

continued on the following page

General Research Tips/Strategies
  http://www.jtasd.k12.pa.us/highschool/library/LibraryWebQuest
Researchpaper.com
  http://www.researchpaper.com/
Writing Research Papers: A Step-by-Step Procedure
  http://www.jtasd.k12.pa.us/highschool/library/writing_research_paper.htm

continued from the previous page

Activity	Date Due	Date Completed
Do Focused Research and Take Notes 5e	_____	_____
Outline Your Paper 5f1	_____	_____
Draft Your Paper 5f2	_____	_____
Revise Your Paper 5f3	_____	_____

5a   Choosing a Topic

The first step in the research process is finding a topic that you can explore within the boundaries of your assignment. Finding a topic is a process of working from broad to narrow: you begin with a relatively broad subject area (for example, "World War II" or "civil rights") that you then narrow until you zero in on a topic suitable for treatment in a short paper.

✔ CHECKLIST: CHOOSING A RESEARCH TOPIC

✔ **Are you genuinely interested in your research topic?** Remember that you will be deeply involved with the topic you select for weeks—perhaps even for an entire semester. If you lose interest in your topic, you are likely to see your research as a tedious chore rather than as an opportunity to discover new information, new associations, and new insights.

✔ **Is your topic suitable for research?** Topics limited to your personal experience and those based on value judgments are not suitable for research. For example, "The superiority of Freud's work to Jung's" might sound promising, but no amount of research can establish that one person's work is "better" than another's.

✔ **Are the boundaries of your research topic appropriate?** A research topic should be neither too broad nor too narrow.

continued on the following page

Researchpaper.com's "Idea (topic) Directory"
    http://www.researchpaper.com/directory.html
Steps in the Research Process (Ohiolink)
    http://karn.ohiolink.edu/~sg-ysu/process.html

"Julius and Ethel Rosenberg: Atomic Spies or FBI Scapegoats?" is far too broad a topic for a 10-page—or even a 100-page—treatment, and "One piece of evidence that played a decisive role in establishing the Rosenbergs' guilt" would probably be too narrow for a 10-page research paper. But how one newspaper reported the Rosenbergs' espionage trial or how a particular group of people (government employees, peace activists, or college students, for example) reacted at the time to the couple's 1953 execution might work well.

✔ **Can your topic be researched in a library to which you have access?** For instance, the library of an engineering or business school may not have a large collection of books of literary criticism; the library of a small liberal arts college may not have extensive resources for researching technical or medical topics. (Of course, if you have access to the Internet or to specialized databases, your options are greatly increased.)

5b   Mapping Out a Search Strategy

Once you have found a topic to write about, plan your search strategy. A **search strategy,** a systematic process of locating and evaluating source material, reflects the way research works: you begin by doing <u>exploratory research</u>, looking at general reference works that give you a broad overview of your topic, and progress to <u>focused research</u>, consulting more specialized reference works as well as books and articles on your topic.

See 5c, 6a

See 5e, 6b

Not so long ago, searching for source material meant spending long hours in the library flipping through card catalogs, examining heavy reference volumes, and hunting for books in the stacks. Technology, however, has dramatically changed the way research is conducted. For example, library card catalogs have largely given way to computerized or <u>online catalogs</u> that can be searched at terminals located throughout the library or, in some cases, at home on a personal computer. In addition, many reference works—indexes, bibliographies, encyclopedias, and other works that serve as starting points for research—have been "translated" into

See 6a1

Research and Writing, Step-by-Step (Internet Public Library)
    http://www.ipl.org/teen/aplus/stepfirst.htm
The Research Rubric
    http://www.bham.wednet.edu/mod8cyl.htm

computerized or electronic formats. The "wiring" of school and community libraries means that today, students and professionals engaged in research find themselves spending a great deal of time in front of a computer, particularly during the exploratory stage of the research process. Note, however, that although the way in which research materials are located and accessed has changed, the research process itself has not. Whether you are working with **print sources** (books, journals, magazines) or **electronic**

See
6a4

SEARCH STRATEGY: THE PROCESS OF RESEARCH

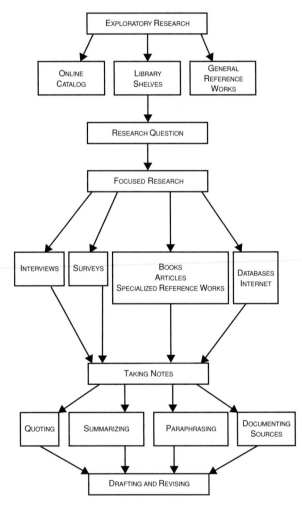

resources (online catalogs, databases, the Internet), in the library or at your home computer, you need to follow the same systematic process.

The diagram on page 82 is a general model of a search strategy that you can customize (perhaps with the help of your instructor or reference librarian) so that it suits the research project you are working on.

5c Doing Exploratory Research and Formulating a Research Question

Doing **exploratory research**—for example, looking through the online catalog, the library shelves, or general reference works—helps you get an overview of your topic and an understanding of its possibilities. As you do exploratory research, you familiarize yourself with key terms, people, and events related to your topic. Your goal is to formulate a **research question,** the question you want your research paper to answer. A research question helps you to decide which sources to seek out, which to examine first, which to examine in depth, and which to skip entirely. The answer to your research question will be your paper's **thesis statement**.

See
1c
2-5

5d Assembling a Working Bibliography

As soon as you begin the process of exploratory research, begin assembling a **working bibliography** for your paper. As you examine each source, record *complete* bibliographic information as well as a brief evaluation on

CLOSE
UP   **ASSEMBLING A WORKING BIBLIOGRAPHY**

As you record bibliographic information for your sources, include the following information:

Book Author(s); title (underlined or in italics); call number (for future reference); city of publication; publisher; date of publication; brief evaluation

continued on the following page

continued from the previous page

> **Article** Author(s); title of article (in quotation marks); title of journal (underlined or in italics); volume number; date; inclusive page numbers; electronic address (if applicable); brief evaluation

See 9a2

an index card or in a computer file. Continue to add this kind of information for each source as you move from exploratory to focused research. This working bibliography will be the basis for your **Works Cited list**, the complete, detailed listing of all the books, articles, and other materials that you have cited in your paper.

Also keep records of interviews (including telephone and e-mail interviews), meetings, lectures, films, and other nonprint sources of information, as well as of electronic sources. For each source, include not only basic identifying details—such as the date of an interview, the call number of a library book, the address (URL) of an Internet source, or the author of an article accessed from a database—but also a brief evaluation. You might also include comments about the kind of information the source contains, the amount of information offered, its relevance to your topic, and its limitations—whether it is biased or outdated, for instance.

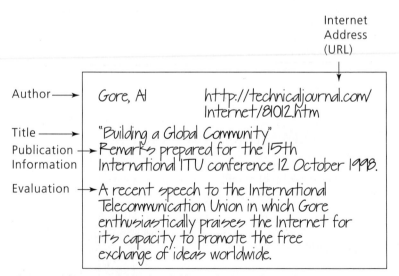

Figure 1   Information for working bibliography (on index card)

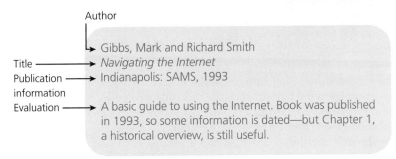

Author

Gibbs, Mark and Richard Smith

Title → *Navigating the Internet*

Publication → Indianapolis: SAMS, 1993
information

Evaluation → A basic guide to using the Internet. Book was published
in 1993, so some information is dated—but Chapter 1,
a historical overview, is still useful.

Figure 2 *Information for working bibliography (in computer file)*

As you go about collecting sources and building your working bibliography, be careful to monitor the quality and relevance of all the materials you examine. For more on evaluating sources, see 6c; for specific guidelines on evaluating Internet sources, see 7c.

5e Doing Focused Research and Taking Notes

During exploratory research, you build your basic knowledge of your topic as you work toward formulating a research question. During **focused research,** keep this research question in mind as you approach your source material with more narrowly focused objectives. Now you fill in the specific details—facts, examples, statistics, definitions, quotations—you will need to support your ideas. You do this by consulting **specialized reference works** as well as books and journal articles written by experts on your topic. You may also have to conduct an **interview** or a **survey**. The nature, depth, and scope of your focused research will depend on your assignment and your topic as well as on more practical matters, such as the amount of time you have and the availability of research materials.

See
6b1

See
6d
1-2

As you do focused research, take notes. Your goal is flexibility: you want to be able to arrange and rearrange information easily and efficiently. If you take notes by hand, you may decide to use the time-tested system of arranging your notes on index cards. If you do, be sure to use a separate index card for each piece of information rather than jotting comments down in the margins of photocopied pages or running several ideas together on a single card. (You may also take notes on your computer.)

TAKING NOTES

Note-taking software can make it easy for you to record and organize information, allowing you to enter notes (quotations, summaries, paraphrases, or your own comments), pictures, or tables; to sort and categorize your material; and even to print out the information in order on computerized note cards. If you do not have access to such software, type each note under an appropriate heading on a separate page. When you finish taking notes and print out the individual pages, you will find that keeping notes distinct from one another makes it easy for you to sort notes into categories as well as to add and delete bits of information and to experiment with different sequences of ideas.

Each piece of information you record—in the form of **summary, paraphrase,** or **quotation**—should be accompanied by a short descriptive heading that indicates its relevance to some aspect of your topic. You

Source

Short ——→
heading

Unequal access to Internet   Belluck

Note ——→
(summary,
paraphrase,
or
quotation)

According to Belluck, a recent Commerce Dept. survey indicates that African American and Hispanic families are "less than half as likely as white families to have access to the Internet from home, work, or school."

Your ——→
comments
(opinions,
reactions,
purpose of
note, con-
nections
with other
sources, etc.)

[This inequality suggests Gore's optimism may not be justified.]

Figure 3 Notes (on note card)

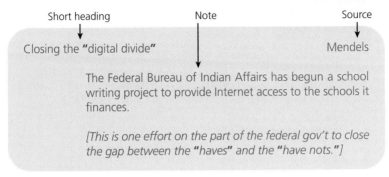

Figure 4 Notes (in computer file)

should also include a brief comment that makes clear your rationale for recording the information and identifies what you think it will add to your paper—and, of course, always include enough information to enable you to identify its source. For example, *Gibbs and Smith 5* would be enough to send you back to your working bibliography card or file, where you can find the complete documentation for Mark Gibbs and Richard Smith's *Navigating the Internet*. (If you use more than one source by the same author, you need a more complete reference.)

✔ CHECKLIST: TAKING NOTES

- ✔ **Identify the source of each piece of information clearly and completely.** Even if the source is sitting on your bookshelf or stored in your computer's hard drive, include full source information with each note.
- ✔ **Include everything now that you will need later** to understand your note—names, dates, places, connections with other notes—and to remember why you recorded it.
- ✔ **Distinguish quotations from paraphrases and summaries and your own ideas from those of your sources.** If you copy a source's words, place them in quotation marks. (If you take notes by hand, circle the quotation marks; if you type your notes, put the quotation marks in boldface.) If you write down your own ideas, enclose them in brackets—and, if you are taking notes on a computer, italicize them as well.
- ✔ **Put an author's comments into your own words whenever possible,** summarizing and paraphrasing material as well as

continued on the following page

continued from the previous page

adding your own observations and analysis. Not only will this strategy save you time later on, but it will also help you understand your sources and evaluate their usefulness now, when you still have time to find additional sources to substitute for if necessary.

✔ If you do record an author's comments, be sure to copy them accurately, using the exact words, spelling, punctuation marks, and capitalization.

 MANAGING SOURCES

Making informed choices early in the research process will save you a lot of time in the long run, so don't collect sources first and assess their usefulness later. Before you check a book out of the library, photocopy a journal article, or download a block of text, take the time to consider its relevance to your topic. Resist the temptation to check out every book that mentions your subject, photocopy page after page of perhaps only marginally useful articles, or download material from every electronic source to which you have access. After all, you will eventually have to read all these sources and take detailed notes on them. If you have too many sources, you will be overwhelmed, unable to remember why a particular idea or a certain article seemed important.

(1) Summarizing Sources

A **summary** is a brief restatement in your own words of the main idea of a passage or article. When you write a summary, you condense the author's ideas into a few concise sentences. A summary is always much shorter than the original because it omits the examples, asides, analogies, and rhetorical strategies that writers use to add emphasis and interest.

Summarizing (USCA)
　　http://www.usca.sc.edu/uscaonlinewr/hos/sum.html#summarizing

When you summarize, use your own words, not the exact language or phrasing of your source. If you think it is necessary to reproduce a distinctive word or phrase, place it in quotation marks; otherwise, you will be committing **plagiarism**. Finally, remember that your summary should accurately represent the author's ideas and should include only the ideas of your source, not your own interpretations or opinions.

See 8b

Original Source

Today, the First Amendment faces challenges from groups who seek to limit expressions of racism and bigotry. A growing number of legislatures have passed rules against "hate speech"—[speech] that is offensive on the basis of race, ethnicity, gender, or sexual orientation. The rules are intended to promote respect for all people and protect the targets of hurtful words, gestures, or actions.

Legal experts fear these rules may wind up diminishing the rights of all citizens. "The bedrock principle [of our society] is that government may never suppress free speech simply because it goes against what the community would like to hear," says Nadine Strossen, president of the American Civil Liberties Union and professor of constitutional law at New York University Law School. In recent years, for example, the courts have upheld the right of neo-Nazis to march in Jewish neighborhoods; protected cross-burning as a form of free expression; and allowed protesters to burn the American flag. The offensive, ugly, distasteful, or repugnant nature of expression is not reason enough to ban it, courts have said.

But advocates of limits on hate speech note that certain kinds of expression fall outside of First Amendment protection. Courts have ruled that "fighting words"—words intended to provoke immediate violence—or speech that creates a clear and present danger are not protected forms of expression. As the classic argument goes, freedom of speech does not give you the right to yell "Fire!" in a crowded theater.

Sudo, Phil. "Freedom of Hate Speech?"
Scholastic Update 124.14 (1992): 17–20.

Summary

The right to freedom of speech, guaranteed by the First Amendment, is becoming more difficult to defend. Some people think stronger laws against the use of "hate speech" weaken the First Amendment, but those who support these laws argue that some kinds of speech remain exempt from this protection (Sudo 17).

✔ CHECKLIST: SUMMARIZING A SOURCE

✔ Reread your source until you understand it.
✔ Write a one-sentence restatement of the main idea.
✔ Write your summary, using the one-sentence restatement as your topic sentence. Use your own words and phrasing, not those of your source. Include quotation marks where necessary.
✔ Add appropriate documentation.

(2) Paraphrasing Sources

A summary conveys just the essence of a source; a **paraphrase** gives a *detailed* restatement of all a source's important ideas. It not only indicates the source's main points, but it also reflects its order, tone, and emphasis. Consequently, a paraphrase can sometimes be as long as the source itself. Make certain that you use your own words in paraphrasing, except when you want to quote to give readers a sense of the original. If you do include quotations, circle the quotation marks in your notes so that you will not forget them later. Try not to look at the source as you paraphrase—use language and syntax that come naturally to you, and avoid duplicating the wording or sentence structure of the original. Whenever possible, use synonyms that accurately convey the meaning of the original word or phrase. If you cannot think of a synonym for an important term, quote—and remember to document all direct quotations from your source as well as the entire paraphrase. Finally, be sure that your paraphrase reflects only the ideas of your source—not your analysis or interpretation of those ideas.

Compare the following paraphrase with the summary of the same source on page 89.

Paraphrase

Many groups want to limit the right of free speech guaranteed by the First Amendment to the Constitution. They believe this is necessary to protect certain groups of people from "hate speech." Women, people of color, and gay men and lesbians, for example, may find that hate speech is used to intimidate them. Legal scholars are afraid that even though the rules against hate speech are well intentioned, they undermine our freedom of speech. As Nadine Strossen, president of the American Civil Liberties Union, says, "The bedrock principle [of our society] is that government may never suppress free speech simply because it goes against what the community would like to hear" (Sudo 17). People who support speech codes point out, however, that certain types of speech are not protected by the First Amendment—for example, words that create a "clear and present danger" or that would lead directly to violence (Sudo 17).

✔ CHECKLIST: PARAPHRASING A SOURCE

✔ Reread your source until you understand it.
✔ Outline your source if necessary.
✔ Write your paraphrase, following the order, tone, and emphasis of the original and making sure that you do not use the words or phrasing of the original without enclosing the borrowed material within quotation marks.
✔ Add appropriate documentation.

(3) Quoting Sources

When you **quote,** you copy an author's remarks exactly as they appear in a source, word for word and punctuation mark for punctuation mark, enclosing the borrowed words in quotation marks. As a rule, do not quote extensively in a research paper. The use of numerous quotations interrupts the flow of your discussion and gives readers the impression that your paper is just an unassimilated collection of other people's ideas.

 WHEN TO QUOTE

- Quote when a source's wording or phrasing is so distinctive that a summary or paraphrase would diminish its impact.
- Quote when a source's words—particularly those of a recognized expert on your subject—will lend authority to your presentation.
- Quote when an author's words are so concise that paraphrasing would create a long, clumsy, or incoherent phrase or would change the meaning of the original.
- Quote when you expect to disagree with a source. Using a source's exact words helps convince readers you are being fair.

91

5f Outlining, Drafting, and Revising

See
1c3

After you have finished your focused research and note taking, go on to develop a **thesis**, a carefully worded statement that expresses a conclusion your research can support.

(1) Outlining

See
1c6

Once you have a thesis, you may prepare a **formal outline**. Although not necessary for short essays, formal outlines are almost essential for longer or more complex writing projects. A formal outline indicates not only the order in which you will present your ideas but also the relationship of main ideas to supporting details.

Formal outlines conform to specific conventions of structure, content, and style. (An example of a formal outline appears at the beginning of the sample research paper on page 167.) If you follow the conventions of outlining carefully, your formal outline can help you plan a paper in which you cover all relevant ideas in an effective order, with appropriate emphasis, within a logical system of subordination.

✔ CHECKLIST: PREPARING A FORMAL OUTLINE

✔ Make sure that each note expresses only one general idea. If this is not the case, recopy any unrelated information, creating a separate note.

✔ Check that the heading for each note specifically characterizes the information it includes. If it does not, change the heading.

✔ Sort your notes by their headings, keeping a miscellaneous pile for notes that do not seem to fit under any heading.

✔ Check your categories for balance. If most of your notes fall into one or two categories, rewrite some of your headings to create narrower, more focused categories. If you have only one or two notes in a category, you'll need to do additional research or treat that topic only briefly, perhaps dropping it entirely.

✔ Organize the individual notes within each group, adding more specific subheads to your headings and arranging ideas in an order that highlights the most important points and subordinates lesser ones. Set aside any notes that do not fit into your emerging scheme.

continued on the following page

✔ Decide on a logical order in which to discuss your paper's major points.
✔ Write out your formal outline with divisions and subdivisions corresponding to your headings.
✔ Review your completed outline to determine whether you have placed too much emphasis on a relatively unimportant idea, whether ideas are illogically placed, or whether overlapping discussions turn up at different points.

OUTLINING

Before you begin writing, create a separate file for each major section of your outline. Then, copy your notes into these files in the order in which you intend to use them. You can print out each file as you need it and use it for a guide as you write.

Remember that the outline you construct at this stage is only a guide for you to follow as you draft your paper; it is likely to change as you write and revise. The final outline, written after your paper is complete, will serve as a guide for your readers.

(2) Drafting

When you are ready to write your **rough draft**, arrange your notes in the order in which you intend to use them. Follow your outline as you write, using your notes as you need them.

See 1d1

To make it easy for you to revise later on, triple-space your draft. Be careful to copy your source information fully and accurately on this and every subsequent draft, placing the documentation as close as possible to the material it identifies.

Remember that the purpose of the first draft is to get ideas down on paper so that you can react to them. *Expect* to revise, so postpone making precise word choices and refining style. As you draft, jot down questions to yourself and note points that need further clarification; leave space for material you plan to add; and bracket phrases or whole sections that you think you may later decide to move or delete.

DRAFTING

You can use a split screen or multiple windows to view your notes as you draft your paper. You can also copy the material that you need from your notes, and then insert it into the text of your paper. (As you copy, be especially careful that you do not unintentionally commit plagiarism.)

(3) Revising

A good way to start revising is to check to see that your thesis statement still accurately expresses your paper's central focus. Make an outline of your draft, and compare it with the outline you made before you began the draft. If you find significant differences, you will have to revise your thesis statement or rewrite sections of your paper.

See 1d2

When reconsidering your draft, use the **revision strategies** that apply to any paper. In addition, ask yourself the following questions that apply specifically to research papers.

✔ CHECKLIST: REVISING A RESEARCH PAPER

✔ Should you do more research to find support for certain points?
✔ Do you need to reorder the major sections of your paper?
✔ Should you rearrange the order in which you present your points within those sections?
✔ Do you need to add section headings? transitional paragraphs?

See 8a

✔ Have you **integrated your notes** smoothly into your paper?
✔ Do you introduce source material with running acknowledgments?
✔ Are quotations blended with paraphrase, summary, and your own observations and reactions?

See 8b

✔ Have you avoided **plagiarism** by carefully documenting all borrowed ideas?
✔ Have you analyzed and interpreted the ideas of others rather than simply stringing those ideas together?
✔ Do your own ideas—not those of your sources—define the focus of your discussion?

REVISING

Copy the file containing your working bibliography, and insert it at the end of your paper. Delete any irrelevant entries, and use the bibliographic information to help you compile your Works Cited list. (Make sure that the format of the entries on your Works Cited list conforms to the documentation style you are using.)

You will probably take your paper through several drafts, changing different parts of it each time or working on one part over and over again. After revising each draft thoroughly, print out a corrected version and make additional corrections on that draft before typing the next version.

NOTE: A variety of different Web sites may be useful to you as you go through the research process. Some of these are mentioned in this chapter; for a more complete list see *The Brief Holt Handbook* Web Site http://www.harcourtcollege.com/english/comp/holt/

CHAPTER 6

LIBRARY RESEARCH

6a Doing Exploratory Research

Even though the nature of research has changed and the research options available to you have increased, the traditional place to begin your paper remains the same—the library. Modern college libraries offer you access to many of the print and electronic resources that you will need to begin your research. For example, you can begin your exploratory research in the library by consulting encyclopedias, dictionaries, and bibliographies; it is also the place to find the many specialized resources you will use during focused research —for example, periodical indexes, articles, and books. Your visit to the library will be most successful, however, if you have a clear idea of where to begin once you get there.

During exploratory research, your goal is to find a **research question** for your paper. You begin this process by searching your library's *online catalog* for information about your topic.

(1) Using Online Catalogs

Most college and university libraries—and a growing number of regional and community libraries—have abandoned print cataloging systems in favor of **online catalogs**—computer databases that list all the books, articles, and other materials held by the library.

You access an online catalog by using one of the computer terminals located throughout the library and typing in certain words or phrases— *search terms* or *options*—that enable you to find the information you need. If you have never used an online catalog, ask your reference librarian for help.

Web Resources by Paper Topic (St. Ambrose University, IA)
   http://www.sau.edu/CWIS/Internet/Wild/Hot/hotindex.htm

When you search the online catalog for information about your topic, you may conduct either a *keyword search* or a *subject search*. (Later on in the research process, when you know more precisely what you are looking for, you can search for a particular book by entering its title or author.)

Conducting a Keyword Search When you carry out a **keyword search,** you enter into the computer a term or terms associated with your topic. The computer then retrieves articles that contain those words in their bibliographic citations or abstracts. The more precise your search terms are, the more specific and useful the information you will retrieve. (Combining keywords with AND, OR, and NOT allows you to narrow or broaden your search. This technique is called conducting a **Boolean search**.)

See
7c3

✔ CHECKLIST: KEYWORD DOS AND DON'TS

When conducting a keyword search, remember the following hints:

✔ Use precise, specific keywords to differentiate your topic from similar topics.

✔ Enter both singular and plural keywords when appropriate—*the printing press* and *printing presses,* for example.

✔ Enter both abbreviations and their full-word equivalents (for example, *U.S.* and *United States*).

✔ Remember to try variant spellings (for example, *color* and *colour*).

✔ Don't use too long a string of keywords. You will retrieve large amounts of irrelevant material.

Conducting a Subject Search When you carry out a **subject search,** you enter specific subject headings into the computer. The subject categories in a library are most often arranged according to headings established in the five-volume manual, *The Library of Congress Subject Headings,* sometimes referred to as the "big red books," which are held at the reference desk of your library. Although it may be possible to guess at a subject heading, your search will be more successful if you consult these volumes to help you identify the exact words you need.

**KEYWORD SEARCHING VS.
SUBJECT SEARCHING**

Keyword Searching

- Searches many fields

- Any significant word or
  phrase can be used

- Retrieves large number of
  items
- May retrieve many
  irrelevant items

Subject Searching

- Searches only a specific
  field
- Only the specific words
  listed in the *Library of
  Congress Subject Headings*
  can be used
- Retrieves small number of
  items
- Retrieves few irrelevant
  items

USING LIBRARY WEB PAGES

Many college and university libraries have Web pages that enable users to access their online catalogs from a dorm room or
from any computer connected to the Internet. Ask at your library
for the appropriate Web address.

You can also browse the online catalogs of major research libraries,
such as the Library of Congress, the New York Public Library, or
the list of academic libraries maintained by the University of
California. Although you will not be able to access subscription-
only databases or indexes, searching a research library's catalog
can give you an overview of the sources available for your topic
and the bibliographic information you can use to request material via **interlibrary loan**.

See
6b4

(2) Browsing

Browsing through the stacks in your library can help you narrow your topic to a research question. Knowing how libraries arrange their books will enable you to find the area in which you are interested.

CLOSE UP — LIBRARY MATERIALS

The Circulating Collection

- Books (hardback and paperback)—novels, how-to, biographies, and so on
- Periodicals—newspapers, magazines, and journals in hard copy and online indexes
- CDs, audiotapes, and videotapes—music, films, speeches, and so on
- Large-print books and books-on-tape

The Reference Collection

- Dictionaries, encyclopedias, handbooks, and atlases provide facts and background information
- Bibliographies and indexes tell you what source material is available for the subject you are researching
- Special subject guides help you find detailed information quickly

---

The Dewey Decimal Classification System   Some community libraries as well as some smaller college libraries arrange books according to the **Dewey Decimal Classification System** (DDC). This organizational system arranges all holdings in the library into ten broad areas and then assigns them numbers.

Library of Congress Searchable Catalog
   http://lcweb.loc.gov/catalog/
Academic Libraries—U.S. (searchable)
   http://sunsite.berkeley.edu/Libweb/usa-acad.html
Public Libraries—U.S.
   http://www.capecod.net/epl/public.libraries.html

DEWEY DECIMAL SUBJECT NUMBERS

000–099	General knowledge
100–199	Philosophy
200–299	Religion
300–399	Social sciences
400–499	Language
500–599	Pure sciences
600–699	Technology (applied sciences)
700–799	Fine arts
800–899	Literature
900–999	History

Thus, if you are working on a science-related topic, browsing through the books on the 500 shelves may help you find useful information about your topic.

The Library of Congress Classification System   Another classification system is the **Library of Congress Classification System** (LC). Because the Library of Congress in Washington, D.C., contains almost every book ever published in the United States, it uses a flexible system that can accommodate an ever-growing base of knowledge. Most large public libraries and large college and university libraries now use this cataloging system.

LIBRARY OF CONGRESS CLASSIFICATION SYSTEM

A	General works
B	Philosophy, psychology, and religion
C–F	History
G	Geography, anthropology, recreation
H	Social science
J	Political science

continued on the following page

K	Law
L	Education
M	Music
N	Fine arts
P	Language and literature
Q	Science
R	Medicine
S	Agriculture
T	Technology
U	Military science
V	Naval science
Z	Bibliography and library sciences

Once you know the classification system your library uses, you can browse through its shelves with a better sense of what materials are there and where they are located.

(3) Consulting General Reference Works

General reference works, which provide a broad overview of a particular subject, can be helpful when you are exploring possible research topics. You can learn key facts and specific terminology as well as find dates, places, and people. In addition, general reference works often include bibliographies that you can use later on when you do focused research. The following kinds of reference works, many of which are available in electronic form as well as print, are useful for exploratory research.

CLOSE UP   GENERAL REFERENCE WORKS

- **General encyclopedias,** such as *Encyclopedia Americana, Collier's Encyclopedia,* and *The New Encyclopaedia Britannica*
- **General bibliographies,** such as *Books in Print;* its *Subject Guide,* which indexes books according to subject area; and *The Bibliographic Index,* a tool for locating bibliographies

continued on the following page

continued from the previous page

- **Specialized encyclopedias, dictionaries,** and **bibliographies,** many of which are listed in Robert Balay's *Guide to Reference Books,* available at the reference desk in most libraries.
- **General biographical references,** such as *Who's Who in America, The Dictionary of American Biography,* and *Webster's Biographical Dictionary*

❓ (4) Using Electronic Resources

Today's libraries have electronic resources that enable you to find much more current information than that found in print sources. Computer terminals and printers, located throughout the library, enable you to access this material.

Online databases   **Online databases** offer citations of books; of articles in journals; magazines, and newspapers, and of reports. Once you have searched the databases and found the right information, you can print out the bibliographic citations, abstracts, and sometimes even full text. In some cases, you may be able to download the information onto one of your own disks.

Different libraries offer different databases, and the number of available services can be overwhelming. For example, Lexis focuses on law and Nexis focuses on business. Your library may also offer online services that enable you to access a large number of databases. For example, DIALOG contains ERIC (education), PsychINFO (psychology), the *MLA International Bibliography* (literature), NewsBank (periodicals), and the Government Printing Office Monthly Catalog.

Online Periodical Indexes   **Online periodical indexes** list articles that are available in general interest magazines such as *Time, Newsweek, National Geographic,* or *Harper's.* The most common is the periodical index *Readers' Guide to Periodical Literature,* which you have probably used before. (Be aware that because the *Readers' Guide* indexes only periodicals aimed at a popular audience, it may not be appropriate for your research. Remember, however, that although you may not be able to use articles from this index in your research paper, you can use them to help gather background information about your topic.) Other general indexes include the *Magazine Index,* the *New York Times Index,* and *InfoTrac.*

Date   Volume   Number   Page

Title: A year of Web pages for every class. (UCLA policy reviewed)

Periodical: The Chronicle of Higher Education, May 15, 1998 v44 n36 pA29.

Author: Jeffrey R. Young

Abstract: The University of California at Los Angeles debates the use of Web pages for classroom use, unwilling to force instructors to offer online course descriptions and discussions with students. Some administrators and students argue Web pages are not worth the money they cost while others support the "Instructional Enhancement Initiative" which strives to intertwine technology and university life.

Subjects: Internet - Usage
Universities and colleges - Innovations

Features: photograph; illustration

Figure 1 Database Printout

CD-ROMs   Many of the databases available online are also available on CD-ROM. In some cases, libraries subscribe to a CD-ROM service or database the same way they do to a printed index or journal and receive updates periodically. In other cases, reference books available in print are also published on CD-ROMs—for example, *The Oxford English Dictionary* and *The Encyclopaedia Britannica.* Many libraries offer individual workstations where CD-ROMs can be loaded and the information can be viewed and printed out.

```
TI:  Curfews and delinquency in major american cities
AU:  Ruefle, -William; Reynolds, -Kenneth-Mike
SO:  Crime-and-Delinquency.  V.41 July 95 p. 347-63
PY:  1995
AN:  95035204
```
Figure 2 CD-ROM Database Printout

CLOSE UP — ONLINE DATABASES VS. CD-ROMS

Online Database	*CD-ROM*
• Frequently updated	• Infrequently updated
• Great number of specialized databases available	• Only as many databases as library owns
• Selected information can be printed out	• Selected information can be printed out
• Low cost to library (some libraries may charge users a fee)	• Each CD-ROM is expensive, and its cost can be prohibitive to libraries with smaller budgets
• Restrictions may apply for number of simultaneous users	• Use is only restricted by number of workstations and CD-ROMS

6b   Doing Focused Research

See 5c

See 5e

Once you have completed your exploratory research and formulated your **research question**, it is time to move to focused research. During **focused research**, you examine the specialized reference works, books, and articles devoted specifically to your topic. You may also need to make use of the special services that many college libraries provide.

WEB RESOURCES FOR FOCUSED RESEARCH

If you have access to the Internet, you can use the following library Web sites to find resources for your focused research:

General Reference Resources (Carnegie-Mellon U.)
http://eserver.org/reference/

continued on the following page

How to Find Articles (U. of Toronto)
http://library.scar.utoronto.ca/Bladen_Library/Research101/
findart.htm

Finding Books (U. of Dayton Libraries—some restrictions)
http://www.udayton.edu/~library/daynet

Internet Public Library—Newspapers
http://aristotle.ipl.org/cgi-bin/reading/news.out.p1

Internet Public Library—Magazines
http://aristotle.ipl.org/reading/serials/

Primary vs. Secondary Sources (U. of Toronto)
http://library.scar.utoronto.ca/Bladen_Library/Research101/
primary.htm

Library Catalogs—Terminology
http://www.nucat.library.nwu.edu

Library Catalogs—Dewey Decimal System
http://www.oclc.org/fp/

(1) Consulting Specialized Reference Works

During your exploratory research, you use general reference works to help you narrow your topic and formulate your research question. Now you can access specialized works to find facts, examples, statistics, definitions, and quotations. The reference works most useful for focused research are unabridged dictionaries, such as the *Oxford English Dictionary;* special dictionaries on topics such as usage, synonyms, slang and idioms, etymologies, and foreign terms; yearbooks and almanacs, such as *Facts on File* and *Statistical Abstract of the United States;* atlases; and quotation books, such as *Bartlett's Familiar Quotations.* Many of these are available in both print and electronic form.

(2) Consulting Books

The online catalog gives you the information you need—specifically, the call numbers—for locating specific titles. A **call number** is like a book's address in the library: it tells you exactly where to find the book you are looking for.

The Dewey Decimal Classification System call number and the Library of Congress Classification System call number, which appear in the catalog and on the book's spine, both work the same way: they start with the book's broad classification numbers and then further divide these numbers for accuracy. Books are arranged alphabetically within each classification by the first letters of the author's last name.

CLOSE UP   **EXAMPLE OF A DDC CALL NUMBER**

Broad knowledge category:	500	Natural sciences and math
Subcategory:	520	Astronomy and allied sciences
Specialized topic:	523	Specific celestial bodies
Decimal points further specialize:	523.3	Moon

The library arranges all books with call number 523.3 together, alphabetized by first letters of the authors' last names.

The Library of Congress Classification System is slightly different, but follows the same principle.

(3) Consulting Articles

A **periodical** is a newspaper, magazine, scholarly journal, or other publication that is published at regular intervals (weekly, monthly, or quarterly). Articles in scholarly journals can be the best, most reliable, sources you can find on a subject; they provide current information and are written by experts on the topic. Because these journals focus on a particular subject area, they can provide in-depth analysis.

Periodical indexes list articles from a selected group of magazines, newspapers, or scholarly journals. These indexes may be available in your

Internet Public Library—Newspapers
  http://aristotle.ipl.org/cgi-bin/reading/news.out.pl
Encyclopedia Britannica Online
  http://www.eb.com:180/

library in bound volumes, on microfilm or microfiche, and on CD-ROM; however, many libraries offer them online. These online indexes are updated frequently and provide the most current information available.

There are two basic types of indexes and abstracts: general indexes and specialized indexes. **General indexes** lead you to articles in newspapers and popular magazines. Because these periodicals are aimed at general audiences and assume no expert knowledge, they are most useful during exploratory research. More useful at the focused research stage are **specialized indexes,** which lead you to articles in professional and scholarly journals. Many of the articles listed in such indexes assume expert knowledge, but some are accessible to general readers.

Abstracting services are a type of specialized index. In addition to providing citations for journal articles, abstracting services include **abstracts,** brief summaries of the articles' major points.

CLOSE UP — CHOOSING THE RIGHT INDEX

Choosing the right index for your research saves you time and energy by allowing you to view articles written about your subject. Following is a selection of indexes (available in electronic and in print form) for specific discipline categories:

Category	Description
Readers' Guide to Periodical Literature	General index, all topics
Social Science Index	Political science, psychology, sociology, history, sports
Humanities Index	Music, literature, film, arts
General Science Index	Science, nursing, medicine, health
Business Index	Business
Biology and Agricultural Index	Agriculture, ecology, forestry

General Reference Resources (CMU)
   http://eserver.org/reference/
Selected Web Resources by Academic Subject (Georgetown U.)
   http://gulib.lausun.georgetown.edu/swr/
Internet Public Library—Serials (Magazines)
   http://aristotle.ipl.org/reading/serials/

FREQUENTLY USED ONLINE INDEXES

Index	Description
Dow Jones Interactive	Full text of articles from U.S. newspapers and trade journals
Ebscohost	Database system for thousands of periodical articles
ERIC	Largest index of education-related journal articles and reports in the world
FirstSearch	Abstracts and some full-text files in news and current events
LEXIS-NEXIS	Wide range of full-text local, national, and international publications on law and business
New York Times Index	Article summaries, 1918+
Reuters Business Briefings	Full-text articles from newspapers, newswires, and magazines
SearchBank	General reference and academic topic databases
Uncover	Tables of contents for 14,000 periodicals
Wall Street Journal Index	Article citations, 1955–1992 (continued by Dow Jones Interactive)

Remember to examine your library's print as well as electronic indexes. Many important articles predate the present computer indexes. Check with your librarian if you are unsure where to find these volumes.

(4) Using Special Library Services

As you do focused research, ask your librarian about any of the following special services you plan to use.

(U.S.) Government Information Locator Service
http://www.gils.net/

SPECIAL LIBRARY SERVICES

- **Interlibrary Loans** Your library may be part of a library system that allows loans of books from one location to another. If this is the case, a loan of a book usually takes no more than a day or two. However, be sure to check with your librarian. If the loan takes longer, you may not be able to take advantage of this service unless you initiate the loan early in your research.
- **Special Collections** Your library may house special collections of books, manuscripts, or documents. In addition, churches, ethnic societies, historical trusts, and museums sometimes have material that you cannot find anywhere else.
- **Government Documents** Federal, state, and local governments publish a variety of print and electronic materials, ranging from consumer information to detailed statistical reports. A large university library may have a separate government documents area with its own catalog or index. The *Monthly Catalog of U.S. Government Publications* may be located either there or among the indexes in the reference area.
- **Vertical Files** The vertical files include pamphlets from a variety of organizations and interest groups, newspaper clippings, and other material collected by librarians because of its relevance to the research interests of your college's population.

6c Evaluating Library Sources

Whenever you find information in the library, take the time to determine whether or not the source is reliable. In other words, you have to **evaluate** it—to assess its usefulness and its reliability. One way to do this is to ask your librarian or your instructor for an opinion. Another way is to try to answer the questions listed in the following Checklist.

✔ CHECKLIST: EVALUATING LIBRARY SOURCES

✔ How relevant is your source to your needs?
   How detailed is its treatment of your subject?
   Is your topic a major focus of your source?

continued on the following page

continued from previous page

✔ How current is your source?
 Have recent developments made any parts of your source dated?
 Does your source rely on information from earlier works?

✔ How reliable is your source?

See 4a

 Is your source largely **fact or opinion**? Are its opinions based on fact?

See 4b

 Is the **supporting evidence** accurate? Does the writer present enough evidence to support his or her position? Does the writer select representative examples?
 Does the author of your source reveal any bias?
 How respected is your source?
 Do other scholars mention your source in their work?

6d   Doing Research Outside the Library

(1) Conducting an Interview

Interviews often give you material that you cannot get by any other means—for instance, biographical information, a firsthand account of an event, or the opinions of an expert on a particular subject.

 CONDUCTING AN E-MAIL INTERVIEW

Using e-mail to conduct an interview can save you a great deal of time because your message is transmitted instantly. Before you send an e-mail message, make sure that the person you want to contact is willing to cooperate. If the person agrees to be interviewed, send a short list of specific questions. After you have received the answers, send a message thanking the person for his or her cooperation.

The kinds of questions you ask in an interview depend on the information you are seeking. **Open-ended questions,** designed to elicit general information, allow a respondent great flexibility in answering: *"Do* *you think students today are motivated? Why or why not?"* **Closed-ended questions**—questions intended to elicit specific information—enable you to zero in on a particular aspect of a subject: *"How much money did the government's cost-cutting programs actually save?"*

✔ CHECKLIST: CONDUCTING AN INTERVIEW

- ✔ Always make an appointment.
- ✔ Prepare a list of specific questions tailored to the subject matter and the time limit of your interview.
- ✔ Do background reading about your topic. Be sure that you do not ask for information that you can easily find elsewhere.
- ✔ Have a pen and paper with you. If you want to tape the interview, get the respondent's permission in advance.
- ✔ Allow the person you are interviewing to complete an answer before you ask another question.
- ✔ Take notes, but continue to pay attention as you do so. Occasionally nod or make comments that show you are interested and that encourage the respondent to continue.
- ✔ Pay attention to the reactions of the respondent.
- ✔ Be willing to depart from your prepared list of questions to ask follow-up questions.
- ✔ At the end of the interview, thank the respondent for his or her time and cooperation.
- ✔ Send a brief note of thanks.

(2) Conducting a Survey

If you are examining a contemporary social, psychological, or economic issue—the level of racism on your college campus, for instance—a **survey** of attitudes or opinions could be indispensable. Begin by identifying the group of people you will poll. This group can be a **convenient sample**—for example, people in your chemistry lecture—or a **random sample**—names chosen from a telephone directory, for instance. When you choose a sample, your goal is to designate a population that is *representative*. You must also have enough respondents to convince readers that your sample is *significant*. If you poll ten people in your French class about an issue of college policy, and your university has ten thousand students, you cannot expect your readers to be convinced by your results.

You should also be sure that your questions are worded clearly and specifically designed to elicit the particular information you wish to get. Short-answer or multiple-choice questions, whose responses can be quantified, are much easier to handle than questions that call for paragraph-length answers. Also, be sure that you do not ask so many questions that respondents lose interest and stop answering. Finally, be careful not to ask biased or leading questions.

If your population is your fellow students, you can slip questionnaires under their doors in the residence hall, or you can distribute them in class, if your instructor permits. If your questionnaire is brief, allow respondents a specific amount of time and collect the forms yourself. If filling out forms on the spot will be time consuming, request that responses be returned to you—placed in a box set up in a central location, for instance.

 CONDUCTING AN E-MAIL SURVEY

If the students at your school have computers and e-mail accounts, you can distribute questionnaires electronically. Students can then send their completed questionnaires back to you by e-mail.

Determining exactly what your results tell you is challenging and sometimes unpredictable. For example, even though only 20 percent of your respondents may be fraternity members, the fact that nearly all fraternity members favor restrictions on hazing would be a fairly significant finding.

✔ CHECKLIST: CONDUCTING A SURVEY

- ✔ Determine what you want to know.
- ✔ Select your sample.
- ✔ Design your questions.
- ✔ Type and duplicate the questionnaire.
- ✔ Distribute the questionnaires.
- ✔ Collect the questionnaires.
- ✔ Analyze your responses.
- ✔ Decide how to use the results in your paper.

CHAPTER 7

INTERNET RESEARCH

7a Understanding the Internet

The **Internet** is a vast system of networks that links millions of computers. Because of its size, diversity, and the technology by which it is driven, the Internet enables people from all over the world to share information and communicate with one another quickly and easily.

Furthermore, because it is inexpensive to publish text, pictures, and sound online (via the Internet), companies, government agencies, libraries, and universities are able to make available to the public vast amounts of information: years' worth of newspaper articles, thousands of pages of scientific papers or government studies, images of all the paintings in a museum—even an entire library of literature. All of this information can be accessed and searched for quickly and easily on the Internet.

7b Using the Internet

As you might imagine, the Internet has revolutionized the way scholars and students conduct research. However, as one scientist put it, the Internet is "like a vast library with all the books strewn on the floor." This chapter will help you understand how the various components of the Internet work and how to use the tools available for searching and accessing the Net's wealth of information.

Guide to Internet Research and Resources
   http://www.miracosta.cc.ca.us/home/gfloren/INTNET.HTM
Internet Research FAQ
   http://www.purefiction.com/pages/res1.htm
Internet Tutorials
   http://www.albany.edu/library/internet/index.html
Internet Research Tips
   http://www.albany.edu/library/internet/checklist.html

INFORMATION AVAILABLE ON THE INTERNET

- Pending legislation, stock market quotes, research study findings, and other current information
- Information disseminated by individuals, institutions, and corporations that is not published by traditional media
- Online editions of newspapers, magazines, and books
- Internet-only publications about a wide variety of topics, including the Internet itself
- Library catalogs and periodical indexes that can help you locate print resources
- Reference material, including many encyclopedias and almanacs

(1) E-mail

E-mail (electronic mail) is the most familiar and widely used way to communicate via the Internet. All you need to send and receive e-mail messages is e-mail software and an account with an **Internet Service Provider,** or **ISP** (for example, AOL, Microsoft Network, or ATT World-Net).

NOTE: As a student, you may have access to e-mail through your college or university. Because e-mail is economical and easy to use, it is an excellent way to conduct interviews, request information, or transfer files from one computer to another by attaching them to an e-mail message.

CONDUCTING AN E-MAIL INTERVIEW

Using e-mail to conduct an interview can save you a great deal of time because your message is transmitted instantly. Before you

continued on the following page

Glenn Bacal's Ten Rules for Searching the Internet
http://www.ali-aba.org/aliaba/rules.htm
Starting Points for Internet Research (Purdue)
http://owl.english.purdue.edu/netsearch/research.html

send an e-mail message, make sure that the person you want to contact is willing to cooperate. If the person agrees to be interviewed, send a short list of specific questions. After you have received the answers, send a message thanking the person for his or her cooperation.

(2) Listservs

Another way to use e-mail to get information is to subscribe to a **listserv.** Essentially electronic mailing lists, listservs (moderated or unmoderated) enable you to communicate with a group of people who are interested in a particular topic. In *moderated* listservs, the person who manages or "moderates" the group e-mails information, often in the form of an electronic digest or newsletter, to all subscribers on a weekly or monthly basis; in *unmoderated* listservs, individual subscribers send an e-mail to a main e-mail address and this message is routed to all group members. Anyone who chooses can then continue the discussion or start a new one by sending a message in the same way. With unmoderated listservs, the general rule is "anything goes"; as a result, subscribers sometimes find themselves overwhelmed with information. For this reason, check your listserv messages regularly to make sure they do not accumulate.

NOTE: The material you get from a listserv is only as good as the person or group that is sending it to you. You should evaluate this information just as you would any other source.

 ACCESSING LISTSERVS

To subscribe to a listserv group, you need the electronic address of the group. To find a listserv, visit the Catalist listserv reference resource at http://www.lsoft.com/lists/listref.html. After you have the electronic address, send an e-mail message to the listserv containing the following message:

Subscribe <name of the list> <first name> <last name>

✔ CHECKLIST: OBSERVING NETIQUETTE

Netiquette refers to the guidelines that responsible users of the Internet should follow. When you use the Internet, especially e-mail, keep the following guidelines in mind.

✔ **Don't Shout** All-uppercase letters indicate that a person is SHOUTING. Not only is this immature, but it is also distracting and irritating.

✔ **Watch Your Tone** Make sure you actually send the message you intend to convey. What may sound humorous to you may seem sarcastic or impolite to someone else.

✔ **Be Careful What You Write** Remember, anything you put in writing will be instantly sent to the address or addresses you have designated. Once you hit *Send,* it's often too late to call back your message. For this reason, you should treat an e-mail message or a posting as you would a written letter. Take the time to proofread and to consider carefully what you have written.

✔ **Respect the Privacy of Others** Do not forward or post a message that you have received unless you have permission from the sender to do so.

✔ **Do Not Flame** When you **flame,** you send an insulting electronic message. At best this response is immature; at worst it is disrespectful.

✔ **Make Sure You Use the Correct Electronic Address** Be certain that your message goes to the right person. Nothing is more embarrassing than sending a communication to the wrong address.

✔ **Use Your Computer Facility Ethically and Responsibly** Do not use computers in public labs for personal communications or for entertainment. Not only is this a misuse of the facility, but it also ties up equipment that others may be waiting to use.

(3) Newsgroups

Newsgroups are discussion groups that form part of a network called the **Usenet** system. Currently, thousands of newsgroups enable people from all over the world to carry on discussions about subjects from anthropology to stand-up comedy. These groups function like gigantic bulletin boards where users post messages that others read and respond to.

Newsgroups are organized by topics and subtopics. For example, under the topic *science* are subtopics like *research methods, organic chemistry,* and *numeric analysis.*

Many postings on newsgroups are simply requests for information. As you explore a research topic, you can use newsgroups to get specific information: facts, statistics, and opinions. You can also use newsgroups to get a sense of how others will respond to your ideas before you use them in your paper.

At best, newsgroups provide interesting and current information about a wide variety of subjects. At worst, they supply a daunting amount of information that users have difficulty evaluating. Because the quality of information from newsgroups varies widely, choose your material carefully, remembering to check the reliability of your source the same way you would any information you get from the Internet.

ACCESSING NEWSGROUPS

You need a newsreader program to gain access to newsgroups. Most of the software that enables you to access the World Wide Web (browsers or "clients") now comes with built-in newsreaders.

(4) FTP

FTP (file transfer protocol) is a way of transferring documents at high speed from one computer to another. (Note that because many FTP files are compressed, transferred in a nonreadable form, you must have a program such as *StuffIt Expander* to make them readable.) There are two kinds of FTP, full-service and anonymous. *Full-service* FTP enables you to access a host computer and to transfer documents from it to your own computer if you have a password. *Anonymous* FTP enables anyone (without a password) to access files from thousands of different computers on the Internet.

With FTP, you can get the full text of books and articles as well as pictures. In addition, you can download *freeware,* software in the public domain (which you can use without charge), and *shareware,* software that developers allow people to use for a fee.

ACCESSING FTP FILES

You can use a tool called *Archie* to search the Internet for FTP files. You can also download FTP files through a World Wide Web browser, certain gopher sites (see below), or an FTP transfer program such as *Fetch* for the Macintosh.

(5) Gopher

See 7c

Gopher is a tool for navigating the Internet. Although it is gradually being displaced by the **World Wide Web**, which is easier to use and has a much more exciting visual format (Gopher reads text only), the amount of information that Gopher has access to makes it a valuable research tool.

By presenting items as a series of menu choices, Gopher gives you access to a wide variety of resources all over the world. You can get information about business, medicine, and engineering as well as up-to-the-minute information about the weather. Gopher is also able to provide material from archived newsgroups and electronic books and magazines.

Gopher can be used by individuals who are connected to a mainframe or campus **server** (a computer that provides information to other computers) and can retrieve FTP files. It enables users to retrieve menu information from any server in the worldwide Gopher network.

ACCESSING GOPHER

The tool Veronica (Very Easy Rodent-Oriented Net-wide Index to Computerized Archives) enables users to do a keyword search of the various menus on the Gopher network. After a keyword (or words) is entered into Veronica, it creates a menu of items that contain the keyword or words. When you select an item on the Veronica menu, you are sent to the Gopher site that contains the keyword.

7c Searching the Web

Although the terms *Internet* and *World Wide Web* are often used inter-changeably, they are in fact different. Technically, the **Web** is a smaller network—within the larger network of the **Internet** itself—that consists of millions of hypertext documents or "pages." (**Hypertext** refers to the way in which information in related documents is cross-referenced or "linked.") Most commonly, these pages are written in a computer language called HTML (Hypertext Markup Language) that allows standard text to be combined with images and other media, like audio and video. Also, HTML makes it possible to link individual documents to any number of others. Links are indicated by underlined words in blue (or another color different from a document's body text); when you use a mouse to click on a link, you are connected to other related documents.

The Web enables you to connect to a vast variety of documents. For example, you can call up a **home page** or **Web page** (an individual document), a **Web site** (a collection of Web pages), a newsgroup, or an FTP site. Government agencies, businesses, universities, libraries, newspapers and magazines, journals, and public interest groups, as well as individuals, all operate their own Web sites. Each of these sites contains hypertext links that can take you to other relevant sites. By using these links, you can "surf the Net," following your interests and moving from one document to another.

ACCESSING THE WEB

You access the Web by means of a program called a **Web browser** (or "client") that enables you to find information on the Internet by clicking on icons or buttons instead of by typing commands. Two of the most popular Web browsers, which display the full range of **hypermedia** (some combination of text, photos, graphics, sound, and video files integrated into a document) on the Web, are *Netscape Navigator* and *Microsoft Internet Explorer*.

(1) Beginning a Web Search

Begin your World Wide Web search by clicking on your Web browser icon or selecting the browser from the list of programs on your computer.

After the program has loaded, you will see a screen that looks similar to the Netscape Navigator screen shown in Figure 1 below.

(2) Entering a Web Address

The most basic way to access information on the Web is to direct your browser to a specific Web page address, called a **URL** (uniform resource locator). (This is like looking for a book in the library after you have its call number.) If you are using Netscape Navigator, select "Open" from the file menu at the top of your browser window; a dialog box will appear. Next, enter the address you wish to visit (typically, a combination of letters, numbers, and symbols, such as: http://www.harcourtcollege.com/english/comp/holt/). Click "Open" on the dialog box, and Navigator will connect you to the page located at that address. From there, you can use hypertext links to go to other parts of the document or to other sites that are related to the one you are exploring.

Netscape
Navigator
home page

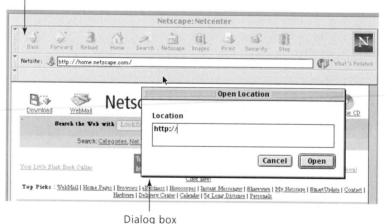

Dialog box

Figure 1 Entering an Address in Navigator

You may also type the URL directly into the "location" text field just below the control panel of your browser window. Use your mouse to highlight the text field, and then type the URL you wish to visit and hit the return key. Your browser will then call up the desired page.

NOTE: Make sure you type the URL *exactly* as it appears, without adding or deleting spaces or punctuation marks. (See 7e for a list of specific Web sites along with their URLs.)

UNDERSTANDING URLs

The first section of a URL indicates the type of file being accessed. In the address http://www.harcourtcollege.com/english/comp/holt/, *http* indicates that the file is in hypertext transfer protocol. After the colon and the two slashes is the name of the host site where the file is stored (www.harcourtcollege.com/). The *www* tells the user that the Web site is on the World Wide Web, *harcourtcollege* is the domain name, and *com* shows that this is a commercial institution. Following this section is the directory path to the file (english/).

(3) Using Subject Guides and Search Engines

Another way to locate information on the Web is to use *subject guides* and *search engines*. Although some Web users do not differentiate between the two, there are important differences.

Subject Guides   Subject guides are Web sites that list or index Web pages according to subject category or subcategories. Yahoo! (www.yahoo.com) is the most popular and well known of the Web's subject guides. Some others are Snap (www.snap.com), about.com (www.about.com), and Look Smart (www.looksmart.com).

When you use a subject guide to help you look for information, you click through a hierarchy of subject headings and subheadings until, eventually, you are presented with a list of specific topics that you want to explore (See Figure 2). Generally speaking, the goal of subject guides is to direct users to the most useful sites relating to any given subject. In many cases, subject guides provide short blurbs about the sites and pages they index so that you can choose between one site and another. In this way, subject guides are subjective: someone has decided whether a particular Web page is indexed or not. Although subject guides are excellent for **exploratory research**, when you move on to **focused research**, you should use a *search engine*.

See
6a, 6b

YAHOO!

What's New   Check Email

Personalize   Help

[Search] advanced search

Shopping - **Auctions** - Yellow Pages - People Search - Maps - Travel - Classifieds - Personals - Games - Chat - **Clubs**
Mail - Calendar - Messenger - **Companion** - My Yahoo! - News - Sports - Weather - TV - Stock Quotes - more...

Yahoo! Shopping - Thousands of stores. Millions of products.

Departments	Stores	Products
· Apparel	· Sports Authority	· Digital cameras
· Bath/Beauty	· Coach	· Pokemon
· Computers	· Toys R Us	· MP3 players
· Electronics	· Banana Republic	· DVD players
· Flowers		
· Sports		
· Music		
· Video/DVD		

Arts & Humanities
Literature, Photography,...

Business & Economy
Companies, Finance, Jobs,...

Computers & Internet
Internet, WWW, Software, Games,...

Education
College and University, K-12,...

Entertainment
Cool Links, Movies, Humor, Music,...

Government
Elections, Military, Law, Taxes,...

Health
Medicine, Diseases, Drugs, Fitness,...

News & Media
Full Coverage, Newspapers, TV,...

Recreation & Sports
Sports, Travel, Autos, Outdoors,...

Reference
Libraries, Dictionaries, Quotations,...

Regional
Countries, Regions, US States,...

Science
Animals, Astronomy, Engineering,...

Social Science
Archaeology, Economics, Languages,...

Society & Culture
People, Environment, Religion,...

In the News
· Israel, Palestinians agree on vital handover
· China warns Taiwanese on pro-independence votes
· Wash. anti-spam law ruled unconstitutional
more...

Marketplace
· Knicks vs. Lakers - charity auction
· Free 56K Internet Access
· Yahoo! Bill Pay - free 3-month trial
more...

Inside Yahoo!
· College Tourney Pick'em - last day to enter!
· Yahoo! Argentina - Mexico - Brazil
· Yahoo! GeoCities - build your free home page
· Oscar Pick'em - make your picks
more...

World Yahoo!s *Europe* : Denmark - France - Germany - Italy - Norway - Spain - Sweden - UK & Ireland
Pacific Rim : Asia - Australia & NZ - China - Chinese - HK - Japan - Korea - Singapore - Taiwan
Americas : Argentina - Brazil - Canada - Mexico - Spanish

Yahoo! Get Local LA - NYC - SF Bay - Chicago - more...   [ ] [Enter Zip Code]

Other Autos - Careers - Digital - Entertainment - Greetings - Health - Invites - Local Events - Net Events
Message Boards - Movies - Music - Real Estate - Small Business - Y! Internet Life - Yahooligans!

How to Suggest a Site - Company Info - Privacy Policy - Terms of Service - Contributors - Openings at Yahoo!

Figure 2 *Yahoo! Home Page*

Search Engines   A **search engine** is much like the online catalog at your college or local library. On the home page of the search engine you have chosen, you will find a box where you can enter a keyword (or words). When you hit the return key, the search engine retrieves and then displays all of the Web pages in its database that match your query. (Note that many search engines offer subject guides on their main pages.)

Alta Vista (www.altavista.com) is perhaps the best known search engine, but there are others as well. Some search engines are more user friendly than others; some allow for more sophisticated searching functions; some are updated more frequently; and some are more comprehensive than others. As you try out a number of search engines, you will probably settle on a favorite that you will turn to first whenever you need to find information.

A GUIDE TO SEARCH ENGINES

Hotbot (www.hotbot.com): Excellent and fast search engine for locating specific information. Good search options that allow you to fine-tune your searches.

Alta Vista (www.altavista.com): Good engine for precise searches. Fast and fairly easy to use.

Excite (www.excite.com): Good for general topics. Search results not always useful.

Infoseek (www.infoseek.com): Very accurate for Web pages, news, and Usenet. Smaller index of Web pages than other search engines.

Lycos (www.lycos.com): Lycos enables you to search for specific media (graphics, for example). Somewhat small index of Web pages.

Ask Jeeves (www.askjeeves.com): Good beginner's site. Allows you to ask questions to narrow your search. Easy to use, but wording precise questions can be difficult.

Northern Light (www.northernlight.com): Searches Web pages but also lists pay-for-view articles not always listed by other search engines. Arranges results under subject headings.

Because even the best search engines search only a fraction of what is on the Web, if you use only one search engine, you will most likely miss much valuable information.

It is therefore a good idea to repeat each search with several different search engines or to use one of the **metasearch** or **metacrawler** sites that enable you to use several search engines simultaneously.

METASEARCH SITES

Dogpile (www.dogpile.com)

GoHip (www5.gohip.com/hipsearch/)

Metacrawler (www.metacrawler.com)

SavySearch (www.savysearch.com/)

In addition to the popular, general-purpose search engines and meta-sites, there are also numerous search engines devoted entirely to specific subject areas, such as literature, business, sports, and women's issues. Hundreds of specialized search engines are indexed at Allsearchengines.com (www.allsearchengines.com).

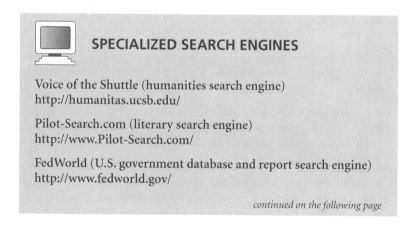

SPECIALIZED SEARCH ENGINES

Voice of the Shuttle (humanities search engine)
http://humanitas.ucsb.edu/

Pilot-Search.com (literary search engine)
http://www.Pilot-Search.com/

FedWorld (U.S. government database and report search engine)
http://www.fedworld.gov/

continued on the following page

HealthFinder (health, nutrition, and diseases information for consumers)
http://www.healthfinder.org/default.htm

The Internet Movie Database (search engine and database for film facts, reviews, and so on)
http://www.imdb.com

Newsbot (news search engine)
http://www.newsbot.com/

SportQuest (sports search engine)
http://www.sportquest.com/

FindLaw (legal search engine)
http://www.findlaw.com/

Bizbot (business search engine)
http://www.bizbot.net/

Keep in mind that a search engine retrieves any site in its database on which the keyword (or words) you have typed appear. If, for example, you simply type *Baltimore* (say, in hope of finding information on the city's economy), the search engine will generate an enormous list of pages—well over a million. This list will likely include, along with pages that might be relevant to your research, the home page of the Baltimore Orioles baseball team, as well as many home pages of people who happen to live in Baltimore.

Because searching this way is inefficient and time consuming, you need to *focus* your search, just as you would with your library's online catalog. You do this by using **search operators,** words and symbols that tell a search engine how to interpret your keywords. One way to use operators to focus your search is to put quotation marks around your search term (type *"Baltimore economy"* rather than *Baltimore economy*). This will direct the search engine to locate only documents containing this phrase.

Another way to focus your search is to carry out a **Boolean search,** combining keywords with AND, OR, NOT (typed in all capital letters), or a plus or minus sign to restrict the field of titles accessed. (To do this type of searching, you may have to select a search engine's *advanced search* option.) For example, to find Web pages that have to do with Baltimore's economy, type *Baltimore* AND *economy* or *Baltimore* + *economy*. By doing this, you make sure the documents you receive contain both the keywords *Baltimore* and *economy*. Some search engines allow you to search using three or four keywords (*Baltimore* AND *economy* NOT agriculture, for example). Focusing your searches in this way helps you eliminate irrelevant Web pages from your search.

 USING SEARCH OPERATORS

" "   Use quotation marks to search for a phrase: *"Baltimore Economy"*

AND   Use *and* to search for sites that contain both words: *Baltimore* and *Economy*

OR   Use *or* to search for sites that contain either word: *Baltimore* or *Economy*

NOT   Use *not* to exclude the word that comes after the *not*: *Baltimore* and *Economy* not *Agriculture*

+ (plus sign)   Use a plus sign to include the word that comes after it: *Baltimore + Economy*

− (minus sign)   Use a minus sign to exclude the word that comes after it: *Baltimore + Economy − Agriculture*

✔ CHECKLIST: TIPS FOR EFFECTIVE SEARCHING

✔ *Choose the Right Search Site*

No one all-purpose search site exists. Make sure you review the tips for choosing a search site on pages 121–123. Remember, use a subject guide, like Yahoo!, for exploratory research and a search engine, like Alta Vista, for more focused research. Also, don't forget to do a metasearch with a search engine like Metacrawler.

continued on the following page

✔ *Choose Your Keywords Carefully*

A search engine is only as good as the keywords you use. Choose keywords carefully.

✔ *Narrow Your Search*

Use quotation marks and operators to make your searches more productive. Review the box on page 124 before you use any search engine.

✔ *Check Your Spelling*

If your search does not yield the results you expect, check to make sure you have spelled your search terms correctly. Even a one-letter mistake can confuse a search engine and cause it to retrieve the wrong information—or no information at all.

✔ *Include Enough Terms*

If you are looking for information on housing, for example, search for several different variations of your keyword: *housing, houses, house buyer, buying houses, residential real estate,* and so on. Some search engines, like Infoseek, automatically search plurals; others do not. Some others, like Alta Vista, automatically search variants of your keyword. Others require you to think of the variants by yourself.

✔ *Consult the Help Screen*

Most search engines have a "help" screen. If you have trouble with your search, do not hesitate to consult it. A little time here can save you a lot of time later.

✔ *Use More Than One Subject Guide or Search Engine*

Because different subject guides and search engines index differ-ent sites, try several when you are looking for results. If one does not yield results after a few tries, switch to another.

7d   Evaluating Internet Sources

Web sites vary greatly in quality and reliability. Those operated by well-known institutions (the Smithsonian or the Library of Congress, for example) tend to have highly reliable information. Those operated by individuals (private Web pages or commercial advertisements, for example) are less reliable. Because it is so easy for anyone to establish a Web site and thereby publish anything, regardless of quality, critical evaluation of Web-based material is even more important than evaluation of more traditional sources of information, such as books and journal articles.

Sources you find on the Web (and on the Internet in general) may present theories, rumors, hearsay, speculation, or even lies as fact. Sometimes it is hard to distinguish such questionable material from legitimate information because you do not know your source as you would if you were dealing with a reputable journal or magazine. To complicate matters further, unscrupulous individuals can represent themselves as respected authorities with impressive credentials, even using the names of other people, and make claims that seem credible but are not. Therefore, when you find information on the Web that seems useful for your research, you need to evaluate it carefully.

✔ CHECKLIST: EVALUATING INTERNET SOURCES

✔ Where does the information come from? An article, for example, may be from a scholarly source, or it may be the personal opinion of a person with no expertise in the area he or she is discussing.

✔ Is the sponsoring institution reputable? Can you trust the institution to be fair and impartial?

✔ Is the author trying to sell something? Is the information biased, slanted, or intentionally misleading?

✔ Is the source current? Does the site have a date assigned to it? Does the site have several dates, indicating that it has been updated?

continued on the following page

Information on Evaluating Internet Sources (U. VT)
   http://www.lib.vt.edu/research/libinst/evaluating.html
Hoax? Scholarly Research? Personal Opinion? You Decide! (UCLA)
   http://www.library.ucla.edu/libraries/college/instruct/hoax/
   evlinfo.htm

✔ Is the text itself credible? Does it include evidence to support its claims? If authorities are quoted or paraphrased, does the text supply information about the credentials of the authorities?

✔ Do slick graphics, sound, or video connected to a Web page mask uninformed opinion or faulty logic? Do not be misled by technologically sophisticated sites that do not offer you any way to evaluate the accuracy of the information presented.

✔ CHECKLIST: STRATEGIES FOR DETERMINING THE LEGITIMACY OF A SOURCE

Sometimes—when a source is anonymous or when you are not familiar with the author, for example—you have to take measures to determine the legitimacy of a source. The following strategies can help you to get information about a questionable document:

✔ Post a query: If you get information from a newsgroup or a listserv, ask others in the group what they know about the source and its author.

✔ Follow the links: Follow the hypertext links in a document to other documents. If the links take you to legitimate sources, you know that the writer is aware of these sources of information.

✔ Do a keyword search: Do a keyword search using the name of the writer or the organization as keywords. Other documents by the same writer or citations in other works can give you an idea of the legitimacy of your source.

✔ Look at the URL: The last part of an electronic address can tell you whether a site is sponsored by a commercial entity (*.com*), a nonprofit organization (*.org*), an educational institution (*.edu*), or a governmental agency (*.gov*). Knowing this information can help you tell whether an organization is trying to sell you something (*.com*) or just giving useful information (*.edu* or *.org*).

Tips and Self-test: Evaluating Internet Sources (Georgetown U. Libraries): http://www.library.georgetown.edu/internet/eval.htm#test

The Evaluating Web Resources Homepage (Widener U.) http://www2.widener.edu/Wolfgram-Memorial-Library/webeval.htm

7e   Useful Web Sites

The Web sites listed below should prove particularly useful to you as you do Internet research.

Guide to Internet Research and Resources
http://www.miracosta.cc.ca.us/home/gfloren/INTNET.HTM

Information on Evaluating Internet Sources (U. VT)
http://www.lib.vt.edu/research/libinst/evaluating.html

Internet Research FAQ
http://www.purefiction.com/pages/res1.htm

Internet Tutorials
http://www.albany.edu/library/internet/index.html

Internet Research Tips
http://www.albany.edu/library/internet/checklist.html

Glenn Bacal's Ten Rules for Searching the Internet
http://www.ali-aba.org/aliaba/rules.htm

Starting Points for Internet Research (Purdue)
http://owl.english.purdue.edu/netsearch/research.html

General Reference Resources (CMU)
http://eserver.org/reference/

Selected Web Resources by Academic Subject (Georgetown U.)
http://gulib.lausun.georgetown.edu/swr/

(U.S.) Government Information Locator Service
http://www.gils.net/

Internet Public Library—Serials (Magazines)
http://aristotle.ipl.org/reading/serials/

Internet Public Library—Newspapers
http://aristotle.ipl.org/cgi-bin/reading/news.out.pl

Encyclopaedia Britannica Online
www.Britannica.com

Web Resources by Paper Topic (St. Ambrose University, IA)
http://www.sau.edu/CWIS/Internet/Wild/Hot/hotindex.htm

Citing Electronic Sources (APA and MLA)
http://www.uvm.edu/~ncrane/estyles/

The World Fact Book
http://www.odci.gov/cia/publications/Factbook/index.html

Library of Congress
http://lcweb.loc.gov

Research-It!
http://www.iTools.com/research-it/research-it.html

7f Glossary of Internet Terminology

archive Collection of several files compressed and combined into one file. Used to save storage space and file transfer time.

back up To duplicate a document, usually on a portable disk. You should always back up your documents.

baud The speed, measured in bits per second, at which information goes through a modem.

bit Binary digit, the smallest unit of information in a binary computer, usually represented by *on* or *off*, or numerically by *0* or *1*.

boot To start a computer and initialize the operating system.

browser Software program (application) necessary for viewing Web pages. Browsers, also referred to as "clients," read the **HTML** "code" in which Web pages are written and display that code as text and images. The two most popular browsers are Netscape Navigator and Microsoft Internet Explorer.

bug Problem in a software application or system program that causes malfunctions.

crash Sudden, catastrophic system or program failure.

cursor Blinking marker on a computer screen. The cursor is the entry point for all text you create on a computer screen. As you type, text appears immediately to the left of the cursor.

document Series of computer-generated characters—usually letters and numbers—stored on a *disk*. Each document is given a name so the computer can find it when commanded to do so. When you write an essay (or part of an essay) and *save* it, you create a *document* (sometimes called a *file*) that remains on the floppy disk as well as in the computer's hard drive and can be accessed again later when you want to edit, display, or print it.

download   To transfer a file or other data from a remote system to the local system; a means of receiving data or files.

e-mail   Abbreviation for "electronic mail."

emoticons   Symbols used in informal e-mail communication to indicate emotions.

FAQ   Abbreviation for "Frequently Asked Questions".

forum   A bulletin board system (BBS) discussion group.

FTP   "File transfer protocol." Process by which files can be moved from one computer to another.

GIF   Image format for displaying graphics (pictures and other images) on the WWW. Stands for "Graphical Interchange Format." Web graphics are uploaded and displayed in either GIF or JPEG format.

hard copy   Printed version of material produced on a computer. A hard copy enables you to reconstruct your work if you lose or damage your floppy disk or accidentally erase or destroy your file.

hard drive   The internal storage medium in a computer.

http   Stands for hypertext transfer protocol; indicates the file being viewed is hypertext.

HTML   Hypertext Markup Language, the computer programming language used to create Web pages.

ISP   Internet Service Provider. A company that, for a monthly fee, provides subscribers with access to the Internet. Some ISPs include AOL (America Online), Concentric Network, ATT WorldNet, and Earthlink.

modem   Modulator-demodulator; a device used to transmit data over telephone lines.

network   Two or more computers connected to one another to enable users to exchange information.

post   To send a message to a mailing list or newsgroup on a public bulletin board system.

RAM   Acronym for "Random Access Memory."

server   Computer that performs a service for other computers, such as file storage and distribution of e-mail.

upload   To transfer a file or other data from the local system to a remote system; a means of sending data or files.

virus   A computer program, transferred from one user to another via a disk or over a network, that has been created solely to "infect" (disable, cause malfunctions with, or in other ways harm) computer hardware or software. Because viruses are spread easily via downloadable files and e-mail messages, Internet and WWW users should use virus protection software to protect their computers.

WYSIWYG   Acronym for "what you see is what you get." Graphic interface that shows documents as they will appear printed, with all special characters and fonts, on the screen.

CHAPTER 8

INTEGRATING SOURCES AND AVOIDING PLAGIARISM

See 5e

As you move through the research process and consult various sources, you take notes in the format of **paraphrase**, **summary**, or **quotation**. When your work is complete, these notes will be integrated into your research paper.

8a Integrating Your Notes into Your Writing

Weave paraphrases, summaries, and quotations smoothly into your discussion, adding analysis or explanation to increase coherence and to show why you are using each source. Remember that you are orchestrating a conversation among different speakers, and your own voice should dominate.

CLOSE UP   **INTEGRATING YOUR NOTES INTO YOUR WRITING**

To avoid monotonous sentence structure, experiment with different methods of integrating source material into your paper.

- Vary the verbs you use to introduce a source's words or ideas (rather than use *says* each time).

acknowledges	discloses	implies
suggests	observes	notes
concludes	believes	comments
insists	explains	claims
predicts	summarizes	illustrates
reports	finds	proposes

continued on the following page

warns	concurs	speculates
admits	affirms	indicates

- Vary the placement of the **identifying tag** (the phrase that identifies the source), putting it in the middle or at the end of the quoted material instead of always at the beginning.

QUOTATION WITH IDENTIFYING TAG IN MIDDLE: "A serious problem confronting Amish society from the viewpoint of the Amish themselves," observes Hostetler, "is the threat of absorption into mass society through the values promoted in the public school system" (193).

PARAPHRASE WITH IDENTIFYING TAG AT END: The Amish are also concerned about their children's exposure to the public school system's values, notes Hostetler (193).

(1) Integrating Quotations

Work quotations smoothly into your sentences, and introduce them with identifying tags. Quotations should never be awkwardly dropped into the paper, leaving the exact relationship between the quoted words and your point unclear. Instead, use a brief introductory remark to provide a context for a quotation, quoting only those words you need to make your point.

UNACCEPTABLE: For the Amish, the public school system represents a problem. "A serious problem confronting Amish society from the viewpoint of the Amish themselves is the threat of absorption into mass society through the values promoted in the public school system" (Hostetler 193).

ACCEPTABLE: For the Amish, the public school system is a problem because it represents "the threat of absorption into mass society" (Hostetler 193).

Whenever possible, use a **running acknowledgment** to introduce the source of the quotation.

RUNNING ACKNOWLEDGMENT: As John Hostetler points out, the Amish see the public school system as a problem because it represents "the threat of absorption into mass society" (193).

Substitutions or Additions within Quotations When you make changes or additions to make a quotation fit into your paper, acknowledge your changes by enclosing them in brackets (not parentheses).

ORIGINAL QUOTATION: "Immediately after her wedding, she and her husband followed tradition and went to visit almost everyone who attended the wedding" (Hostetler 122).

QUOTATION REVISED TO MAKE VERB TENSES CONSISTENT: Nowhere is the Amish dedication to tradition more obvious than in the events surrounding marriage. Right after the wedding celebration the Amish bride and groom "visit almost everyone who [has] attended the wedding" (Hostetler 122).

QUOTATION REVISED TO SUPPLY AN ANTECEDENT FOR A PRONOUN: "Immediately after her wedding, [Sarah] and her husband followed tradition and went to visit almost everyone who attended the wedding" (Hostetler 122).

QUOTATION REVISED TO CHANGE AN UPPERCASE TO A LOWERCASE LETTER: The strength of the Amish community is illustrated by the fact that "[i]mmediately after her wedding, she and her husband followed tradition and went to visit almost everyone who attended the wedding" (Hostetler 122).

See
36f1

Omissions within Quotations When you delete unnecessary or irrelevant words, substitute an **ellipsis** (three spaced periods) for the deleted words.

ORIGINAL: "Not only have the Amish built and staffed their own elementary and vocational schools, but they have gradually organized on local, state, and national levels to cope with the task of educating their children" (Hostetler 206).

QUOTATION REVISED TO ELIMINATE UNNECESSARY WORDS: "Not only have the Amish built and staffed their own elementary and vocational schools, but they have gradually organized [. . .] to cope with the task of educating their children" (Hostetler 206).

NOTE: MLA style requires square brackets around ellipses you add to distinguish them from those that appear in the quotation.

CLOSE UP OMISSIONS WITHIN QUOTATIONS

Be sure you do not misrepresent or distort the meaning of quoted material when you shorten it. For example, do not say, "the Amish have managed to maintain [. . .] their culture" when the original quotation is "the Amish have managed to maintain *parts of* their culture."

Long Quotations   Set off a quotation of more than four typed lines of **prose** or more than three lines of **poetry** by indenting it one inch (ten spaces) from the margin. Double-space, do not use quotation marks, and introduce the long quotation with a colon. If you are quoting a single paragraph, do not indent the first line. If you are quoting more than one paragraph, indent the first line of each complete paragraph (including the first one) an additional one-quarter inch (three spaces).

See 35b 2 & 3

According to Hostetler, the Amish were not always hostile to public education:

> The one-room rural elementary school served the Amish community well in a number of ways. As long as it was a public school, it stood midway between the Amish community and the world. Its influence was tolerable, depending upon the degree of influence the Amish were able to bring to the situation. (196)

(2) Integrating Paraphrases and Summaries

Introduce your paraphrases and summaries with running acknowledgments, and end them with appropriate documentation. By doing so, you make certain that your readers are able to differentiate your own ideas from the ideas of your sources.

MISLEADING (IDEAS OF SOURCE BLEND WITH IDEAS OF WRITER): Art can be used to uncover many problems that children have at home, in school, or with their friends. For this reason, many therapists use art therapy extensively. Children's views of themselves in society are often reflected by their art style. For example, a cramped, crowded art style using only a portion of the paper shows their limited role (Alschuler 260).

REVISED WITH RUNNING ACKNOWLEDGMENT (IDEAS OF SOURCE DIFFERENTIATED FROM IDEAS OF WRITER): Art can be used to uncover many problems that children have at home, in school, or with their friends. For this reason, many therapists use art therapy extensively. According to William Alschuler in *Art and Self-Image,* children's views of themselves in society are often reflected by their art style. For example, a cramped, crowded art style using only a portion of the paper shows a child's limited role (260).

(3) Synthesizing Sources

A **synthesis** uses paraphrase, summary, and quotation to combine materials from two or more sources, along with your own ideas, to express an original viewpoint. (In this sense, an entire **research paper** is a synthesis.) You begin synthesizing material by comparing your sources and determining how they are alike and different, where they agree and disagree, and whether they reach the same conclusions. As you identify connections between one source and another or between a source and your own ideas, you develop your own perspective on your subject. It is this viewpoint, summarized in a thesis statement (in the case of an entire paper) or in a topic sentence (in the case of a paragraph), that becomes the focus of your synthesis.

As you write your synthesis, make your points one at a time, and use material from your sources to support these points. Make certain you use running acknowledgments as well as the transitional words and phrases that your readers will need to follow your discussion. Finally, remember that your distinctive viewpoint, not the ideas of your sources, should be central to your discussion.

Following is a synthesis written by a student as part of a research paper:

Computers have already changed our lives. They carry out (at incredible speed) many of the everyday tasks that make our way of life possible. For example, computer billing, with all its faults, makes modern business possible, and without computers we would not have access to the telephone services or television reception that we take for

continued on the following page

See 9b

granted. But computers are more than fast calculators. According to one computer expert, they are well on their way to learning, creating, and someday even thinking (Raphael 21). Another computer expert, Douglas Hofstadter, agrees, saying that someday a computer will have both "will . . . and consciousness" (423). It seems likely, then, that as a result of the computer, our culture will change profoundly (Turkle 15).

8b Avoiding Plagiarism

Plagiarism is taking credit for ideas or words that are not your own. Sometimes plagiarism is intentional, but often it is unintentional—occurring, for example, when a student pastes a quoted passage from a computer file directly into a paper and forgets to use quotation marks and documentation. The best way to avoid plagiarism is to take careful notes, to distinguish between your ideas and those of your sources, and to give credit to your sources with __documentation__.

See Ch 9 & Ch 10

In general, document words and ideas borrowed from your sources. (This rule applies to both print and electronic sources.) Of course, certain items need not be documented: **common knowledge** (information every reader probably knows), facts available from a variety of reference sources, familiar sayings and well-known quotations, and your own original research (interviews and surveys, for example).

Information in dispute or that is one person's original contribution, however, must be acknowledged. You need not, for example, document the fact that John F. Kennedy graduated from Harvard in 1940 or that he was elected president in 1960. You must, however, document a historian's evaluation of Kennedy's performance as president or one researcher's recent statements about his private life.

Plagiarism
   http://www2.rscc.cc.tn.us/~jordan_jj/OWL/Plagiarism.html
Plagiarism
   http://www.indiana.edu/~wts/wts/plagiarism.html

You can avoid plagiarism by using documentation wherever it is required and by adhering to the guidelines that follow.

(1) Enclose Borrowed Words in Quotation Marks

ORIGINAL: Historically, only a handful of families have dominated the fireworks industry in the West. Details such as chemical recipes and mixing procedures were cloaked in secrecy and passed down from one generation to the next. [. . .] One effect of familial secretiveness is that, until recent decades, basic pyrotechnic research was rarely performed, and even when it was, the results were not generally reported in scientific journals. (Conkling, John A. "Pyrotechnics." *Scientific American* July 1990: 96)

PLAGIARISM: John A. Conkling points out that until recently, little scientific research was done on the chemical properties of fireworks, and when it was, <u>the results were not generally reported in scientific journals</u> (96).

The preceding passage does cite the source, but it irresponsibly uses the source's exact words without placing them in quotation marks.

CORRECT (BORROWED WORDS IN QUOTATION MARKS): John A. Conkling points out that until recently, little scientific research was done on the chemical properties of fireworks, and when it was, "<u>the results were not generally reported in scientific journals</u>" (96).

CORRECT (PARAPHRASE): John A. Conkling points out that <u>the little research conducted on the chemical composition of fireworks was seldom reported in the scientific literature</u> (96).

PLAGIARISM AND THE INTERNET

See Ch. 7

Any time you download text from the **Internet**, you risk committing plagiarism. To avoid this possibility, do not simply cut and paste blocks of downloaded text directly into your paper. Take the time to summarize or paraphrase this material, copying it into your notes (which may be stored in another file) before you use it in a paper. If you do use the exact words of your source, enclose them in quotation marks. Remember to include documentation for all Internet sources that you use in your paper.

(2) Do Not Imitate a Source's Syntax and Phrasing

ORIGINAL: Let's be clear: this wish for politically correct casting goes only one way, the way designed to redress the injuries of centuries. When Pat Carroll, who is a woman, plays Falstaff, who is not, casting is considered a stroke of brilliance. When Josette Simon, who is black, plays Maggie in *After the Fall,* a part Arthur Miller patterned after Marilyn Monroe and which has traditionally been played not by white women, but by blonde white women, it is hailed as a breakthrough.

But when the pendulum moves the other way, the actors' union balks. (Quindlen, Anna. "Error, Stage Left." *New York Times* 12 Aug. 1990, sec. 1: 21)

PLAGIARISM: Let us be honest. The desire for politically appropriate casting goes in only one direction, the direction intended to make up for the damage done over hundreds of years. When Pat Carroll, a female, is cast as Falstaff, a male, the decision is a brilliant one. When Josette Simon, a black woman, is cast as Maggie in *After the Fall,* a role that Arthur Miller based on Marilyn Monroe and that has usually been played by a woman who is not only white but also blonde, it is considered a major advance.

But when the shoe is on the other foot, the actors' union resists (Quindlen 21).

Although the preceding passage does not use the exact words of the source, it closely imitates the original's syntax and phrasing, simply substituting synonyms for the author's words.

CORRECT (PARAPHRASE; ONE DISTINCTIVE PHRASE PLACED IN QUOTATION MARKS): According to Anna Quindlen, the actors' union supports "politically correct casting" (21) only when it means casting a woman or minority group member in a role created for a male or a Caucasian. Thus, it is acceptable for actress Pat Carroll to play Falstaff or for black actress Josette Simon to play Marilyn Monroe; in fact, casting decisions such as these are praised. But when it comes to casting a Caucasian in a role intended for an African American, Asian, or Hispanic, the union objects (21).

NOTE: Although the parenthetical documentation at the end identifies the passage's source, the quotation requires separate documentation.

(3) Document Statistics Obtained from a Source

Although many people assume that statistics are common knowledge, accepted by many experts in a field, they are usually the result of original research and must therefore be documented. Moreover, providing the source of statistics allows readers to assess their reliability.

CORRECT: According to one study, male drivers between the ages of sixteen and twenty-four accounted for the majority of accidents. Of 303 accidents recorded almost one-half took place before the drivers were legally allowed to drive at eighteen (Schuman et al., 1027).

(4) Differentiate Your Words and Ideas from Those of the Source

ORIGINAL: At some colleges and universities traditional survey courses of world and English literature [. . .] have been scrapped or diluted. At others they are in peril. At still others they will be. What replaces them is sometimes a mere option of electives, sometimes "multicultural" courses introducing material from Third World cultures and thinning out an already thin sampling of Western writings, and sometimes courses geared especially to issues of class, race, and gender. Given the notorious lethargy of academic decision-making, there has probably been more clamor than change; but if there's enough clamor, there will be change (Howe, Irving. "The Value of the Canon." *The New Republic* 2 Feb. 1991: 40–47).

PLAGIARISM: Debates about expanding the literary canon take place at many colleges and universities across the United States. At many universities the Western literature survey courses have been edged out by courses that emphasize minority concerns. These courses are "thinning out an already thin sampling of Western writings" in favor of courses geared especially to issues of "class, race, and gender" (Howe 40).

Here it appears that only the quotation in the last sentence is borrowed when, in fact, the second sentence of the passage also owes a debt to the original. A running acknowledgment should come *before* the borrowed material to mark where it begins.

CORRECT: Debates about expanding the literary canon take place at many colleges and universities across the United States. According to critic Irving Howe, at many universities the Western literature survey courses have been edged out by courses that emphasize minority concerns (41). These courses, says Howe, are "thinning out an already thin sampling of Western writings" in favor of "courses geared especially to issues of class, race, and gender" (40).

Documenting Sources: MLA Style

PART 4

MLA

? FREQUENTLY ASKED QUESTIONS

CHAPTER 9   MLA DOCUMENTATION

PART 4

MLA

DIRECTORY OF MLA IN-TEXT CITATIONS

1. A work by a single author
2. A work by two or three authors
3. A work by more than three authors
4. A work in multiple volumes
5. A work without a listed author
6. A work that is one page long
7. An indirect source
8. More than one work
9. A literary work
10. An entire work
11. Two or more authors with the same last name
12. A government document or a corporate author
13. An electronic source

DIRECTORY OF MLA WORKS CITED ENTRIES

Entries for Books

1. A book by one author
2. A book by two or three authors
3. A book by more than three authors
4. Two or more books by the same author
5. An edited book
6. A selection in an anthology
7. More than one essay from the same anthology
8. A multivolume work
9. The foreword, preface, or afterword of a book
10. A short story, play, or poem in an anthology
11. A short story, play, or poem in a collection of an author's work
12. A book with a title within its title
13. A translation
14. A republished book
15. A dissertation (published/unpublished)
16. An article in a reference book (signed/unsigned)
17. A pamphlet
18. A government publication

Entries for Articles

19. An article in a scholarly journal with continuous pagination through an annual volume

20. An article in a scholarly journal with separate pagination in each issue
21. An article in a weekly magazine (signed/unsigned)
22. An article in a monthly magazine
23. An article that does not appear on consecutive pages
24. An article in a newspaper (signed/unsigned)
25. An editorial
26. A letter to the editor
27. A book review
28. An article with a title within its title

Entries for Other Sources
29. A lecture
30. A personal interview
31. A published interview
32. A personal letter
33. A published letter
34. A letter in a library's archives
35. A film
36. A videotape, DVD, or laser disc
37. A radio or television program
38. A recording
39. A cartoon
40. An advertisement

Entries for Electronic Sources
41. A scholarly project or information database
42. A document within a scholarly project or information database
43. A Web page or home page
44. An online book
45. An article in an online scholarly journal
46. An article in an online newspaper
47. An article in an online newsletter
48. An article in an online magazine
49. A review
50. A letter to the editor
51. An article in an online encyclopedia
52. A work from an online service
53. A nonperiodical publication on CD-ROM or diskette
54. A periodical publication on CD-ROM
55. A painting or photograph
56. A map
57. An e-mail
58. An online posting
59. A synchronous communication (MOO or MUD)

CHAPTER 9

MLA DOCUMENTATION

Documentation, the formal acknowledgment of the sources you use in your paper, enables your readers to judge the quality and originality of your work. Different academic disciplines use different documentation styles. This chapter explains and illustrates the documentation style recommended by the Modern Language Association (MLA). Chapter 10 discusses the documentation styles of the American Psychological Association (APA), *The Chicago Manual of Style (CMS),* and the Council of Biology Editors (CBE).

9a   Using MLA Style*

MLA style is required by many teachers of English and other languages as well as teachers in other humanities disciplines. This method of documentation has three parts: *parenthetical references in the text* (also known as *in-text citations*), a *list of works cited,* and *content notes.*

(1) Parenthetical References in the Text

MLA documentation uses **parenthetical references** within the text keyed to a Works Cited list at the end of the paper. A typical reference consists of the author's last name and a page number.

> MLA Style Guide (Capital Comm.-Tech. College, CT)
>   http://webster.commnet.edu/mla.htm
> MLA Homepage
>   http://www.mla.org/set_stl.htm
> Dan Kies' Guide to the MLA Style (College of DuPage)
>   http://www.cod.edu/dept/kiesdan/engl_101/mla.htm
> MLA Style Documentation (U. Wisc.)
>   http://www.wisc.edu/writing/Handbook/DocMLA.html

*MLA documentation style follows the guidelines set in the *MLA Handbook for Writers of Research Papers,* 5th ed. New York: MLA, 1999.

The colony's religious and political freedom appealed to many idealists in Europe (Ripley 132).

To distinguish two or more sources by the same author, include an appropriate shortened title in the parenthetical reference after the author's name.

Penn emphasized his religious motivation (Kelley, <u>William Penn</u> 116).

If you state the author's name or the title of the work in your sentence, do not include it in the parenthetical reference that follows.

Penn's political motivation is discussed by Joseph P. Kelley in <u>Pennsylvania, The Colonial Years, 1681–1776</u> (44).

A period or other punctuation mark follows the parenthetical reference except when a quoted **long prose passage** is set off from the text, in which case the parenthetical reference appears one space *after* the final punctuation.

Sample MLA Parenthetical References

1. A Work by a Single Author

Fairy tales reflect the emotions and fears of children (Bettelheim 23).

2. A Work by Two or Three Authors

The historian's main job is to search for clues and solve mysteries (Davidson and Lytle 6).

With the advent of behaviorism, psychology began a new phase of inquiry (Cowen, Barbo, and Crum 31–34).

Big Dog Grammar's Quick MLA Guide
   http://gabiscott.com/bigdog/mla.htm
Downloadable MLA Style Guide pdf file (Montana State U.)
   http://www.lib.montana.edu/instruct/styles/
Sample Citations in MLA Style
   http://perth.uwlax.edu/MurphyLibrary/guides/mla.html
Citing Electronic Sources (APA and MLA)
   http://www.uvm.edu/~ncrane/estyles/

3. A Work by More Than Three Authors

List only the first author, followed by *et al.* ("and others").

The European powers believed they could change the fundamentals of Muslim existence (Bull et al. 395).

4. A Work in Multiple Volumes

If you list more than one volume of a multivolume work in your Works Cited list, include the appropriate volume and page number (separated by a colon).

The French Revolution had a great influence on William Blake (Raine 1: 52–53).

5. A Work without a Listed Author

Use a shortened version of the title in the parenthetical reference, beginning with the word by which it is alphabetized in the Works Cited list.

In spite of political unrest, Soviet television remained fairly conservative, ignoring all challenges to the system ("Soviet").

6. A Work That Is One Page Long

Do not include a page reference for a one-page article.

Sixty percent of Arab Americans work in white-collar jobs (El-Badru).

7. An Indirect Source

If you must use a statement by one author that is quoted in the work of another author, indicate that the material is from an indirect source with the abbreviation *qtd. in* ("quoted in").

Wagner stated that myth and history stood before him "with opposing claims" (qtd. in Thomas 65).

8. More Than One Work

Cite each work as you normally would, separating one from another with a semicolon.

The Brooklyn Bridge has been used as a subject by many American artists (McCullough 144; Tashjian 58).

Long parenthetical references distract readers. Whenever possible, present them as **content notes**.

See 9a3

9. A Literary Work

When citing a literary work, it is often helpful to include more than just the author's name and the page number.

In a parenthetical reference to a prose work, begin with the page number, follow it with a semicolon, and then add any additional information that might be necessary.

> In <u>Moby Dick</u>, Melville refers to a whaling expedition funded by Louis XIV of France (151; ch. 24).

In parenthetical references to long poems, cite both division and line numbers, separating them with a period.

> In the <u>Aeneid</u> Virgil describes the ships as cleaving the "green woods reflected in the calm water" (8.124).

(In this citation, the reference is to book 8, line 124 of the *Aeneid.*)

In citing classic verse plays, omit page numbers and include the act, scene, and line numbers, separated by periods (*Macbeth* 2.2.14–16). In biblical citations include an abbreviated title, the chapter, and the verse (Gen 5.12).

NOTE: Use arabic rather than roman numerals for act and scene numbers of plays.

10. An Entire Work

When citing an entire work, include the author's name and the work's title in the text of your paper rather than in a parenthetical reference.

> Herbert Gans's <u>The Urban Villagers</u> is a study of an Italian-American neighborhood in Boston.

11. Two or More Authors with the Same Last Name

To distinguish authors with the same last name, include their initials in the parenthetical references.

> Recent increases in crime have probably caused thousands of urban homeowners to install alarms (Weishoff, R. 115). Some of these alarms use sophisticated sensors that were developed by the army (Weishoff, C. 76).

12. A Government Document or a Corporate Author

Cite such works using the organization's name followed by the page number (American Automobile Association 34). You can avoid long parenthetical references by working the organization's name into the text of your paper.

According to the President's Commission for the Study of Ethical Problems in Medicine and Biomedical and Behavioral Research, the issues relating to euthanasia are complicated (76).

13. An Electronic Source

If a reference to an electronic source includes paragraph numbers rather than page numbers, use the abbreviation *par.* or *pars.* followed by the author's name, a comma, and the paragraph number or numbers. If the electronic source has no page or paragraph numbers, cite the work in the text of your paper rather than in a parenthetical reference.

The earliest type of movie censorship came in the form of licensing fees, and in Deer River, Minnesota, "a licensing fee of $200 was deemed not excessive for a town of 1000" (Ernst, par. 20).

In her article "Limited Horizons," Lynne Cheney says that schools do best when students read literature not for what it tells about the workplace, but for its insights into the human condition.

(2) Works Cited List

The **Works Cited list,** which appears at the end of your paper, gives publication information for all the research materials you cite. If your instructor tells you to list all the sources you read, whether you actually cited them or not, give this list the title *Works Consulted.*

✔ CHECKLIST: PREPARING THE MLA WORKS CITED LIST ❓

> ✔ Begin the list of works cited on a new page after the last page of text or content notes, numbered as the next page of the paper.

continued on the following page

continued from the previous page

✔ The title *Works Cited* should be centered one inch from the top of the page. Double-space between the title and the first entry.

✔ Each item has three divisions—author, title, and publication information. The separation between major divisions is marked by a period and one space.

✔ List entries alphabetically according to the author's last name. List the author's full name as it appears on the title page. Alphabetize unsigned sources by the first main word of the title.

✔ Type the first line of each entry flush with left-hand margin; indent subsequent lines five spaces (or one-half inch).

✔ Double-space within and between entries.

Sample MLA Works Cited Entries: Books   Book citations include the author's name; book title (underlined); and publication information (place, publisher, date). Capitalize all major words of the title except articles, coordinating conjunctions, prepositions, and the *to* of an infinitive (unless such a word is the first or last word of the title or subtitle).

NOTE: Do not underline the period that follows a book's title.

1. A Book by One Author
Use a short form of the publisher's name; *Alfred A. Knopf, Inc.,* for example, is shortened to *Knopf*, and *Oxford University Press* becomes *Oxford UP*.

Bettelheim, Bruno. The Uses of Enchantment: The Meaning and Importance of Fairy Tales. New York: Knopf, 1976.

When citing an edition other than the first, indicate the edition number as it appears on the work's title page.

Gans, Herbert J. The Urban Villagers. 2nd ed. New York: Free, 1982.

2. A Book by Two or Three Authors
List the first author last name first. Subsequent authors are listed first name first in the order in which they appear on the title page.

Davidson, James West, and Mark Hamilton Lytle. After the Fact: The Art of Historical Detection. New York: Knopf, 1982.

3. A Book by More Than Three Authors
List only the first author, followed by *et al.* ("and others").

> Bull, H., et al. The Near East. New York: Oxford UP, 1990.

4. Two or More Books by the Same Author
List books by the same author in alphabetical order by title. Three un-spaced hyphens followed by a period take the place of the author's name after the first entry.

> Thomas, Lewis. The Lives of a Cell: Notes of a Biology Watcher. New
>
> York: Viking, 1974.
>
> ---. The Medusa and the Snail: More Notes of a Biology Watcher. New
>
> York: Viking, 1979.

If the author is the editor or translator of the second entry, place a comma and the appropriate abbreviation after the hyphens (---, ed.).

5. An Edited Book
An edited book is a work prepared for publication by a person other than the author. If your emphasis is on the *author's* work, begin your citation with the author's name. After the title, include the abbreviation *Ed.* ("Edited by") followed by the name of the editor or editors.

> Bartram, William. The Travels of William Bartram. Ed. Mark Van Doren.
>
> New York: Dover, 1955.

If your emphasis is on the *editor's* work, begin your citation with the editor's name followed by the abbreviation *ed.* ("editor") if there is one editor or *eds.* ("editors") if there is more than one.

> Van Doren, Mark, ed. The Travels of William Bartram. By William Bar-
>
> tram. New York: Dover, 1955.

6. A Selection in an Anthology
Supply inclusive page numbers for the entire essay even if you cite only one page in your paper.

> Lloyd, G.E.R. "Science and Mathematics." The Legacy of Greece. Ed.
>
> Moses I. Finley. New York: Oxford UP, 1981. 256–300.

7. More Than One Essay from the Same Anthology

List each essay from the same anthology separately, followed by a cross-reference to the entire anthology. You may also list complete publication information for the anthology itself.

Bolgar, Robert R. "The Greek Legacy." Finley 429–72.

Finley, Moses I., ed. <u>The Legacy of Greece</u>. New York: Oxford UP, 1981.

Williams, Bernard. "Philosophy." Finley 202–55.

8. A Multivolume Work

When all volumes of a multivolume work have the same title, include the number of the volume you are using.

Raine, Kathleen. <u>Blake and Tradition</u>. Vol. 1. Princeton: Princeton UP, 1968.

When you use two or more volumes, cite the entire work.

Raine, Kathleen. <u>Blake and Tradition</u>. 2 vols. Princeton: Princeton UP, 1968.

If the volume you are using has an individual title, you may cite the title without mentioning any other volumes.

Durant, Will, and Ariel Durant. <u>The Age of Napoleon</u>. New York:

Simon, 1975.

If you wish, however, you may include supplemental information such as the number of the volume, the title of the entire work, the total number of volumes, and the inclusive publication dates.

Durant, Will, and Ariel Durant. <u>The Age of Napoleon</u>. New York: Simon,

1975. Vol. 11 of <u>The Story of Civilization</u>. 11 vols. 1935–75.

9. The Foreword, Preface, or Afterword of a Book

Taylor, Telford. Preface. <u>Less than Slaves</u>. By Benjamin B. Ferencz. Cam-

bridge: Harvard UP, 1979. xiii–xxii.

10. A Short Story, Play, or Poem in an Anthology

Chopin, Kate. "The Storm." <u>Literature: Reading, Reacting, Writing</u>. Ed.

Laurie G. Kirszner and Stephen R. Mandell. Compact 4th ed. Fort

Worth: Harcourt, 2000. 138–42.

Shakespeare, William. Othello, The Moor of Venice. Shakespeare: Six

Plays and the Sonnets. Ed. Thomas Marc Parrott and Edward

Hubler. New York: Scribner's, 1956. 145–91.

11. A Short Story, Play, or Poem in a Collection of an Author's Work

Walcott, Derek. "Nearing La Guaira." Selected Poems. New York:

Farrar, 1964. 47–48.

12. A Book with a Title within Its Title

If the book you are citing contains a title that is normally underlined to indicate italics (a novel, play, or long poem, for example), do *not* underline the interior title.

Knoll, Robert E., ed. Storm over The Waste Land. Chicago: Scott, 1964.

If the book you are citing contains a title that is normally enclosed within quotation marks, keep the quotation marks.

Herzog, Alan, ed. Twentieth Century Interpretations of "To a Skylark."

Englewood Cliffs: Prentice, 1975.

13. A Translation

García Márquez, Gabriel. One Hundred Years of Solitude. Trans. Gre-

gory Rabassa. New York: Avon, 1991.

14. A Republished Book

Include the original publication date after the title of a republished book—for example, a paperback version of a hardcover book.

Wharton, Edith. The House of Mirth. 1905. New York: Scribner's, 1975.

15. A Dissertation (Published/Unpublished)

For dissertations published by University Microfilms International (UMI), include the order number.

Peterson, Shawn. Loving Mothers and Lost Daughters: Images of

Female Kinship Relations in Selected Novels of Toni Morrison. Diss.

U of Oregon, 1993. Ann Arbor: UMI, 1994. 9322935.

NOTE: University Microfilms, which publishes most of the dissertations in the United States, also publishes in CD-ROM. You will find the proper format for citing CD-ROMs on page 163.

Use quotation marks for the title of an unpublished dissertation.

Romero, Yolanda Garcia. "The American Frontier Experience in Twentieth-

Century Northwest Texas." Diss. Texas Tech U, 1993.

16. An Article in a Reference Book (Signed/Unsigned)

For a signed article, begin with the author's name. When citing relatively unfamiliar encyclopedias, give full publication information.

Drabble, Margaret. "Expressionism." The Oxford Companion to English

Literature. 5th ed. New York: Oxford UP, 1985.

When citing familiar encyclopedias, do not include publication information. Enter the title of an unsigned article just as it is listed in the reference book. No volume or page numbers are needed.

"Cubism." The Encyclopedia Americana. 1994 ed.

17. A Pamphlet

If no author is listed, enter the underlined title first.

Existing Light Photography. Rochester: Kodak, 1989.

18. A Government Publication

If the publication has no listed author, begin with the name of the government, followed by the name of the agency.

United States. Office of Consumer Affairs. 1999 Consumer's Resource

Handbook. Washington: GPO, 1999.

Sample MLA Works Cited Entries: Articles   Article citations include the author's name; the title of the article (in quotation marks); the underlined name of the periodical; the month and the year; and the pages on which the full article appears, without the abbreviations *p.* or *pp.*

NOTE: Abbreviate the names of months—except for May, June, and July—in the Works Cited list (Jan., Feb., Mar., Apr., Aug., Sept., Oct., Nov., Dec.). Write them out in full in the text of your paper.

19. An Article in a Scholarly Journal with Continuous Pagination through an Annual Volume

For an article in a journal with continuous pagination—for example, one in which an issue ends on page 172 and the next issue begins with page 173—include the volume number, followed by the date of publication (in parentheses). Follow the publication date with a colon, a space, and the page numbers.

Huntington, John. "Science Fiction and the Future." College English 37

(1975): 340–58.

20. An Article in a Scholarly Journal with Separate Pagination in Each Issue

For a journal in which each issue begins with page 1, add a period and the issue number after the volume number.

Sipes, R. G. "War, Sports, and Aggression: An Empirical Test of Two

Rival Theories." American Anthropologist 4.2 (1973): 65–84.

21. An Article in a Weekly Magazine (Signed/Unsigned)

In dates, the day precedes the month. For unsigned articles, start with the title of the article.

Traub, James. "The Hearts and Minds of City College." New Yorker 7

June 1993: 42–53.

"Solzhenitsyn: A Candle in the Wind." Time 23 Mar. 1970: 70.

22. An Article in a Monthly Magazine

Roll, Lori. "Careers in Engineering." Working Woman Nov. 1982: 62.

23. An Article That Does Not Appear on Consecutive Pages

When, for example, an article begins on page 15, continues on page 16, and then skips to page 86, include only the first page number and a plus sign.

Griska, Linda. "Stress and Job Performance." Psychology Today

Nov.–Dec. 1995: 120+.

24. An Article in a Newspaper (Signed/Unsigned)

Oates, Joyce Carol. "When Characters from the Page Are Made Flesh

on the Screen." New York Times 23 Mar. 1986, late ed.: C1+.

"Soviet Television." Los Angeles Times 13 Dec. 1990, sec. 2: 3+.

25. An Editorial

"Tough Cops, Not Brutal Cops." Editorial. New York Times 5 May

1994, late ed.: A26.

26. A Letter to the Editor

Bishop, Jennifer. Letter. Philadelphia Inquirer 10 Dec. 1995: A17.

27. A Book Review

Begin with the reviewer's name, followed by the title of the review (if any); then write *Rev. of,* the title of the book reviewed, a comma, the word *by,* and the name of the author. End with publication information.

Fox-Genovese, Elizabeth. "Big Mess on Campus." Rev. of Illiberal

Education: The Politics of Race and Sex on Campus, by Dinesh

D'Souza. Washington Post 15 Apr. 1991, ntnl. weekly ed.: 32.

28. An Article with a Title within Its Title

If the article you are citing contains a title that is normally enclosed within quotation marks, use single quotation marks for the interior title.

Nash, Robert. "About 'The Emperor of Ice Cream.'" Perspectives 7

(1954): 122–24.

If the article you are citing contains a title that is normally underlined to indicate italics, underline it in your Works Cited entry.

Leicester, H. Marshall, Jr. "The Art of Impersonation: A General Prologue

to The Canterbury Tales." PMLA 95 (1980): 213–24.

Sample MLA Works Cited Entries: Other Sources

29. A Lecture

Sandman, Peter. "Communicating Scientific Information." Communications Seminar, Dept. of Humanities and Communications. Drexel
U, 26 Oct. 1999.

30. A Personal Interview

West, Cornel. Personal interview. 28 Dec. 1998.

Tannen, Deborah. Telephone interview. 8 June 1999.

31. A Published Interview

Stavros, George. "An Interview with Gwendolyn Brooks." Contemporary
Literature 11.1 (Winter 1970): 1–20.

32. A Personal Letter

Tan, Amy. Letter to the author. 7 Apr. 1997.

33. A Published Letter

Joyce, James. "Letter to Louis Gillet." 20 Aug. 1931. James Joyce. By
Richard Ellmann. New York: Oxford UP, 1965. 631.

34. A Letter in a Library's Archives

Stieglitz, Alfred. Letter to Paul Rosenberg. 5 Sept. 1923. Stieglitz
Archive. Yale, New Haven.

35. A Film
Include the title of the film (underlined), the distributor, and the date,
along with other information of use to readers, such as the names of the
performers, the director, and the writer.

Citizen Kane. Dir. Orson Welles. Perf. Orson Welles, Joseph Cotten,
Dorothy Comingore, and Agnes Moorehead. RKO, 1941.

If you are focusing on the contribution of a particular person, begin with that person's name.

Welles, Orson, dir. <u>Citizen Kane</u>. . . .

36. A Videotape, DVD, or Laser Disc

Cite a videotape, DVD (digital videodisc), or laser disc like a film, but include the medium before the name of the distributor.

<u>Interview with Arthur Miller</u>. Dir. William Schiff. Videocassette. The Mosaic Group, 1987.

37. A Radio or Television Program

"Prime Suspect 3." Writ. Lynda La Plante. Perf. Helen Mirren. <u>Mystery!</u> PBS. WNET, New York. 28 Apr. 1994.

38. A Recording

List the composer, conductor, or performer (whichever you are emphasizing), followed by the title (and, when citing jacket notes, a description of the material), manufacturer, and year of issue.

Boubill, Alain, and Claude-Michel Schönberg. <u>Miss Saigon</u>. Perf. Lea Salonga, Claire Moore, and Jonathan Pryce. Cond. Martin Koch. Geffen, 1989.

Marley, Bob. "Crisis." Lyrics. <u>Bob Marley and the Wailers</u>. Kava Island Records, 1978.

39. A Cartoon

Trudeau, Garry. "Doonesbury." Cartoon. <u>The Philadelphia Inquirer</u> 19 July 1999: E 13.

40. An Advertisement

Microsoft. Advertisement. <u>National Review</u> 28 June 1999: 11.

Sample MLA Works Cited Entries: Electronic Sources The documentation style for electronic sources presented here conforms to the most recent guidelines published in the *MLA Handbook for Writers of Research Papers* (5th ed.) or found online at <http://mla.org>. (If your instructor prefers that you use Columbia Online Style for citing electronic sources, you can find it at <http://www.cas.usf.edu/english/walker/mla.html>.)

Because the information in electronic sources can change frequently, the version you accessed at the time of your research may not be the version that readers see later. For this reason, MLA recommends that you include *both* the date of the electronic publication (if available) and the date you accessed the source. In addition, MLA suggests that you print out and save the version of the electronic source that you accessed during your research. Finally, MLA recommends that you print the electronic address inside angle brackets to distinguish the address from the punctuation in the rest of the citation. (If you have to carry an electronic address over to the next line, divide it after a slash or at some other logical place—after a punctuation mark, for example. Never insert a hyphen or permit your word processor to insert one.)

NOTE: MLA style recognizes that full source information is not always available. Include in your citation whatever information you can reasonably obtain.

41. A Scholarly Project or Information Database

Philadelphia Writers Project. Ed. Miriam Kotzen Green. May 1998.

　　Drexel U. 12 June 1999. <http://www.Drexel.edu/letrs/wwp/>.

NOTE: Be sure to give the complete electronic address. Include the **access mode identifier** (*http, ftp, gopher, telnet,* or *news*) and all appropriate path and file names.

42. A Document within a Scholarly Project or Information Database

"'D' Day: June 7th, 1944." The History Channel Online. 1999. History

　　Channel. 7 June 1999 <http://historychannel.com/thisday/today/

　　997690.html>.

43. A Web Page or Home Page

Wilton, D. D. Wilton's Etymology Page. 15 June 1999 <http://www.

　　wilton.net/Etyma1.htm>.

Gainor, Charles. Home page. 22 July 1999 <http://

　　www.chass.utoronto.ca:9094/~char/>.

44. An Online Book

Douglass, Frederick. <u>My Bondage and My Freedom</u>. Boston, 1855.

8 June 1999 <gopher://gopher.vt.edu:10024/22/178/3>.

45. An Article in an Online Scholarly Journal

Dekoven, Marianne. "Utopias Limited: Post-Sixties and Postmodern

American Fiction." <u>Modern Fiction Studies</u> 41.1 (1995): 13 pp.

17 Mar. 1999 <http://muse.jhu.edu/journals/mfs.v041/

41.1dwkovwn.html>.

When you cite information from the print version of an online source, include the publication information for the printed source, the number of pages or paragraphs (if available), and the date you accessed it.

46. An Article in an Online Newspaper

Lohr, Steve. "Microsoft Goes to Court." <u>New York Times on the Web</u>

19 Oct. 1998. 29 Apr. 1999 <http://www.nytimes.com/web/

docroot/library.cyber/week/1019business.html>.

47. An Article in an Online Newsletter

"Unprecedented Cutbacks in History of Science Funding." <u>AIP Center

for History of Physics</u> 27.2 (Fall 1995). 26 Feb. 1996 <http://

www.aip.org/history/fall95.html>.

48. An Article in an Online Magazine

Weiser, Jay. "The Tyranny of Informality." <u>Time</u> 26 Feb. 1996. 1 Mar.

1999. <http://www.enews.com/magazines.tnr/current/

022696.3.html>.

49. A Review

Ebert, Roger. Rev. of <u>Star Wars: Episode I—The Phantom Menace</u>, dir.

George Lucas. <u>Chicago Sun-Times Online</u> 8 June 1999. 22 June

1999 <http://www.suntimes.com/output/ebert/08show.html>.

50. A Letter to the Editor

Chen-Cheng, Henry H. Letter. New York Times on the Web 19 July

1999. 19 July 1999 <http://www.nytimes.com/yr/mo/day/letters/

lchen-cheng.html>.

51. An Article in an Online Encyclopedia

"Hawthorne, Nathaniel." Britannica Online. Vers. 98.2. Apr. 1998.

Encyclopaedia Britannica. 16 May 1998 <http://www.eb.com/>.

52. A Work from an Online Service

You can often access material from online services like America On-line and Lexis-Nexis without using a URL. If you access such material by using a keyword, provide the keyword you used at the end of the entry (following the date of access).

"Kafka, Franz." Compton's Encyclopedia Online. Vers. 2.0. 1997.

America Online. 8 June 1998. Keyword: Compton's.

If, instead of using a keyword, you follow a series of paths, list the paths (separated by semicolons).

"Elizabeth Adams." History Resources. 11 Nov. 1997. America Online.

28 June 1999. Path: Research; Biography; Women in Science;

Biographies.

53. A Nonperiodical Publication on CD-ROM or Diskette

Cite a nonperiodical publication on CD-ROM or diskette the same way you would a book, except include a description of the medium of publication—*CD-ROM* or *Diskette.*

"Windhover." The Oxford English Dictionary. 2nd ed. CD-ROM. Oxford:

Oxford UP, 1992.

"Whitman, Walt." DiscLit: American Authors. Diskette. Boston: Hall, 1993.

54. A Periodical Publication on CD-ROM

Zurbach, Kate. "The Linguistic Roots of Three Terms." Linguistic Quar-

terly 37 (1994): 12–47. InfoTrac: Magazine Index Plus. CD-ROM.

Information Access. Jan. 1996.

55. A Painting or Photograph

Lange, Dorothea. Looking at Pictures. 1936. Museum of Mod. Art,

New York. 28 June 1999 <http://moma.org/exhibitions/

lookingatphotographs/lang-fr.html>.

56. A Map

"Philadelphia, Pennsylvania." Map. U. S. Gazetteer. US Census Bureau.

17 July 1999 <http://www.census.gov/cgi-bin/gazetteer>.

57. An E-Mail

Adkins, Camille. E-mail to the author. 28 June 1999.

58. An Online Posting

Gilford, Mary. "Dog Heroes in Children's Literature." Online posting. 17

Mar. 1999. 12 Apr. 1999 <news: alt.animals.dogs>.

Schiller, Stephen. "Paper Cost and Publishing Costs." Online posting.

24 Apr. 1999. 17 May 1999. Book Forum. 11 May 1999

<www.nytimes.com/webin/webx?13A^41356.ee765e/0>.

WARNING: Using information from Internet sources—especially newsgroups and online forums—is risky. Contributors are not necessarily experts, and frequently they are incorrect and misinformed. Unless you can be certain that the information you are obtaining from these sources is reliable, do not use it. You can check the reliability of an Internet source by consulting the checklist for **evaluating Internet sources** or by asking your instructor or reference librarian for guidance.

See 7d

59. A Synchronous Communication (MOO or MUD)

MOOs (multiuser domain, object oriented) and MUDs (multiuser domain) are Internet software that enables users to communicate in real time. To cite a communication obtained on a MOO or a MUD, give the name (or names) of the writer, a description of the situation, and the form of communication (LinguaMOO).

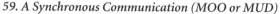

Guitar, Gwen. Online discussion of Cathy in Emily Brontë's Wuthering

Heights. 17 Mar. 1999. LinguaMOO. 17 Mar. 1999 <telnet://

lingua.utdallas.edu:8888>.

(3) Content Notes

Content notes—multiple bibliographical citations or other material that does not fit smoothly into the text—are indicated by a superscript (raised numeral) in the paper. Notes can appear either as footnotes at the bottom of the page or as endnotes on a separate numbered sheet entitled *Notes,* placed after the last page of the paper and before the Works Cited list. Content notes are double-spaced within and between entries.

For Multiple Citations

In the Paper

Many researchers emphasize the necessity of having dying patients share their experiences.[1]

In the Note

[1]Kübler-Ross 27; Stinnette 43; Poston 70; Cohen and Cohen 31–34; Burke 1:91–95.

For Explanations

In the Paper

The massacre of the Armenians during World War I is an event the survivors could not easily forget.[2]

In the Note

[2]For a firsthand account of these events, see Bedoukian 178–81.

9b Sample Research Paper: MLA Style

The following paper, which uses MLA documentation style, includes a title page, a formal outline, a notes page, and a list of works cited. (If your instructor does not require a separate title page, use the format illustrated in **4d.**) Annotations comment on the paper's style and structure and explains various methods of incorporating source material.

When and What to Footnote (from Harvard)
http://www.fas.harvard.edu/~wricntr/footnote.html

About ½ page
down

Title   The Great Digital Divide

|

2 inches

|

| By

Name   Kimberly Larsen Romney

|

2 inches

|

Instructor   Professor Wilson

Course   Double-space   English 1302

Date submitted   April 28, 2000

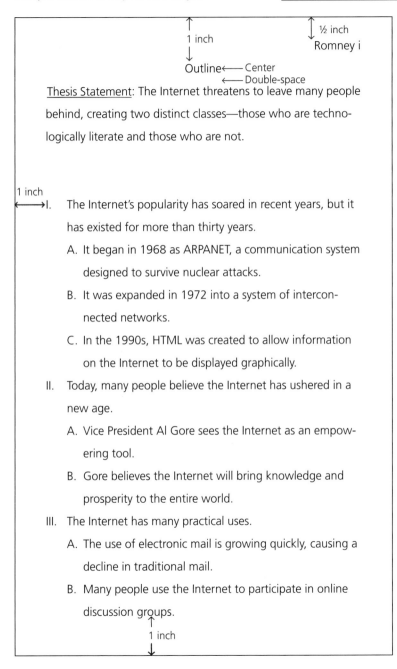

½ inch
1 inch
Romney i

Outline ⟵— Center
⟵— Double-space

<u>Thesis Statement</u>: The Internet threatens to leave many people behind, creating two distinct classes—those who are technologically literate and those who are not.

1 inch

I. The Internet's popularity has soared in recent years, but it has existed for more than thirty years.

A. It began in 1968 as ARPANET, a communication system designed to survive nuclear attacks.

B. It was expanded in 1972 into a system of interconnected networks.

C. In the 1990s, HTML was created to allow information on the Internet to be displayed graphically.

II. Today, many people believe the Internet has ushered in a new age.

A. Vice President Al Gore sees the Internet as an empowering tool.

B. Gore believes the Internet will bring knowledge and prosperity to the entire world.

III. The Internet has many practical uses.

A. The use of electronic mail is growing quickly, causing a decline in traditional mail.

B. Many people use the Internet to participate in online discussion groups.

1 inch

C. The Internet also provides access to information databases.

IV. Along with these uses, however, come problems.

A. E-mail communications are often badly written.

B. E-mail—and the other services provided by the Internet—can also encourage antisocial behavior.

C. It is often difficult to evaluate the material posted on
Web sites.

V. The most serious problem associated with the Internet is
the widening gap between those who have access to this
new technology and those who do not.

A. The Internet is still out of reach for many Americans.

B. Problems facing people without Internet access include
difficulties at school, trouble obtaining employment,
and fewer opportunities to save money and time as
consumers.

C. The people who are "digitally dispossessed" may not
even realize what they are missing.

D. The Internet is widening the economic and social divide that already separates us.

VI. Many public officials recognize the potential danger of the
"digital divide" and are taking steps to narrow the gap.

A. President Clinton "mandated that every school and
public library be connected to the Internet by the year
2000."

    B. Library professionals also recognize the seriousness of the problem.

    C. The federal government has launched a school writing project to set up Internet connections in all schools run by the Federal Bureau of Indian Affairs.

    D. Congress is also making efforts to decrease the gap between the "haves" and the "have nots."

VII. Despite these efforts, much still needs to be done.

    A. We must make the Internet available to the widest possible audience.

    B. We must provide training to people unfamiliar with the new technology.

    C. We must target low-income and minority families (particularly those in rural areas) and the elderly for this training.

½ inch

1 inch

Romney 1

The Great Digital Divide ←— Center

←— Double-space

Indent
1/2 inch —→ Today, a basic understanding of computers and how to

use them is necessary if one is to succeed. For this reason,

1 inch those who are unfamiliar with modern digital technology find   1 inch

←———→ themselves at a great disadvantage when it comes to educa- ←———→

tion and employment. One of the newest digital technologies

available is the information superhighway—better known as

the Internet. The Internet, with its accompanying software

and services, is rapidly changing the way we access and see in-

formation. Although the Internet offers great promise, how-

ever, it has also created some problems. Perhaps the most

Thesis serious of these problems is that the Internet threatens to
statement

leave many people behind, creating two distinct classes—

those who are technologically literate and those who are not.

Paragraph   The Internet's popularity has soared in recent years, but it
summarizes
material from has existed for more than thirty years. It began in 1969 under
a book
chapter that the name ARPANET (ARPA stood for Advanced Research Pro-
presents a
historical jects Agency, which was part of the United States Department
overview.
of Defense). During the Cold War, the United States govern-

ment allocated funds to establish a communication system

that would survive a nuclear attack, and ARPANET was created

to serve this purpose. The goal was to build a network that

would function even if part of it were destroyed. The first

ARPANET system consisted of just four connected computers,

but by 1972, fifty universities and research facilities (all doing

1 inch

research for the military) were linked. This system enabled
users to send messages over a number of available routes, not
just one (Gibbs and Smith 5).

Beginning in 1972, researchers decided to expand the
scope of this project. They wanted to find a way to increase
the number of computers that could be on ARPANET. To ac-
complish this goal, researchers established a collection of pro-
tocols called TCP/IP (Transmission Control Protocol/Internet
Protocol).[1] The conversion to TCP/IP, which was completed in
1983, allowed ARPANET to serve as the "nerve center" that
connected all the new networks (UNIX, USENET, and BITNET,
for example) that had come into existence since 1972. This
new system of interconnected networks was given the name
Internet (Wendall).

Finally, in the 1990s, a computer language called HTML
(HyperText Markup Language) was created to allow information on the Internet to be displayed graphically. Whereas the
older networks on Internet looked like typed pages, HTML displayed information in a more visually stimulating format. This
advance gave rise to the World Wide Web, which allowed
users to access text, graphics, and even sound while moving
from one site to another simply by clicking on a hypertext link.
This in turn made the Internet more accessible and useful to
the general public and aroused unprecedented interest in the
new digital technology (Wendall).

Superscript (raised numeral) refers to content note. See Notes page following text of paper.

Paragraphs 3 and 4 combine paraphrase and summary from a source.

Romney 3

Today, many people believe the Internet has ushered in a new age, one in which this instant communication will bring people closer together and eventually even eliminate national boundaries. Vice President Al Gore takes this optimistic view, observing that the Internet is a means "to deepen and extend our oldest and most cherished global values: rising standards of living and literacy, an ever-widening circle of freedom, and individual empowerment." Gore goes on to say that he can see the day when we will "extend our knowledge and our prosperity to our most isolated inner cities, to the barrios, the favelas, the colonias, and our most remote rural villages." For many people, however, the benefits of the Internet are not nearly this obvious or far reaching.

Certainly the Internet has many practical uses, not the least of which is its ability to help people communicate with one another almost instantaneously. In fact, the use of electronic mail (e-mail), both personal and business-related, is growing so fast that the United States Post Office is predicting a sharp decline in traditional mail over the next ten years. As Sarah Sklaroff observes, "Where once Americans depended on the vagaries of the post office to communicate in personalized, written messages, now we send 2.2 billion e-mail messages a day, compared with at most 293 million pieces of first-class mail."

Many people use the Internet to participate in online discussion groups, engaging in two-way conversations in real

Material from Internet source, introduced by author's name, does not include a parenthetical reference directing reader to a paragraph or page number because this information was not provided in the electronic text.

Running acknowledgment introduces quotation.

Romney 4

time or conducting business around the world without even leaving their desks. In addition to these discussion groups, electronic bulletin boards enable users to "exchange information on hobbies, buy and sell goods and services, and exchange programs" ("Telecommunications").

Finally, a use of the Internet that is helpful both in the classroom and in the workplace is its ability to provide access to information databases. At present, researchers can use the Internet to view encyclopedia articles, yearbooks, almanacs, journal and magazine articles, and even whole books. Jazlin V. Ebenezer and Eddy Lau, two teachers who combine classroom instruction with the Internet, observe that systems like Wide Area Information Server (WAIS) are changing the classroom forever. With WAIS, users can get connected, type in any topic they wish to research, and within fifteen seconds, have a list of articles from various sources that deal specifically with their topic. Although WAIS does not include as many databases as some other commercial servers, it already has thousands, and more are coming online all the time (27–28). With resources such as these, students and professionals alike can use the Internet as a tool for serious research.

Along with these uses, however, come problems. For example, just a glance at the average e-mail communication will show that it is usually badly written. The same is true for the writing on electronic bulletin boards and on many Web sites.

Title alone used in parenthetical reference because source does not identify author.

Running acknowledgment introduces combination of paraphrase and summary of two pages in source.

Romney 5

As Philip Elmer-DeWitt observes, much of online writing is simply awful: "sloppy, meandering, puerile, ungrammatical, poorly spelled, badly structured, and at times virtually content free." Of course, e-mail is not like ordinary writing; the established rules of mechanics and grammar do not seem to apply, and there is often no penalty for poor writing. (In fact, with its abbreviations and smiley-faced emoticons, e-mail seems to encourage it.)

This paragraph and the following one include no documentation because they present the student's own ideas.

E-mail—and the other services provided by the Internet—can also encourage antisocial behavior. Eventually, everything we require will be available online at the click of a mouse. Soon, there will be no need to leave our homes to buy clothes or purchase a book, or to meet someone over coffee to have a conversation. Already, people who feel uncomfortable talking to others face-to-face find the Internet an easy and comfortable place to hide. As people begin to rely more and more on the Internet as a means of communication, their social skills will decline, and we will become more isolated from one another than we are already.

Even the great amount of information that people can access through the Internet can create problems. It is often difficult to evaluate material posted on Web sites. A search for information about a topic sometimes will yield thousands of sites. At present, however, no Web browser evaluates Web sites or the information they contain. For this reason, distin-

Romney 6

guishing between fact and opinion, or between truth and pro-
paganda, becomes extremely difficult—sometimes even impossible.

The most serious problem associated with the Internet,
however, is the widening gap between those who have access
to this new technology and those who do not. Despite Vice
President Gore's optimistic predictions, the Internet is still out
of reach for many Americans, and this has created what the
NAACP and others have called the "digital divide" ("NAACP
Targets Minority Gap"). A large percentage of the poor, elderly, and members of many minority groups are excluded
from current technological advancements. For example, one
recent survey by the Commerce Department shows that
African-American and Hispanic families are "less than half as
likely as white families to have access to the Internet from
home, work, or school" (Belluck). This disparity exists even at
low income levels. According to Belluck, "At the lowest income levels, the gap is great—a child in a low-income white
family is three times as likely to have Internet access as a child
in a low-income black family."

Problems facing people without Internet access include
difficulty at school, trouble obtaining employment, and fewer
opportunities to save money and time as consumers. For example, those to whom the Internet is not available are denied access to the research materials and jobs posted on the Web as

Paragraph synthesizes material from two sources.

Two references to the same source. Note that each quotation requires a separate parenthetical reference.

Romney 7

well as to opportunities for special airline discounts, savings on long-distance carriers, and lower prices on computer software. With access to only a portion of available goods and services, people who are off-line do not have the advantages that people who are online routinely get:

Quotation of more than four lines is typed as a block, indented ten spaces (or one inch) and double-spaced, with no quotation marks. Parenthetical documentation is placed one space after end punctuation.

> Their choices will be restricted, and they're going to pay a little bit more for things and they'll have fewer options. [. . .] and it's not going to be one of these things where you see the digital homeless on the street, or sleeping on the steps of City Hall. It's going to be an invisible problem. The people who are digitally dispossessed may not even appreciate that they are dispossessed. (Belluck)

Clearly, the Internet is widening the economic and social divide that already separates people in this country.

Many public officials recognize the potential danger of the "digital divide" and are taking steps to narrow the gap. For example, President Clinton, in his Internet initiative, mandated that "every school and public library be connected to the Internet by the year 2000" (Fulton 18). The chairperson of the United States National Commission on Libraries and Information Science also recognizes the complexity and seriousness of the problem:

Ellipses within brackets indicate that the student deleted some material from the quotation.

> The 1998 survey [. . .] based on a sample of 2,500 of the nation's 15,718 public library outlets [. . .]

Romney 8

found that 73.3% of public library outlets now offer public access to the Internet. However, only 68.6% offer graphical public Internet access to the World Wide Web, and only 45.3% offer graphical public access to the Web at speeds of 56 kbps or greater (Simon) .

No page number is used when referring to a one-page source.

The federal government is also making efforts to narrow the "digital divide." One example of their efforts is the school writing project launched by the Federal Bureau of Indian Affairs. The goal of this program is to set up Internet connections in the one hundred eighty-five schools the Bureau finances. By giving these schools Internet access, the Bureau hopes to lessen the sense of isolation Native American students experience because they live in remote rural areas. One concern, however, is that teachers at these Native American schools will not be adequately trained in using the Internet; another is that there will not be enough technical support to keep the computer screen running smoothly (Mendels).

Congress is also making efforts to decrease the gap between the "haves" and the "have-nots." In the Telecommunications Act of 1996, the Federal Communications Commission was directed to "set rules requiring telephone and cable television companies to provide 'universal access' to new services, like the Internet" (Lohr). Legislators hope this language will encourage regulators to "mandate access and cut-rate service for schools and public libraries" (Lohr).

Conclusion recommends solutions for problem of "digital divide."

Despite these efforts, however, much still needs to be done to ensure that everyone has access to the Internet. Even Vice President Al Gore, an enthusiastic advocate of the digital revolution, admits that several challenges remain. First, we must make the Internet available to the widest possible audience. In other words, access in public places must be increased. If people cannot afford computers, they will not have access to the Internet unless computers are made available in public schools, libraries, and community centers. Second, we must provide training to people unfamiliar with the new technology. Finally, we must target low-income and minority families (particularly those in rural areas) for this training because these are the most likely "have-nots." Unless we take steps to make the Internet available to all, we will quickly become two separate and unequal societies: one "plugged-in" and privileged and one "unplugged" and marginalized.

Note

[1]A *protocol* is an agreed-upon method of communication between computers.

↑ 1 inch

↕ ½ inch

Romney 11

Works Cited ←— Center

←— Double-space

Belluck, Pam. "What Price Will Be Paid by Those Not on the

Indent
1/2 inch ⟶ Net?" New York Times on the Web 22 Sept. 1999. 15

Oct. 1999 <http://search.nytimes.com/search/daily/bin/

fastweb?getdoc+site+site+88705+68+wAA+Internet%

7Eand%7Esocity>.

Ebenezer, Jazlin V., and Eddy Lau. Science on the Internet: A

Resource for K-12 Teachers. New Jersey: Simon, 1999.

Elmer-DeWitt, Phillip. "Bards of the Internet." Time 4 July

1994. 20 Nov. 1999 <http://www.pathfinder.com/time/

magazine/archive/1994/940704/940704.technology.htm>.

Fulton, Michael. Exploring Careers in Cyberspace. New York:

Rosen, 1998.

1 inch ←——→ Gibbs, Mark and Richard Smith. Navigating the Internet. ←——→ 1 inch

Indianapolis: SAMS, 1993.

Gore, Al. "Building a Global Community." Remarks Prepared

for the 15th International ITU Conference. 12 Oct. 1998.

69 pars. 8 Oct. 1999 <http://technicaljournal.com/

Internet/81012.htm>.

Lohr, Steve. "The Great Unplugged Masses Confront the Fu-

ture." New York Times on the Web 21 Apr. 1996. 16

Oct. 1999 <http://search.nytimes.com/search/daily/bin/

fastweb?getdoc+site+site+82132+35+wAAA+>.

Mendels, Pamela. "U. S. Program Wires Remote Native Reser-

vations. New York Times on the Web 6 May 1998.

1 inch

Romney 12

11 Oct. 1999 <http://search.nytimes.com/search/daily/bin/

fastweb?getdoc+site+site+82132+35+wAA+>.

"NAACP Targets Minority Gap in Internet Use, TV Roles."

CNN.Com 13 July 1999. 11 Oct. 1999 <http://search.cnn.

com:80/querry.html?col=cnni&qp=&qs=&qc=&pw=460&

ws=0&la=fs=&qt=Internet&qm=0&ql=&st=11&nh=10&

1k=1&rf=1>.

Sklaroff, Sara. "E-Mail: Americans Are Connecting Online Like

Never Before, and It's Changing the Way We Live and

Love." U. S. News and World Report Mar. 1999: 54–62.

Simon, Jeanne Hurley. "Moving Toward More Effective Public

Internet Access: The 1998 National Survey." Journal of

the U. S. National Commission on Libraries and Informa-

tion Science 65 (1999): 14.

"Telecommunications." Encarta 1994. CD-ROM. Redmond,

WA: Microsoft, 1995.

Wendall, Kyla. "Internet History." University of Regina Student

Connection Program. 18 Aug. 1997. 10 Oct. 1999

<http://tdi.uregina.ca/~ursc/internet/history.html>.

Long URL cannot be divided after a slash. For this reason, URL is broken in logical places.

Documenting Sources:
APA and Other Styles

APA & OTHER STYLES

PART 5

CHAPTER 10

APA AND OTHER DOCUMENTATION STYLES

10a Using APA Style

APA style,* which is used extensively in the social sciences, relies on short parenthetical citations, consisting of the last name of the author, the year of publication, and—for direct quotations only—the page number. These references are keyed to an alphabetical list of references that follows the paper. APA style also permits content notes placed after the last page of the text.

(1) Parenthetical References in the Text

When introducing a quotation, include the author's name and the date in the introductory phrase. Put the page number in parentheses after the quotation.

According to Weston (1996), children from one-parent homes read

at "a significantly lower level than those from two-parent homes"

(p. 58).

American Psychological Association Extension Webpage (WEAPAS)
  http://www.beadsland.com/weapas/
Using APA Sources Wisely (Roane St. CC)
  http://rscc3.rscc.cc.tn.us/~jordan_jj/OWL/UsingSources_APA.html
List of APA Style Resources
  http://www.psychwww.com/resource/apacrib.htm
Downloadable APA Style Guide, pdf file (Montana State U.)
  http://www.lib.montana.edu/instruct/styles/
Citing Electronic Sources (APA and MLA)
  http://www.uvm.edu/~ncrane/estyles/

*APA documentation style follows the guidelines set in the *Publication Manual of the American Psychological Association,* 4th ed. Washington, DC: APA., 1994.

When introducing a paraphrase or summary, include the author's name and the date either in the introductory phrase or in parentheses at the end of the paraphrase or summary.

> According to Zinn (1995), this program has had success in training teenage
>
> fathers to take financial and emotional responsibility for their offspring.

> This program has had success in training teenage fathers to take financial
>
> and emotional responsibility for their offspring (Zinn, 1995).

Long quotations (forty words or more) are double-spaced and indented five spaces from the left margin. Parenthetical documentation is placed after the final punctuation.

DIRECTORY OF APA IN-TEXT CITATIONS

1. A work by two authors
2. A work by three to five authors
3. A work by six or more authors
4. A work by a corporate author
5. A work with no listed author
6. A personal communication
7. An indirect source
8. A specific part of a source
9. Two or more works within the same parenthetical reference
10. A table

Sample APA In-Text Citations

1. A Work by Two Authors

> There is growing concern over the use of psychological testing in ele-
>
> mentary schools (Albright & Glennon, 1982).

2. A Work by Three to Five Authors

 If a work has more than two but fewer than six authors, mention all names in the first reference, and in subsequent references cite only the first author followed by *et al.* and the year.

First Reference

> (Sparks, Wilson, & Hewitt)

Subsequent Reference

(Sparks et al., 1984).

3. A Work by Six or More Authors

When a work has six or more authors, cite the name of the first author followed by *et al.* and the year in all references.

(Miller et al., 1995).

CLOSE UP   CITING WORKS BY MULTIPLE AUTHORS

When referring to multiple authors in the text of your paper, join the last two names with *and.*

According to Rosen, Wolfe, and Ziff (1988). . . .

In parenthetical documentation, however, use an **ampersand.**

(Rosen, Wolfe, & Ziff, 1988).

---

4. A Work by a Corporate Author

If the name of a corporate author is long, abbreviate it after the first citation.

First Reference

(National Institute of Mental Health [NIMH], 1994)

Subsequent Reference

(NIMH, 1994)

5. A Work with No Listed Author

If a work has no listed author, cite the first two or three words of the title and the year.

("New Immigration," 1994).

6. A Personal Communication

(R. Takaki, personal communication, October 17, 1996).

NOTE: Cite letters, memos, telephone conversations, personal interviews, e-mail, messages from electronic bulletin boards, and so on, only in the text—*not* in the reference list.

7. An Indirect Source

Cogan and Howe offer very different interpretations of the problem (as cited in Swenson, 1990).

8. A Specific Part of a Source
Use abbreviations for the words *page* (p.), *chapter* (chap.), and *section* (sec.).

These theories have an interesting history (Lee, 1966, chap. 2).

9. Two or More Works within the Same Parenthetical Reference
List works by different authors in alphabetical order.

This theory is supported by several studies (Barson & Roth, 1985; Rose, 1987; Tedesco, 1982).

List works by the same author or authors in order of date of publication.

This theory is supported by several studies (Weiss & Elliot, 1982, 1984, 1985).

For works by the same author published in the same year, designate the work whose title comes first alphabetically *a*, the one whose title comes next *b*, and so on; repeat the year in each citation.

This theory is supported by several studies (Hossack, 1985a, 1985b).

10. A Table
If you use a table from a source, give credit to the author in a note at the bottom of the table.

Note. From "Predictors of Employment and Earnings Among JOBS Participants," P. A. Neenan and D. K. Orthner, 1996, Social Work Research, 20(4), p. 233.

(2) Reference List

The list of all the sources cited in your paper falls at the end on a new numbered page headed *References* (or *Bibliography* if you are listing all the works you consulted, whether or not you cited them).

✔ CHECKLIST: PREPARING THE APA REFERENCE LIST

✔ Begin the reference list on a new page after the last page of text or content notes, numbered as the next page of the paper.

✔ List the items on the reference list alphabetically (with author's last name first).

✔ Indent the first line of each entry five to seven spaces; type subsequent lines flush with the left-hand margin.*

✔ Separate the major divisions of each entry with a period and one space.

✔ Double-space the reference list within and between entries.

✔ CHECKLIST: ARRANGING WORKS IN THE APA REFERENCE LIST

✔ Single-author entries precede multiple-author entries that begin with the same name.

Field, S. (1987).

Field, S., & Levitt, M. P. (1984).

✔ Entries by the same author or authors are arranged according to date of publication, starting with the earliest date.

Ruthenberg, H., & Rubin, R. (1985).

Ruthenberg, H., & Rubin, R. (1987).

✔ Entries with the same author or authors and date of publication are arranged alphabetically according to title.

Wolk, E. M. (1986a). Analysis . . .

Wolk, E. M. (1986b). Hormonal . . .

*This format is now recommended by the APA for all manuscripts submitted for publication. If your instructor prefers, you may instead type the first line of each entry flush with the left-hand margin and indent subsequent lines three spaces.

DIRECTORY OF APA REFERENCE LIST ENTRIES

Entries for Books

1. A book with one author
2. A book with more than one author
3. An edited book
4. A book with no listed author or editor
5. A work in several volumes
6. A work with a corporate author
7. A government report
8. One selection from an anthology
9. An article in a reference book
10. The foreword, preface, or afterword of a book

Entries for Articles

11. An article in a scholarly journal with continuous pagination through an annual volume
12. An article in a scholarly journal with separate pagination in each issue
13. A magazine article
14. A newspaper article (signed/unsigned)
15. A letter to the editor
16. A published letter

Entries for Electronic Sources

17. Online article
18. Abstract on CD-ROM
19. Abstract online
20. Computer software

Sample APA Reference List Entries: Books Capitalize only the first word of the title and subtitle. Underline the entire title, including punctuation, and enclose the date, volume number, and edition number in parentheses. Write out the publisher's name in full.

1. A Book with One Author

Maslow, A. H. (1974). <u>Toward a psychology of being.</u> Princeton: Van Nostrand.

2. A Book with More Than One Author
List all the authors—by last name and initials—regardless of how many there are.

Wolfinger, D., Knable, P., Richards, H. L., & Silberger, R. (1990). <u>The chronically unemployed.</u> New York: Berman Press.

3. An Edited Book

Lewin, K., Lippitt, R., & White, R. K. (Eds.). (1985). <u>Social learning and imitation.</u> New York: Basic Books.

4. A Book with No Listed Author or Editor

<u>Writing with a computer.</u> (1993). Philadelphia: Drexel Publications.

5. A Work in Several Volumes

Jones, P. R., & Williams, T. C. (Eds.). (1990–1993). <u>Handbook of therapy</u> (Vols. 1–2). Princeton: Princeton University Press.

6. A Work with a Corporate Author

League of Women Voters of the United States. (1991). <u>Local league handbook.</u> Washington, DC: Author.

NOTE: When the author and publisher are the same, list *Author* at the end of the citation instead of repeating the publisher's name.

7. A Government Report

National Institute of Mental Health. (1987). <u>Motion pictures and violence: A summary report of research</u> (DHHS Publication No. ADM 91-22187). Washington, DC: U.S. Government Printing Office.

8. One Selection from an Anthology

Lorde, A. (1984). Age, race, and class. In P. S. Rothenberg (Ed.), <u>Racism and sexism: An integrated study</u> (pp. 352–360). New York: St. Martin's.

NOTE: A title of a selection in an anthology is not underlined or enclosed in quotation marks. If you cite two or more selections from the same anthology, give the full citation for the anthology in each entry.

9. An Article in a Reference Book

Edwards, P. (Ed.). (1987). Determinism. In The encyclopedia of philosophy (Vol. 2, pp. 359–373). New York: Macmillan.

10. The Foreword, Preface, or Afterword of a Book

Taylor, T. (1979). Preface. In Less than slaves by Benjamin B. Ferencz. Cambridge: Harvard University Press.

Sample APA Reference List Entries: Articles   Capitalize only the first word of the title and subtitle. Do not underline the title of the article or enclose it in quotation marks. Give the periodical title in full; underline the title and capitalize all major words. Underline the volume number, as well as the comma that follows it, but not the issue number in parentheses. Give inclusive page numbers. Use *pp.* when referring to page numbers in newspapers and popular magazines, but omit this abbreviation when referring to page numbers in periodicals with volume numbers.

11. An Article in a Scholarly Journal with Continuous Pagination through an Annual Volume

Miller, W. (1969). Violent crimes in city gangs. Journal of Social Issues, 27, 581–593.

12. An Article in a Scholarly Journal with Separate Pagination in Each Issue

Williams, S., & Cohen, L. R. (1984). Child stress in early learning situations. American Psychologist, 21 (10), 1–28.

13. A Magazine Article

McCurdy, H. G. (1983, June). Brain mechanisms and intelligence. Psychology Today, pp. 61–63.

14. A Newspaper Article (Signed/Unsigned)

James, W. R. (1993, November 16). The uninsured and health care. The Wall Street Journal, pp. A1, A14.

NOTE: Article appears on two separate pages.

Study finds many street people mentally ill. (1993, June 7). New York Times, p. A7.

15. A Letter to the Editor

Williams, P. (1993, July 19). Self-fulfilling stereotypes [Letter to the editor]. Los Angeles Times, p. A22.

16. A Published Letter

Joyce, J. (1931). Letter to Louis Gillet. In Richard Ellmann, James Joyce (p. 631). New York: Oxford University Press.

Sample APA Reference List Entries: Electronic Sources

17. Online Article

Farrell, P. D. (1997, March). New high-tech stresses hit traders and investors on the information superhighway. [14 paragraphs.] Wall Street News [Online serial]. Available http: wall-street-news.com/forecasts/stress/stress.html

NOTE: No period follows the electronic address.

18. Abstract on CD-ROM

Guiot, A., & Peterson, B. R. (1995). Forgetfulness and partial cognition. [CD-ROM]. Memory and Cognition, 23, 643–652. Abstract from: SilverPlatter File: PsycLit Item: 90-14321

19. Abstract Online

Guiot, A., & Peterson, B. R. (1995). Forgetfulness and partial cognition. [Online]. Memory and Cognition, 23, 643–652. Abstract from: DIALOG file: PsycINFO Item: 90-14321

20. Computer Software

Sharp, S. (1995). Career Selection Tests (Version 5.0) [Computer software]. Chico, CA: Avocation Software.

(3) Content Notes

APA format allows, but does not encourage, the use of content notes, indicated by **superscripts** (raised numerals) in the text. The notes are listed on a separate numbered page, entitled *Footnotes,* following the last page of text. Double-space all notes, indenting the first line of each note five to seven spaces and beginning subsequent lines flush left.

10b   Sample Research Paper: APA Style

The following paper, which uses APA documentation style, includes a title page and a reference list.

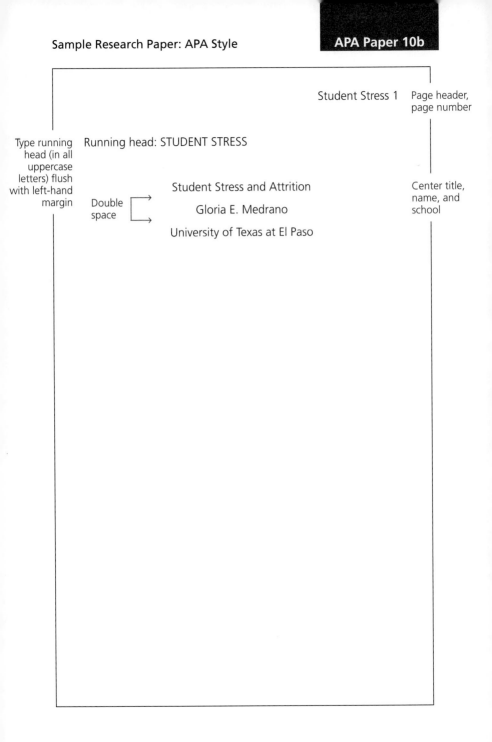

Student Stress 1   Page header, page number

Type running head (in all uppercase letters) flush with left-hand margin

Running head: STUDENT STRESS

Double space

Student Stress and Attrition

Gloria E. Medrano

University of Texas at El Paso

Center title, name, and school

Full title

Student Stress and Attrition

Ecklund and Henderson (1981), in their national longitudi-   Statistic used in introduction

nal study of the high school class of 1972, documented that

46% of enrolling college freshmen had at one point or another

dropped out of college. Thirty-four percent dropped out within

Author's name in parentheses when not mentioned in text

their first two years (Ecklund & Henderson, 1981). The high

dropout rate, along with a decreasing student population (Dusek

& Renteria, 1984), is still directly affecting the state of our educa-

tional system today. Although there is little that can be done

about the lower numbers of incoming freshmen, something can

be done to lessen the problem of college attrition.

The ideal approach to combating this problem is to deal

with the group of students closest in proximity to the university--

the residence hall population. Many of their reasons for with-

drawing from the university are traced to a fundamental cause:

Thesis statement

stress. In this case, stress is the psychological phenomenon that

contributes to the high attrition rates of resident students.

Headings included in the text. See 14c for format.

Statement of the Problem

The on-campus resident student population is very differ-   Identifies and describes the group to be studied, distinguishing it from other groups.

ent from other groups of individuals. They cannot be com-

pared to such groups as nonstudents, noncommuters, and

commuters. Aside from such student-related stressors as aca-

demics and personal, financial, and emotional problems, on-

campus residents must also contend with adjusting to their

new environment, living away from home and in a new community, having a roommate, and being disturbed by the overall noise level in the dormitories.

Bishop and Snyder (1976) noted grades and money as the major pressures that account for the differences between residents and commuters. Commuters ranked time management next on their list, and residents listed social pressures and concerns about their future as their next most prominent problem. Residents cited peer pressure more often as a source of stress, while commuters were more concerned with difficulties of scheduling.

Year in parentheses, authors' names in text

Background of the Problem

Resident students at the University of Texas at El Paso experience problems that are different and distinct from those at other major universities. Of the more than 15,000 students attending this university, slightly more than 700 live on campus. This is a relatively small percentage compared to the neighboring campus of New Mexico State University, where over 1,500 of the 12,000 students live on campus (R. Hanke, personal communication, December 2, 1996). U.T. El Paso is a commuter campus, which means that after 6 p.m. the campus is virtually deserted. Many other universities, like NMSU, have campus-oriented communities. The students have many activities with which to fill their time. As stated earlier, the social atmosphere is directly related to student stress levels. Many of

Profile of the group to be studied

Personal communication cited in text but not on reference list our on-campus residents are from out of town, with no means of transportation to get them off campus, and there is no real community around the campus. They are therefore unable to develop social outlets. Another factor that relates to UTEP is that many of our residents are freshmen; they are often unfamiliar with campus activities that would break the monotony of campus living. Because of the low numbers of on-campus residents and the high numbers of commuting students, residents are also limited in terms of the potential number of people they can interact with.

The new system of integrating athletes into the regular student housing system has been particularly traumatic for nonathlete residents. Previously, athletes were housed in a separate dormitory, Burges Hall; however, because that hall has fallen into disrepair, the incoming freshman football players have been moved into Barry Hall's third floor. This floor is between two other nonacademic floors. A nonacademic floor is one that is not especially designated for honors students or other students requiring special study hours. As such, nonacademic floors do not have designated quiet hours or rules and regulations that foster study and quiet. Aside from the usual noise related to living in a nonacademic dormitory, additional problems, such as the dropping of weights on the floor and disciplinary problems related to the rowdiness of athletes in general, also occur.

Student Stress 5

Description of the Problem

At the beginning of the fall semester of 1996, Barry

Hall's second floor had 22 residents. Three residents dropped

out of school because of personal and family problems, and

2 residents moved to other floors because of roommate con-

flicts that could not be resolved. Of the remaining 17 resi-

dents, 11 will be returning to the university in the spring

semester. Five students are leaving the system to study at a

university closer to home, and 1 is moving out of the dormi-

tory into an apartment. Five of the returning students will

move back to Barry Hall's second floor, while 6 will be moving

to other floors after having been seriously frustrated by living

on a nonacademic floor. Table 1, which summarizes the

changes in population on Barry Hall's second floor after the

fall 1996 semester, suggests the variety of stressful situations

that face resident students.

Solutions

Although the dropout rate caused by stress in the dormi-

tories does not significantly affect the university because most

students are commuters, it is a problem that, if alleviated, will

help to solve the institution's overall retention problem. At a

time when UTEP is concerned with decreasing enrollment,

maintaining enrollment is important. The implementation of a

wide range of educational and social programs within the resi-

dence halls, strengthening the programs of recruitment,

APA style recommends using figures to express numbers 10 and above and words to express numbers below 10. Use figures to express all numbers below 10 that are grouped for comparison with numbers 10 and above.

Generalized description of the problem related to the specific case

Table 1, included as an appendix, is referred to in the text. See 14c for format.

Recommendations for solving the problem

Student Stress 6

admissions, counseling services, financial aid, career planning and placement, and health services, will also contribute to decreased stress and improved retention.

It is important that those individuals who have the closest contact with students--resident assistants--be well trained.

List inserted in text. See 14c for format.

1. Resident assistants should be trained in handling stress.

2. Resident assistants should be introduced to the student services available on campus--for example, the Financial Aid Office, The Career Information Center, and the Health Center.

3. Resident assistants should be involved in freshman orientation.

Resident assistants should pay particular attention to their residents and watch for signs that warn them if students are having stress-related problems. If a resident assistant suspects that a resident is having a special problem, the resident can be referred to an appropriate program or department for help.

Brief concluding paragraph summarizes recommendations.

With proper training, resident advisors can take the necessary steps to control the 50% attrition rate among on-campus resident students.

Student Stress 7

Reference page numbered consecutively

Center
Double-space

References

Bishop, J. B., & Snyder, G. S. (1976). Commuters and

residents. Pressures, helps, and psychological services. Journal

of College Student Personnel, 17, 232–235.

Journal article by two authors

Indent first
line of each
entry five to
seven spaces*

Dusek, R., & Renteria, R. (1984, December 13). Plan

slashes UTEP budget by 28%. El Paso Times, p. A1.

Newspaper article

Document
from
computer
database

Ecklund, B. K., & Henderson, L. B. (1981). Longitudinal

study of the high school class of 1972. Washington, DC: Na-

tional Institute of Education. (ERIC Document Reproduction

Service No. ED 311 222)

*This format is now recommended by the APA for all manu-
scripts submitted for publication. If your instructor prefers, you
may instead type the first line of each entry flush with the left margin and indent subsequent lines three spaces.

Table 1

Residents on Barry Hall's Second Floor

Dropouts	Returning Students
3 left school because of personal problems	2 moved because of conflict with roommate
5 transferred to another university	1 moving to an apartment
	5 returning to Barry Hall's second floor
	6 moving to other floors
Total: 8 students	Total: 14 students

10c   Using CMS Style

The Chicago Manual of Style (CMS) is used in history and some social science and humanities disciplines. **CMS format*** has two parts: notes at the end of the paper (endnotes) and a list of bibliographic citations. (Although Chicago style encourages the use of endnotes, it also allows the use of footnotes at the bottom of the page.)

(1) Endnotes and Footnotes

The notes format calls for a **superscript** (raised numeral) in the text after source material you have either quoted or referred to. This numeral, placed after all punctuation marks except dashes, corresponds to the numeral that accompanies the note.

✔ CHECKLIST: PREPARING CMS ENDNOTES

✔ Begin endnotes on a new page after the last page of the paper.
✔ Number the page on which the endnotes appear as the next page of the paper.
✔ Type and number notes in the order in which they appear in the paper, beginning with number 1.
✔ Type the note number on the line, followed by a period and one space.
✔ Indent the first line of each note three spaces; type subsequent lines flush with the left-hand margin.
✔ Double-space within and between entries.

Endnote and Footnote Format: CMS

In the Text

By November of 1942, the Allies had proof that the Nazis were engaged in the systemic killing of Jews.[1]

University of Chicago Press homepage
http://press-www.uchicago.edu

---

*CMS format follows the guidelines set in *The Chicago Manual of Style*, 14th ed. Chicago: U of Chicago P, 1993.

In the Note

> 1. David S. Wyman, *The Abandonment of the Jews: America and the Holocaust 1941–1945* (New York: Pantheon Books, 1984), 65.

CLOSE UP SUBSEQUENT REFERENCES

In the first reference to a work, use the full citation; in subsequent references to the same work, list only the author's last name, followed by a comma and a page number.

First Note on Espinoza

> 1. J. M. Espinoza, *The First Expedition of Vargas in New Mexico, 1692* (Albuquerque: University of New Mexico Press, 1949), 10–12.

Subsequent Note

> 5. Espinoza, 29.

NOTE: *The Chicago Manual of Style* allows the use of the abbreviation *ibid.* ("in the same place") for subsequent references to the same work as long as there are no intervening references. *Ibid.* takes the place of the author's name and the work's title—but not the page number.

First Note on Espinoza

> 1. J. M. Espinoza, *The First Expedition of Vargas in New Mexico, 1692* (Albuquerque: University of New Mexico Press, 1949), 10–12.

Subsequent Note

> 2. Ibid., 23.

Keep in mind, however, that the use of *Ibid.* is giving way to the use of the author's last name and the page number for subsequent references to the same work.

(2) Bibliography

In addition to the heading *Bibliography*, Chicago style allows *Selected Bibliography, Works Cited, Literature Cited, References*, and *Sources Consulted*.

✔ CHECKLIST: PREPARING THE CMS BIBLIOGRAPHY

- ✔ Type entries on a separate page after the endnotes.
- ✔ List entries alphabetically according to the author's last name.
- ✔ Type the first line of each entry flush with the left-hand margin; indent subsequent lines three spaces.
- ✔ Double-space the bibliography within and between entries.

DIRECTORY OF CMS ENDNOTE CITATIONS AND BIBLIOGRAPHY ENTRIES

Entries for Books

1. A book by one author
2. A book by two or three authors
3. A book by more than three authors
4. An edited book
5. A chapter in a book or an essay in an anthology
6. A multivolume work

Entries for Articles

7. An article in a scholarly journal with continuous pagination through an annual volume
8. An article in a scholarly journal with separate pagination in each issue
9. An article in a weekly magazine
10. An article in a monthly magazine
11. An article in a newspaper

Entries for Other Sources

12. A personal interview
13. A published interview
14. A letter
15. A film or videotape
16. A recording

Entries for Electronic Sources

17. Computer software
18. An electronic document

Sample CMS Entries: Books   Although underlining to indicate italics is acceptable, Chicago style recommends the use of italics for titles.

1. A Book by One Author

Endnote

     1. Herbert J. Gans, *The Urban Villagers,* 2d ed. (New York: Free Press, 1982), 100.

Bibliography

Gans, Herbert J. *The Urban Villagers,* 2d ed. New York: Free Press, 1982.

2. A Book by Two or Three Authors

Endnote

     2. James W. Davidson and Mark Hamilton Lytle, *After the Fact: The Art of Historical Detection* (New York: Alfred A. Knopf, 1982), 54.

Bibliography

Davidson, James W., and Mark Hamilton Lytle. *After the Fact: The Art of Historical Detection.* New York: Alfred A. Knopf, 1982.

3. A Book by More than Three Authors

Endnote

     3. Robert E. Spiller et al., eds., *Literary History of the United States* (New York: Macmillan, 1974), 24.

Bibliography

Spiller, Robert E., et al., eds. *Literary History of the United States.* New York: Macmillan, 1974.

4. An Edited Book

Endnote

     4. William Bartram, *The Travels of William Bartram,* ed. Mark Van Doren (New York: Dover Press, 1955), 85.

Bibliography

> Bartam, William. *The Travels of William Bartram.* Edited by Mark Van
> Doren. New York: Dover Press, 1955.

5. A Chapter in a Book or an Essay in an Anthology

Endnote

> 5. Peter Kidson, "Architecture and City Planning," in *The Legacy of
> Greece,* ed. M. I. Finley (New York: Oxford University Press, 1981),
> 376–400.

Bibliography

> Kidson, Peter. "Architecture and City Planning." In *The Legacy of
> Greece,* ed. M. I. Finley, 376–400. New York: Oxford University Press,
> 1981.

6. A Multivolume Work

Endnote

> 6. Kathleen Raine, *Blake and Tradition* (Princeton: Princeton Univer-
> sity Press, 1968), 1: 143.

Bibliography

> Raine, Kathleen. *Blake and Tradition.* Vol. 1. Princeton: Princeton Uni-
> versity Press, 1968.

Sample CMS Entries: Articles

7. An Article in a Scholarly Journal with Continuous Pagination through an Annual Volume

Endnote

> 7. John Huntington, "Science Fiction and the Future," *College Eng-
> lish* 37 (fall 1975): 341.

Bibliography

> Huntington, John. "Science Fiction and the Future." *College English* 37
> (fall 1975): 340–58.

8. An Article in a Scholarly Journal with Separate Pagination in Each Issue

Endnote

8. R. G. Sipes, "War, Sports, and Aggression: An Empirical Test of Two Rival Theories," *American Anthropologist* 4, no. 2 (1973): 80.

Bibliography

Sipes, R. G. "War, Sports, and Aggression: An Empirical Test of Two Rival Theories." *American Anthropologist* 4, no. 2 (1973): 65–84.

9. An Article in a Weekly Magazine

Endnote

9. James Traub, "The Hearts and Minds of City College," *New Yorker,* 7 June 1993, 45.

Bibliography

Traub, James. "The Hearts and Minds of City College." *New Yorker,* 7 June 1993, 42–53.

10. An Article in a Monthly Magazine

Endnote

10. Lori Roll, "Careers in Engineering," *Working Woman,* November 1982, 62.

Bibliography

Roll, Lori. "Careers in Engineering." *Working Woman,* November 1982, 62.

11. An Article in a Newspaper

Endnote

11. Raymond Bonner, "A Guatemalan General's Rise to Power," *New York Times,* 21 July 1982, 3(A).

Bibliography

Bonner, Raymond. "A Guatemalan General's Rise to Power." *New York Times,* 21 July 1982, 3(A).

Sample CMS Entries: Other Sources

12. A Personal Interview

Endnote

12. Cornel West, interview by author, tape recording, St. Louis, Mo., 8 June 1994.

Bibliography

West, Cornel. Interview by author. Tape recording. St. Louis, Mo., 8 June 1994.

13. A Published Interview

Endnote

13. Gwendolyn Brooks, interview by George Stravos, *Contemporary Literature* 11, no. 1 (winter 1970): 12.

Bibliography

Brooks, Gwendolyn. Interview by George Stravos. *Contemporary Literature* 11, no. 1 (winter 1970): 1–20.

14. A Letter

Endnote

14. Amy Tan, letter to author, 7 April 1990.

Bibliography

Tan, Amy. Letter to author. 7 April 1990.

15. A Film or Videotape

Endnote

15. *Interview with Arthur Miller,* dir. William Schiff, 17 min., The Mosaic Group, 1987, videocassette.

Bibliography

Miller, Arthur. *Interview with Arthur Miller.* Directed by William Schiff.

17 min. The Mosaic Group, 1987. Videocassette.

16. A Recording

Endnote

16. Bob Marley, "Crisis," on *Bob Marley and the Wailers,* Kava Island

Records compact disk 423 095-3.

Bibliography

Marley, Bob. "Crisis." On *Bob Marley and the Wailers.* Kava Island

Records compact disk 423 095-3.

Sample CMS Entries: Electronic Sources

17. Computer Software

Endnote

17. *Reunion: The Family Tree Software,* vers. 2.0 for Macintosh,

Lester Productions, Cambridge, Mass.

Bibliography

Reunion: The Family Tree Software. Vers. 2.0 for Macintosh. Lester Pro-

ductions, Cambridge, Mass.

18. An Electronic Document

The Chicago Manual of Style recommends following the guidelines developed by the International Standards Organization (ISO). List the authors, the title, the electronic medium (electronic bulletin board, for example), information about a print version, access dates, and electronic address or location information.

Endnote

18. Arthur Sklar, "Survey of Legal Opinions Regarding the Death

Penalty in New Jersey," in NL-KR (Digest vol. 3, no. 2) [electronic bul-

letin board] (Newark, N.J., 1995 [cited 17 March 1997]); available from

nl-kr@cs.newark.edu; INTERNET.

Bibliography

Sklar, Arthur. "Survey of Legal Opinions Regarding the Death Penalty in New Jersey," in NL-KR (Digest vol. 3, no. 2) [electronic bulletin board]. (Newark, N.J., 1995 [cited 17 March 1997]. Available from nl-kr@cs.newark.edu; INTERNET.

10d Sample Research Paper: CMS Style

Following are examples of various elements of a CMS research paper: two sample pages of the paper, a notes page, and a bibliography.

Page number
on every page

Angela M. Womack

American History 301

December 3, 1999

Double-space   Native Americans and the Reservation System

It is July 7th, and ten thousand Navajo Indians make
ready to leave land in Arizona that they have called home for
generations. This land has been assigned to the Hopi tribe by
the U.S. government to settle a boundary dispute between
the two tribes.[1] Ella Bedonie, a member of the Navajo tribe,   Superscripts
refer to
says, "The Navajo and the Hopi people have no dispute. It's   endnotes
listed on
the government that's doing this to us. I think the Hopis may   "Notes" page
have the land for a while, but then the government . . . will
step in."[2] The Hopis are receiving 250,000 acres to compen-
sate them for the 900,000 acres they will lose in this land
deal; however, the groundwater on this land is suspect because of possible contamination by a uranium mine upstream.
To mitigate this situation the government has sweetened the
deal with incentives of livestock.[3]

This was the fate many Native Americans faced as western
expansion swept across the North American continent. Now consider that the incident mentioned occurred not on July 7, 1886,
but on July 7, 1986. Indian relations with the U.S. government
are as problematic today as ever before, for the federal government's administration of the reservation system both promotes
and restricts the development of the Native American culture.

2

A reservation is an area of land reserved for Indian use. There are approximately 260 reservations in the United States at present.[4] The term *reservation* can be traced back to the time when land was "reserved" for Indian use in treaties between whites and Native Americans. Figures from 1978 by the Bureau of Indian Affairs show that 51,789,249 acres of land are in trust for Native Americans; 41,678,875 acres of this are for tribes, and 10,110,374 acres are for individuals.[5] The Native Americans are by no means restricted to these areas, although this assumption is commonly made. They are as free as any other citizen to leave these areas.

10

Notes

1. Trebbe Johnson, "Indian Land, White Greed," *Nation,* 4 July 1987, 15.

2. Johnson, 17.

3. Johnson, 16.

4. Ted Williams, "On the Reservation: America's Apartheid," *National Review,* 8 May 1987, 28.

5. U.S. Bureau of Indian Affairs, "Information About . . . The Indian People" (Washington, D.C.: GPO, 1981), 6, mimeographed.

Sources listed in order in which they appear in paper. Second and subsequent references to sources include only author's last name and page number.

11

Bibliography   ← Center
   ← Double-
"Adrift in Their Own Land." *Time,* 6 July 1987, 89.   space

Entries are   Arrandale, Tom. "American Indian Economic Development."
listed
alphabetically   *Editorial Research Reports,* 17 Feb. 1984, 127–142.
according to
author's last   Battise, Carol. Personal interview, 25 Sept. 1987.
name
   Cook, J. "Help Wanted--Work, Not Handouts." *Forbes,* 4 May

1987, 68–71.

First line of   Horswell, Cindy. "Alabama-Coushattas See Hope in U.S.
each entry is
flush with   Guardianship." *Houston Chronicle,* 27 May 1987, 11.
left-hand
margin;   Johnson, Trebbe. "Indian Land, White Greed." *Nation,* 4 July
subsequent
lines are   1987, 15–18.
indented 3
spaces   Martin, Howard N. "Alabama-Coushatta Indians of Texas:

Alabama-Coushatta Historical Highlights." Brochure,

Alabama-Coushatta Indian Reservation: Livingston, Tex., n.d.

Article has no   "A New Brand of Tribal Tycoons." *Time,* 16 March 1987, 56.
listed author;
alphabetized   Philp, K. R. "Dillon S. Myer and the Advent of Termination:
according to
first significant   1950–1953." *Western Historical Quarterly* 3 (January
word of title
1988): 37–59.

U.S. Bureau of Indian Affairs. "Information About . . . The Indian

People." Washington, D.C.: GPO, 1981. Mimeographed.

Williams, Ted. "On the Reservation: America's Apartheid."

National Review, 8 May 1987, 28–30.

Young, J., and Williams T. *American Realities: Historical Reali-*

ties from the First Settlements to the Civil War. Boston:

Little, Brown, 1981.

10e   Using CBE Style

(1) Documentation in the Text

Documentation styles recommended by the Council of Biological Editors (CBE) are used in biology, zoology, physiology, anatomy, and genetics. The *CBE Style Manual** recommends two documentation styles: the number-reference system and the author-year (or name-year) system.

The Number-Reference System: The number-reference format calls for either raised numbers in the text of the paper (the preferred form) or numbers inserted parenthetically in the text of the paper.

One study[1] has demonstrated the effect of low dissolved oxygen.

These numbers correspond to a list titled *References, Literature Cited,* or *References Cited* at the end of the paper. If you refer to more than one source in a single note, the numbers are separated by a dash if they are in sequence [2-3] and by a comma if they are not [3,6].

The Author-Year (Or Name-Year) System: This system calls for the author's name and the year of publication to be inserted parenthetically in the text. If the author's name is used to introduce the source material, only the date of publication is needed. When two or more works are cited in the same parentheses, the sources are arranged chronologically (from earliest to latest) and separated by a semicolon.

A great deal of heat is often generated during this process (McGinness 1999).

According to McGinness, a great deal of heat is often generated during this process (1999).

Epidemics can be avoided by taking tissue cultures (Domb 1998) and by intervention with antibiotics (Baldwin and Rigby 1984; Martin and others 1992; Cording 1998).

Council of Biology Editors (CBE) homepage
   http://www.cbe.org

*CBE style follows the guidelines set in the style manual of the Council of Biological editors: *Scientific Style and Format: The CBE Manual for Authors, Editors, and Publishers,* 6th ed. New York: Cambridge U P, 1994.

NOTE: The first citation, *Baldwin and Rigby, 1984,* refers to a work by two authors; the second citation, *Martin and others,* refers to a work by three or more authors.

(2) Reference List

The format of the reference list depends on the documentation style you use. If you use the author-year documentation style, your reference list will resemble the reference list for an APA paper. If you use the number-reference documentation style, your sources will be listed by number, in the order in which they appear in your text, on a *References* page. This section presents guidelines using the number-reference system.

✔ CHECKLIST: PREPARING THE CBE REFERENCE LIST

- ✔ Begin the reference list on a new page after the last page of the paper, numbered as the next page of the paper.
- ✔ List the items in the order in which they appear in the paper, not alphabetically.
- ✔ Number the entries consecutively; type the note numbers on (not above) the line, followed by a period.
- ✔ Type the first line of each entry flush with the left-hand margin; align subsequent lines directly beneath the first letter of the author's last name.
- ✔ Double-space within and between entries.

DIRECTORY OF CBE REFERENCE LIST ENTRIES

1. A book with one author
2. A book with more than one author
3. An edited book
4. A specific section of a book
5. A chapter in a book or an essay in an anthology
6. An article in a journal with continuous pagination
7. An article in a journal with separate pagination in each issue
8. An article with no listed author
9. An electronic source

Sample CBE Reference List Entries: Books   List the author or authors (last name first), the title (not underlined, and with only the first word capitalized), the place of publication (followed by a colon), the full name of the publisher (followed by a semicolon), the year (followed by a period), and the total number of pages (followed by a period).

1. A Book with One Author

1. Key, K. Plant biology. Fort Worth: Harcourt Brace; 1995. 437 p.

2. A Book with More Than One Author

2. Krause, KF, Paterson, MK. Tissue culture: methods and application. New York: Academic Press; 1993. 217 p.

3. An Edited Book

3. Marzacco, MP, editor. A survey of biochemistry. New York: Bowker; 1985. 523 p.

4. A Specific Section of a Book

4. Baldwin, LD, Rigby, CV. A study of animal virology. New York: Wiley; 1984: p 121–133.

5. A Chapter in a Book or an Essay in an Anthology

5. Brydon, RB, Ellis, J, Scott, CD. Cell division and cancer treatment. In Gotlieb, JM. editor. Current research in cancer treatment. New York: Springer-Verlag; 1996: p. 34–47.

Sample CBE Reference List Entries: Articles　List the author or authors (last name first), the title of the article (with only the first word capitalized), the abbreviated name of the journal (with all major words capitalized, but not underlined), the year (followed by a semicolon), the volume number (followed by a colon), and inclusive page numbers. No spaces separate the year, the volume, and the page numbers.

6. An Article in a Journal with Continuous Pagination

6. Bensley, KR. Profiling women physicians. Medica 1985; 1:140–145.

7. An Article in a Journal with Separate Pagination in Each Issue

7. Paul, DR, Wang, AR, Richards, L. The human genome project. Sci Am 1995 Sept;285(2):43–52.

8. An Article with No Listed Author

8. [Anonymous]. Developments in microbiology. Int. J. Microbiol 1987;6:234–248.

9. An Electronic Source

List the author or authors, the title (followed by the journal title, along with the date and volume number, in the case of journal articles), the electronic medium [*serial on-line* for periodicals and *monograph on-line* for books], the date of publication, the words *Available from* followed by a colon and the electronic address, and the date of access.

9. Bensley, KR. Profiling women physicians. Medica [serial on-line] 1985;1. Available from: ftp.lib.nscu.edu via the INTERNET. Accessed 1997 Feb 18.

10f   Sample Research Paper: CBE Style

The following excerpts from a biology research paper uses the number-reference format recommended by the *CBE Style Manual.*

Maternal Smoking

1

June M. Fahrman

Biology 306

April 17, 2000

Maternal Smoking: Deleterious Effects on the Fetus

Introduction

The placenta, lifeline between fetus and mother, has been the subject of various studies aimed at determining the mechanisms by which substances in the mother's bloodstream affect the fetus. For example, cigarette smoking is clearly associated with an increased risk in the incidence of low-birthweight infants,[1] due both to prematurity and to intrauterine growth retardation.[2]

Development of the Placenta

At the morula stage of development, less than one week after fertilization, two types of cells can be distinguished. . . .

Maternal Smoking

10

Conclusion

In summary, abundant evidence exists as to the harmful effects maternal smoking may have on the fetus. These include low birthweight, low IQ scores, minimal brain dysfunction, shorter stature, prenatal mortality, and premature birth. . . .

Maternal Smoking

11

References

1. Rakel, RE. Conn's current therapy 1988. Philadelphia: W. B. Saunders; 1988. 360 p.

2. Meberg, A, Sande, H, Foss, OP, Stenwig, JT. Smoking during pregnancy—effects on the fetus and on thiocyanate levels in mother and baby. Acta. Paediatr Scand 1979; 68:547–552.

3. Lehtovirta, P, Forss, M. The acute effect of smoking on intervillous blood flow of the placenta. Brit Obs Gyn 1978; 85:729–731.

4. Phelan, JP. Diminished fetal reactivity with smoking. Amer Obs Gyn 1980; 136:230–233.

5. VanDerVelde, WJ. Structural changes in the placenta of smoking mothers: a quantitative study. Placenta 1983; 4:231–240.

10g   Using Other Documentation Styles

The following style manuals describe documentation formats used in **?**
other disciplines.

Chemistry

Dodd, Janet S. American Chemical Society. *The ACS Guide: A Manual for Authors and Editors.* 2nd ed. Washington: Amer. Chemical Soc., 1997.

Government Documents

Garner, Diane L. *The Complete Guide to Citing Government Information Resources: A Manual for Writers and Librarians.* Rev. Ed. Bethesda: Congressional Information Service, 1993.

Geology

United States Geological Survey. *Suggestions to Authors of the Reports of the United States Geological Survey.* 7th ed. Washington: GPO, 1991.

History

The Chicago Manual of Style. 14th ed. Chicago: U of Chicago P, 1993.

Journalism

Associated Press Staff. *Associated Press Stylebook and Libel Manual.* 32nd ed. New York: Associated Press, 1997.

Law

The Bluebook: A Uniform System of Citation. Comp. Editors of *Columbia Law Review* et al. 16th ed. Cambridge: Harvard Law Rev. Assn., 1996.

Linguistics

Linguistic Society of America. "LSA Style Sheet." Published annually in December issue of the *LSA Bulletin.*

Mathematics

American Mathematical Society. *AMS Author Handbook.* Providence: Amer. Mathematical Soc., 1997.

Medicine

    Iverson, Cheryl. *Manual of Style: A Guide for Authors and Editors.* 9th
       ed. Chicago: Amer. Medical Assn., 1997.

Music

    Holman D. Kirn, ed. *Writing about Music: A Style Sheet from the Edi-
       tors of 19th-Century Music.* Berkeley: U California P, 1988.

Physics

    American Institute of Physics. *AIP Style Manual.* 4th ed. New York:
       Am. Inst. of Physics, 1990.

Scientific and Technical Writing

    Rubens, Philip, ed. *Science and Technical Writing: A Manual of Style.*
       Fort Worth: Harcourt, 1992.

NOTE: For other guides to style see John Bruce Howell. *Style Manuals of
the English-Speaking World: A Guide.* Phoenix: Oryx, 1983.

PART 6

Academic and Professional Survival Skills

SURVIVAL SKILLS

SURVIVAL SKILLS

PART 6

CHAPTER 11

DEVELOPING READING SKILLS

Knowing how to read effectively is an important skill, one that every college student should master. When you read, your goal should be not just to understand the literal meanings of the words on the page, but also to understand what those words suggest. And, if you are reading a book or article that takes a position on a subject or an issue, you will also have to assess the writer's credibility and evaluate the soundness of his or her ideas. In such cases, you will need to be open to new ideas and willing to question what you read and how you react.

Central to developing effective reading skills is learning the techniques of active reading. **Active reading** means reading with pen in hand, physically marking the text to help you distinguish important points from not-so-important ones. In the process, you learn to identify parallels and to connect causes with effects and generalizations with specific examples.

11a Previewing

The first time you approach a book or article, **preview** it—skim it to gain a sense of the writer's subject and emphasis.

When you preview a book, begin by looking at its table of contents and perhaps skimming its index. Even a quick glance at the index and table of contents will reveal the amount and kind of coverage the book gives to subjects that may be important to you. As you leaf through the chapters, look at pictures, graphs, and tables, reading the captions that appear under them.

When you preview an article, look for headings or boxed material. Then, scan the introductory and concluding paragraphs for summaries of the author's main points. Thesis statements, topic sentences, repeated key terms, and transitional words and phrases can also identify the points the writer is addressing.

The Reading Comprehension Page (Muskingum College)
   http://muskingum.edu/~cal/database/reading.html#Strategies
How to Get the Most Out of Reading Non-Fiction (U. Mich.)
   http://www.si.umich.edu/~pne/read.a.book.htm

11b Highlighting

Once you have finished previewing a work, go on to **highlight** it to identify the writer's key points and their relationships to one another. As you highlight, use symbols and underlining to identify important ideas. (If you are working with library material, photocopy the pages you need and then highlight them.) Be sure to use symbols that you will be able to understand when you reread your material later on.

✓ CHECKLIST: HIGHLIGHTING SYMBOLS

- ✔ Underline to indicate information you will need to read again.
- ✔ Box or circle key words or important phrases.
- ✔ Put a question mark next to confusing passages, unclear points, or words you have to look up.
- ✔ Draw lines or arrows to identify connections between ideas.
- ✔ Number points that appear in sequence.
- ✔ Draw a vertical line in the margin to set off an important section of text.
- ✔ Star especially important ideas.

11c Annotating

After you have read through a reading selection once, start to read more critically. At this stage, you should **annotate** the pages, recording your reactions to what you read. This process of recording notes in the margins or between the lines will help you understand the writer's ideas and your own reactions to those ideas.

Some of your responses may be relatively straightforward. For example, you may define new words, identify unfamiliar references, or jot down brief summaries. Other responses may be more personal. For example, you may identify a parallel between your own experience and one described in the reading selection, or you may record your opinion of the writer's position. Still other annotations may require you to think critically, identifying points that confirm (or dispute) your own ideas, questioning the appropriateness or accuracy of the writer's support, uncovering the writer's biases or **<u>faulty reasoning</u>**, or even questioning (or challenging) the writer's conclusion.

See 3d

The following passage illustrates a student's annotations of a section of an article.

We can see every problem with the schools clearly except one: the fact that our decision to abandon the schools has helped create all the other problems. One small example: In the early 1980s, Massachusetts passed one of those tax cap measures, called Proposition 2½, which has turned out to be a force for genuine evil in the public schools. Would Proposition 2½ have passed had the middle class still had a stake in the schools? I wonder. I also wonder whether 20 years from now, in the next round of breast-beating memoirs, the exodus of the white middle class from the public schools will finally be seen for what it was. Individually, every parent's rationale made impeccable sense—"I can't deprive my children of a decent education"—but collectively, it was a deeply destructive act.

Is this "one small example" enough to support his point?

Also—exodus from city to suburbs

(Do all parents have same motives?)

The main reason the white middle class fled, of course, is race, or more precisely, the complicated admixture of race and class and good intentions gone awry. The fundamental good intention—which even today strikes one as both moral and right—was to integrate the public classroom, and in so doing, to equalize the resources available to all school children. In Boston, this was done through enforced busing. In Washington, it was done through a series of judicial edicts that attempted to spread the good teachers and resources throughout the system. In other big city districts, judges weren't involved; school committees, seeing the handwriting on the wall, tried to do it themselves.

Reasonable assumption?

Why does he assume intent was "good" & "moral"? Is he right?

?

However moral the intent, the result almost always was the same. The white middle class left. The historic parental vigilance I mentioned earlier had had a lot to do with creating the two-tiered system—one in which schools attended by the kids of the white middle class had better teachers, better equipment, better everything than those attended by the kids of the poor. This did not happen because the white middle-class parents were racists, necessarily; it happened because they knew how to manipulate the system and were willing to do so on behalf of their kids. Their neighborhood schools became little havens of decent education, and they didn't much care what happened in the other public schools. (from Joseph Nocera, "How the Middle Class Has Helped Ruin the Public Schools," *Washington Monthly,* February 1989; reprinted in the *Utne Reader,* September/ October 1990)

Where did they go? (Our neighborhood schools = mostly minority now)

How does he know they weren't?

Interesting point—but is it true?

CHAPTER 12

WRITING ESSAY EXAMS

To prepare to write an essay exam, you must do more than memorize facts; you must synthesize information and arrange ideas into clear, well-organized paragraphs and essays.

12a   Planning an Essay Exam Answer

(1) Consider Your Audience and Purpose

The primary audience for any exam is the instructor who prepared it. As you read the questions, then, think about what your instructor has emphasized in class. Keep in mind that your purpose is to demonstrate that you understand the material, not to make clever remarks or to introduce irrelevant information. Also, make every effort to use the vocabulary of the specific academic discipline and to follow any discipline-specific stylistic conventions that your instructor has discussed.

(2) Read through the Entire Exam

Before you begin to write, read the entire exam carefully to determine your priorities and your strategy. First, be sure that your copy of the test is complete and that you understand exactly what each question requires. If you need clarification, ask your instructor or proctor for help. Then plan carefully, deciding how much time you should devote to answering each question. Often the point value of each question or the number of questions on the exam determines how much time you

Answering Essay Questions (successatschool.com)
   http://www.successatschool.com/EssayQ.html
Tips on Essay Exams (UNC)
   http://www.unc.edu/depts/wcweb/handouts/essay-exams.html

should spend on each answer. If an essay question is worth fifty out of one hundred points, for example, you will probably have to spend at least half (and perhaps more) of your time planning, writing, and proof-reading your answer.

Next, decide where to start. Responding first to short answers (or to questions whose answers you are sure of) is usually a good strategy. This tactic ensures that you will not become bogged down in a question that baffles you, left with too little time to write a strong answer to a question that you understand well. Moreover, starting with the questions that you are sure of can help build your confidence.

(3) Read Each Question Carefully

To write an effective answer, you need to understand the question. As you read any essay question, you may find it helpful to underline key words and important terms.

SOCIOLOGY: <u>Distinguish</u> among <u>Social Darwinism</u>, <u>instinct theory</u>, and <u>sociobiology</u>, giving <u>examples</u> of each.

MUSIC: <u>Explain how</u> Milton <u>Babbitt</u> used the <u>computer</u> to expand <u>Schoenberg's twelve-tone</u> method.

PHILOSOPHY: <u>Define existentialism</u> and <u>identify three</u> influential ex-istentialist <u>works</u>, explaining <u>why</u> they are important.

Look carefully at the wording of each question. If the question calls for a *comparison and contrast* of *two* styles of management, a *description* or *analysis* of *one* style, no matter how comprehensive, will not be accept-able. If the question asks for causes *and* effects, a discussion of causes alone will not do.

 KEY WORDS IN EXAM QUESTIONS

• Explain	• Clarify	• Classify
• Compare	• Relate	• Identify
• Contrast	• Justify	• Illustrate
• Trace	• Analyze	• Define
• Evaluate	• Summarize	• Support
• Discuss	• Describe	• Interpret

(4) Brainstorm to Find Ideas

See 1b5

Once you understand the question, begin **brainstorming**, quickly jotting down all the relevant ideas you can remember. Then, determine which points are most useful and delete less promising ones. A quick review of the exam question and your supporting ideas should lead you to a workable thesis for your essay answer.

12b   Developing a Thesis and an Outline

See 1c3

Often you can rephrase the exam question as a **thesis statement**. For example, the American history exam question "Give a detailed summary of the effects of the Great Depression on the United States, briefly discussing the major causes of the economic collapse" suggests the following thesis statement.

> The Great Depression, caused by the American government's economic policies, had major political, economic, and social effects on the United States.

See 1c6

Because time is limited, make an informal **outline** of your major points and supporting points in the order in which you plan to discuss them. (Use the inside cover of your exam book.) Check your completed outline against the exam question to make certain it covers everything the question calls for—and *only* what the question calls for.

12c   Writing and Revising an Essay Exam Answer

Do not waste your valuable time trying to create an elaborate or unusual introduction. A simple statement of your thesis is usually all you need; this approach is economical, and it reminds you to address the question directly. Follow your outline point by point, using clear topic sentences and transitions to indicate your progression and to help your reader see that you are answering the question in full. Such signals, along with **parallel** sentence structure and repeated key words, make your answer easy to follow. Your conclusion should be a clear, simple restatement of the thesis or a brief summary of your essay's main points.

See 15a

Be careful not to repeat yourself or to volunteer unrequested information. Do not express your own feelings or opinions unless they are specifically called for—and be sure to support all your general statements with specific examples.

Finally, leave enough time to reread and revise what you have written. Have you left out words or written illegibly? Is your thesis statement clearly worded? Does your essay support your thesis statement and answer the question? Are your facts correct, and are your ideas presented in a logical order? If a sentence—or even a whole paragraph—seems irrelevant, cross it out. If you suddenly remember something you want to add, insert a few additional words with a caret (∧). A longer addition should be inserted at the end of your answer, boxed and labled so your instructor will know where it belongs. (Do not waste time recopying entire passages unless what you have written is illegible.) Finally, check sentence structure, word choice, spelling, and punctuation. If you have additional time, reread your answer again. It generally pays to use all the time provided.

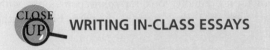

WRITING IN-CLASS ESSAYS

Many of the strategies that can help you to write strong responses to essay exams can also help you plan, write, and revise other kinds of in-class essays.

If you are asked to write an in-class essay, follow the steps outlined in this chapter, and be sure you understand exactly what you are being asked to do and how much time you have in which to do it. Keep in mind, however, that in-class essays, unlike essay exams, may be evaluated as much on their style and structure as on their content. This means, for example, that they should have fully developed introductory and concluding paragraphs.

CHAPTER 13

WRITING ABOUT LITERATURE

13a Reading Literature

See Ch 11

When you read a literary work about which you plan to write, use the same critical thinking skills and active reading strategies you apply to other works you read: **preview** the work and **highlight** it to identify key ideas and cues to meaning; then **annotate** it carefully.

As you read and take notes, focus on the special concerns of literary analysis, considering elements like a short story's plot, a poem's rhyme or meter, or a play's staging. Look for *patterns,* related groups of words, images, or ideas that run through a work. Look for *anomalies,* unusual forms, unique uses of language, unexpected actions by characters, or original treatments of topics. Finally, look for *connections,* links with other literary works, with historical events, or with biographical information.

> **? CLOSE UP READING LITERATURE**
>
> When you read a work of literature, keep in mind that you do not read to discover the one correct meaning the writer has hidden between the lines of the work. The "meaning" of a literary work is created by the interaction between a text and its readers. Do not assume, however, that a work can mean whatever you want it to mean; ultimately, your interpretation must be consistent with the stylistic signals, thematic suggestions, and patterns of imagery in the text.

Reading Poetry (U. Wisc.)
    http://www.wisc.edu/writing/Handbook/main.html
Some Basic Guidelines for Reading Literature (Texas)
    http://uwc-server.fac.utexas.edu/stu/handouts/reading.html
Guide to Literary Resources on The Net (J. Lynch)
    http://andromeda.rutgers.edu/~jlynch/Lit/

✔ CHECKLIST: READING LITERATURE ❓

READING FICTION

✔ **Plot** What happens in the story? What conflicts can you identify? Are they resolved? How are the events arranged? Why are they arranged in this way?

✔ **Character** Who is the protagonist? The antagonist? What role do minor characters play? What are each character's most striking traits? Does the protagonist grow and change during the story? Are the characters portrayed sympathetically? How do characters interact with one another?

✔ **Setting** Where and when is the story set? How does the setting influence the plot? How does it affect the characters?

✔ **Point of View** Is the story told by an anonymous third-person narrator or by a character who uses first-person (*I* or *we*) point of view? Is the first-person narrator trustworthy? Is the narrator a participant in the action or just a witness to the story's events? How would a different point of view change the story?

✔ **Style, Tone, and Language** Is the level of diction formal? Informal? Is the style straightforward or complex? Is the tone intimate or distant? What kind of imagery and figurative language are used?

✔ **Theme** What central theme or themes does the story explore?

READING POETRY

✔ **Voice** Who is the poem's speaker? What is the speaker's attitude toward the poem's subject? How would you characterize the speaker's tone?

✔ **Word Choice and Word Order** What words seem important? Why? What does each word say? What does it suggest? Are any words repeated? Why? Is the poem's diction formal or informal? Is the arrangement of words conventional or unconventional?

✔ **Imagery** What images are used in the poem? To what senses (sight, sound, smell, taste, or touch) do they appeal? Is one central image important? Is there a pattern of related images?

✔ **Figures of Speech** Does the poet use simile? Metaphor? Personification? What do figures of speech contribute to the poem?

✔ **Sound** Does the poem include rhyme? Where? Does it have regular meter (that is, a regular pattern of stressed and unstressed syllables)? Does the poem include repeated consonant or vowel sounds? What do these elements contribute to the poem?

continued on the following page

Writing 13b   Writing about Literature

continued from the previous page

✔ **Form** Is the poem written in open form (with no definite pattern of line length, rhyme, or meter) or in closed form (conforming to a pattern)? Why do you think this kind of form is used?

✔ **Theme** What central theme or themes does the poem explore?

READING DRAMA

✔ **Plot** What happens in the play? What conflicts are developed? How are they resolved? Are there any subplots? What events, if any, occur offstage?

✔ **Character** Who are the major characters? The minor characters? What relationships exist among them? What are their most distinctive traits? What do we learn about characters from their words and actions? From the play's stage directions? From what other characters tell us? Does the main character change or grow during the course of the play?

✔ **Staging** When and where is the play set? How do the scenery, props, costumes, lighting, and music work together to establish this setting? What else do these elements contribute to the play?

✔ **Theme** What central theme or themes does the play explore?

13b   Writing about Literature

When you have finished your reading and annotating, **brainstorm** to discover a topic to write about; then, organize your material. As you arrange related material into categories, you will begin to see a structure for your paper. At this point, you are ready to start drafting your essay.

When you write about literature, your goal is to make a point and support it with appropriate references to the work under discussion or to related works or secondary sources. As you write, you observe the conventions of literary criticism, which has its own specialized vocabulary and formats. You also respond to certain discipline-specific assignments. For instance, you may be asked to **analyze** a work, to take it apart and

Writing About Literature (The Citadel)
   http://www.citadel.edu/citadel/otherserv/wctr/writinglit.html
Sample Literary Essay (U. Victoria)
   http://www.clearcf.uvic.ca/writersguide/Pages/SampleEssaysLit.html

consider one or more of its elements—perhaps the plot or characters in a story or the use of language in a poem. Or, you may be asked to **interpret** a work, to try to discover its possible meanings. Less often, you may be called on to **evaluate** a work, to judge its strengths and weaknesses.

More specifically, you may be asked to trace the critical or popular reception to a work, to compare two works by a single writer (or by two different writers), or to consider the relationship between a work of literature and a literary movement or historical period. You may be asked to analyze a character's motives or the relationship between two characters or to comment on a story's setting or tone. In any case, understanding exactly what you are expected to do will make your writing task easier.

✔ CHECKLIST: WRITING ABOUT LITERATURE

- ✔ Use present-tense verbs when discussing works of literature: "The character of Mrs. Mallard's husband is not developed. . . ."
- ✔ Use past-tense verbs only when discussing historical events ("Owen's poem conveys the destructiveness of World War I, which at the time the poem *was* written *was* considered to be. . . ."), when presenting historical or biographical data ("Her first novel, *published* in 1811 when Austen *was* thirty-six, . . ."), or when identifying events that occurred prior to the time of the story's main action ("Miss Emily is a recluse; since her father *died* she has lived alone except for a servant.").
- ✔ Support all points with specific, concrete examples from the work you are discussing, briefly summarizing key events, quoting dialogue or description, describing characters or setting, or paraphrasing ideas.
- ✔ Combine paraphrase, summary, and quotation with your own interpretations, weaving quotations smoothly into your paper **(see 5e, 8a).**
- ✔ Be careful to acknowledge all sources, including the work or works under discussion. Check to see you have introduced the words or ideas of others with a reference to the source and followed borrowed material with appropriate parenthetical documentation. Also, be sure you have quoted accurately and enclosed the words of others in quotation marks.
- ✔ Use parenthetical documentation **(see 9a1)** and include a Works Cited list **(see 9a2)** in accordance with MLA documentation style.

continued on the following page

continued from the previous page

✔ When citing a part of a short story or novel, supply the page number (168). For a poem, give the line numbers (2–4). For a classic verse play, include act, scene, and line numbers (1.4.29–31). For other plays, supply act and/or scene numbers. (When quoting more than four lines of prose or more than three lines of poetry, be sure you have followed the guidelines outlined in **35b.**)

✔ Avoid subjective expressions like *I feel, I believe, it seems to me,* and *in my opinion.* These weaken your paper by suggesting that its ideas are "only" your opinion and have no validity in themselves.

✔ Avoid unnecessary plot summary. Your goal is to draw a conclusion about one or more works and to support that conclusion with pertinent details. If a plot development supports a point you wish to make, a *brief* summary is acceptable. But plot summary is no substitute for analysis.

✔ Use literary terms accurately. For example, be careful not to confuse *narrator* or *speaker* with *writer* (feelings or opinions expressed by a narrator or character do not necessarily represent those of the writer). You should not say, "In the poem's last stanza, *Frost* expresses his indecision" when you mean the poem's *speaker* is indecisive.

✔ Underline titles of novels and plays **(see 39a);** enclose titles of short stories and poems within quotation marks **(see 35c).**

CHAPTER 14

DOCUMENT DESIGN AND MANUSCRIPT FORMAT

This chapter presents general guidelines for document design as well as specific formatting conventions followed in the humanities and the social sciences and specified by MLA and APA, respectively.

14a   Document Design

Document design refers to the conventions that determine the way a document—a research paper, memo, report, business letter, or résumé, for example—looks on a page. Designing a document often involves making choices that will emphasize key ideas and make your paper easier to read. In many college writing situations, the **format** of your paper—including such matters as how you use headings, how you construct tables and charts, and how you arrange information on a title page—is defined by the discipline in which you are writing. Although formatting conventions differ from discipline to discipline, the basic principles of document design are the same. In general, well-designed documents have the following characteristics:

- Effective format
- Clear headings
- Useful lists
- Attractive visuals

(1) Creating an Effective Format

Margins   Your document should be double-spaced (unless your instructor tells you otherwise) with at least a one-inch margin on all sides. You can either leave a ragged edge on the right, or you can justify your text so that all the words are aligned evenly at the right margin. A ragged edge is recommended because it varies the visual landscape of your document, making it easier to read.

Font Size To create a readable document, use a 10- or 12-point font. Avoid fonts that distract readers (script or cursive fonts, for example).

(2) Using Headings

Headings tell readers what to expect in a section before they actually read it. By breaking up a text and eliminating long, uninterrupted blocks of prose, headings make a document inviting and readable.

Number of Headings You should have enough headings to highlight the most important points of your document. A long, complicated document needs more headings than a shorter, less complex document. Keep in mind, however, that while too few headings may not be of much use, too many headings will make your document look like an outline.

Phrasing Headings should be brief, descriptive, specific, and to the point. They can be single words—*Summary* or *Introduction,* for example—or phrases (always stated in **parallel** terms): *Choosing a dog; Caring for the dog; Housebreaking the dog.* Headings can be phrased as questions (*How do you choose a dog?*) or statements (*Choosing a dog carefully*).

See 27a

Format Headings and subheadings may be *centered,* placed *flush left,* or *indented.* The most important thing to remember is that headings at the same level should have the same format—for example, if one first-level heading is boldfaced and centered, all other first-level headings must be boldfaced and centered.

Typographical Emphasis You can emphasize headings or other important words and phrases by using **boldface,** *italics,* or ALL CAPITAL LETTERS. Used in moderation, these distinctive typefaces make a text more readable. (Notice, for example, how these typefaces are used in this handbook.) Used excessively, however, they slow readers down and make reading more difficult.

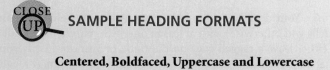

CLOSE UP **SAMPLE HEADING FORMATS**

Centered, Boldfaced, Uppercase and Lowercase

continued on the following page

> Flush Left, Underlined, Uppercase and Lowercase
>   Indented, underlined, lowercase paragraph heading ending with a period.
>   ALL CAPITAL LETTERS, CENTERED

(3) Constructing Lists

A list moves material out of a text, where it may be difficult to read, and enables readers to see it easily. A list can also break up complicated statements into a series of key ideas. Lists are easiest to read when all the elements are **parallel** and about the same length. When rank is important, number the items on the list; when it isn't, use **bullets** (as in the list below). Make sure you introduce the list with a complete sentence followed by a colon.

There are several steps we should take to reduce our spending:
- We should cut our work force by 10%.
- We should utilize less expensive vendors.
- We should decrease overtime.
- We should replace our present health plan with a less expensive HMO.

(Because the items on the list above are complete sentences, each ends with a period. Do not use periods if the items are not sentences.)

NOTE: Lists are useful because they make items stand out from the text around them. Too many lists, however, have the opposite effect, making a document seem choppy and difficult to understand.

(4) Tables, Graphs, Diagrams, and Photographs

Visuals, such as tables, graphs, diagrams, and photographs, can enhance your document by enabling you to present a great deal of information in a limited space. You can create your own tables and graphs by using a computer program like *Excel, Lotus,* or *Microsoft Word.* In addition, you can get diagrams and photographs by photocopying or scanning them from a print source or by downloading them from the Internet or CD-ROMs. Remember, however, that if you use a visual from a source, you *must* use appropriate **documentation**.

Tables   Tables present data in a condensed, visual format—arranged in rows and columns. Tables most often contain numerical data, although occasionally they contain words as well as numbers. When you plan your table, make sure you include only the data that you will need; discard information that is too detailed or difficult to understand (this material is best presented in an appendix). Keep in mind that tables may distract readers, so include only those necessary to support your discussion. The following table summarizes personnel data:

McVay 3

As the following table shows, the Madison location now employs more workers in every site than the St. Paul Location.

Heading   Table 1

Descriptive caption   Number of Employees at Each Location

Employees	Location	
	Madison	St. Paul
Plant	461	254
Warehouse	45	23
Outlet Stores	15	9

Data

Because the Madison location has grown so quickly, steps must be taken to. . . .

Graphs   Like tables, graphs present data in visual form. Whereas tables present specific numerical data, graphs convey the general pattern or trend that the data suggest. Because graphs tend to be more general (and therefore less accurate) than tables, they are frequently accompanied by tables. The following is an example of a bar graph:

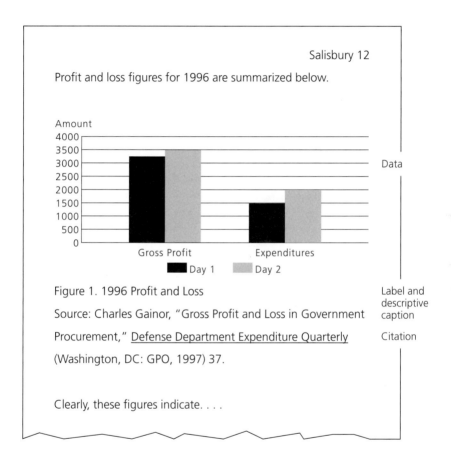

Salisbury 12

Profit and loss figures for 1996 are summarized below.

Figure 1. 1996 Profit and Loss   Label and
                                                            descriptive
Source: Charles Gainor, "Gross Profit and Loss in Government   caption

Procurement," <u>Defense Department Expenditure Quarterly</u>   Citation

(Washington, DC: GPO, 1997) 37.

Clearly, these figures indicate. . . .

Diagrams   A diagram enables you to focus on specific details of a mechanism or object. Diagrams are often used in scientific and technical writing to clarify concepts while eliminating paragraphs of detailed and confusing description. The diagram below, which illustrates the ancient Greek theater, serves a similar purpose in a literature paper.

Dixon 10

The design of the ancient Greek theater is similar to that of a present-day sports stadium, as figure 2 illustrates.

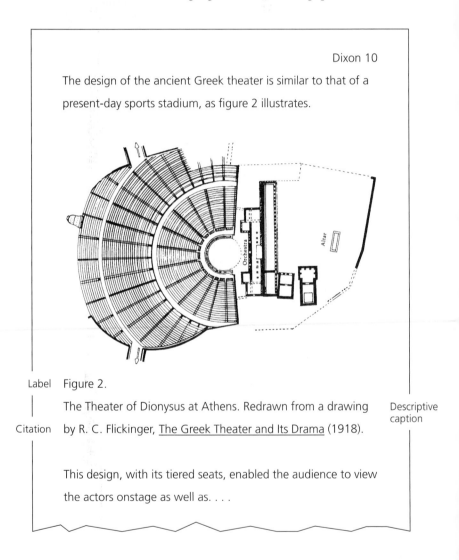

Label   Figure 2.

The Theater of Dionysus at Athens. Redrawn from a drawing   Descriptive caption

Citation   by R. C. Flickinger, <u>The Greek Theater and Its Drama</u> (1918).

This design, with its tiered seats, enabled the audience to view the actors onstage as well as. . . .

Photographs   Photographs enable you to show exactly what something or someone looks like—an animal in its natural habitat, a work of fine art, or an actor in costume, for example. Although computer technology that enables you to paste photographs directly into a text is widely available, use it with restraint. Not every photograph will support or enhance your written text; in fact, an irrelevant photograph distracts readers.

Robes 3

In the later years of his life, Twain was seen more as a personality than as a writer. Figure 3 shows him in a characteristic pose.

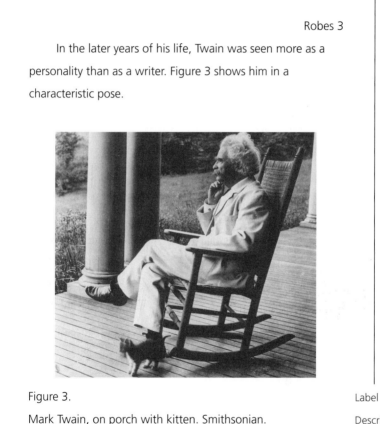

Figure 3.   Label

Mark Twain, on porch with kitten. Smithsonian.   Descriptive
                                                                             caption

The white suit he wears in this photograph. . . .

✔ CHECKLIST: USING VISUALS IN THE TEXT

- ✔ Use a visual only when it contributes something important to the discussion, not for embellishment.
- ✔ Use the visual in the text only if you plan to discuss it in your paper (place the visual in an appendix if you do not).
- ✔ Introduce each visual with a complete sentence.
- ✔ Follow each visual with a discussion of its significance.
- ✔ Leave wide margins around each visual.
- ✔ Place the visual as close as possible to the section of your document in which it is discussed.
- ✔ Label each visual appropriately.
- ✔ Document each visual that is borrowed from a source.

❓ 14b   Creating a Web Site

Because many colleges and universities now provide students with a full range of Internet services, it is possible that over the course of your college career you will have the opportunity to create a Web page. You may even be asked to do so as part of the requirements for a course. Like other documents, Web pages are subject to specific conventions of document design.

Essentially, there are two ways to create Web pages. You can create a Web page from scratch using HTML (hypertext markup language), the programming language by which standard documents are converted to World Wide Web hypertext documents. Or (and this is by far the easier way), you can use Web page creation software that automatically converts text and graphics into HTML so that they can be posted on the Web. Even though these programs allow you to create Web pages quickly and easily, you will still need to devote time to learning them, just as you would with any new software program.

(1) Building a Home Page

If you have never created a Web site, you might begin by building a personal **home page.** Personal home pages usually contain information

---

DTP Jump Station Font Page
   http://www.teleport.com/~eidos/dtpij/old/fonts.html
A Beginner's Guide to HTML
   http://www.ncsa.uiuc.edu/General/Internet/WWW/HTMLPrimerAll.html

about how to contact the author, a brief biography, and links to other Web sites. Later, when you become more proficient, you can expand this home page into a full **Web site** (a group of related web pages).

To create a simple home page from scratch, you will need to know a few of the most basic HTML tags. (**Tags** tell your Web browser how to display text and images.) If you have a document that you want to turn into a Web page, you must code it by placing the proper HTML tags as needed.

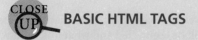

BASIC HTML TAGS

<HTML> Indicates the beginning of an HTML document

<BODY> Indicates the start of a document's body text

<P>, </P> Indicates begin paragraph and end paragraph, respectively

<H1>, <H2>, <H3>, <H4> Heading tags, from largest to smallest

<A HREF= "(Web address here)"> Tag used to create a link to another Web page

</A> Ends linked text

 Indicates a line break

<B> Indicates that the word following will appear in bold

</B> Indicates the end of a word that will appear in bold

</BODY> Indicates the end of a document's body text

</HTML> Indicates the end of a document

If you examined a coded home page, you would notice that it begins with an <HTML> tag at the top and ends with an </HTML> tag at the bottom. Similarly, <BODY> and </BODY> tags indicate the beginning and end of a document's text. Paragraph <P> and heading <H> tags organize body text into headings, subheadings, and paragraphs.

Once you have mastered simple text-only pages, you can move on to design Web pages that include tables, charts, photographs, animation, and even film clips. One way to learn how to do this is to examine the HTML codes for your favorite Web pages. Do this by clicking on *view* in your browser's main menu (at the top of your computer screen) and selecting *page source* from the pull-down menu. Your browser will then display the HTML code for the page you are viewing. You can then "save" the source code in a word processing document and borrow it later as you create pages of your own. Note that although you may borrow code from a Web site, it is never acceptable to **plagiarize** a site's content.

See
8b

(2) Organizing Information

Before creating a Web site, sketch a basic plan on a piece of paper. Consider how your Web pages will be connected and what links you will provide to other Web sites. Your home page should provide an overview of your site and give readers a clear sense of what material the site will contain. Beginning with the home page, users will navigate from one piece of information to another.

As you plan your Web site, consider how your pages will be organized. If your site is relatively simple, you can arrange pages so that one page leads sequentially to the next. For example, your personal Web site could begin with a home page and then progress to a page that presents your interest in sports, then to one that presents your volunteer work, and finally to your résumé. If your site is relatively complicated, however, you will have to group pages according to their order of importance or according to their relevance to a particular category. The *Holt Handbook's* Web site, for example, presents a great deal of information under various headings—Using Your Brief Holt Handbook, Succeeding in First-Year Composition, Tip of the Day, for example (see Figure 1).

(3) Designing Your Web Site

When you design your Web site, lay out text and graphics so that they present your ideas clearly and logically. Because your home page is the first thing readers will encounter, it should be clear and easy to follow. If it is not, readers will lose interest and move on to some other site. Present related items next to each other, and use text sparingly. Make sure you identify items on the same topic by highlighting them in the same color or by using the same font or graphic. Remember, however, that using too many graphics or fancy type styles will confuse readers. In addition, do not use graphics that take too long to download (25 to 30K is a reasonable upper limit). Finally, remember that it is never acceptable to plagiarize the original content of a Web site or to use images without acknowledgment.

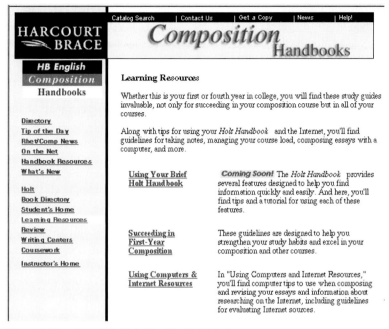

Figure 1 Page from *The Holt Handbook's* Web site

(4) Providing Links

Your home page will contain buttons or links. **Buttons**—graphic icons such as arrows or pictures—enable readers to move from one page of a Web site to another. **Links** (short for hyperlinks)—words or URLs (electronic addresses) highlighted and underlined in blue—enable readers to navigate from one site to another. Keep in mind that when you provide a link, you are directing people to the Web site to which the link refers. For this reason, be certain that the site is up and running and that the information is reliable. In addition, only include links that are relevant to your Web site.

(5) Proofreading Your Text

Before you post your site on the Web, proofread the text of your Web pages just as you would any other document. (Even if you run a spell check and grammar check, you should still proofread carefully.) Then, make sure you have provided both *begin* and *end* tags. If you have included links on your Web site, be sure you have entered the full Web address (beginning with *http://*). If you have used a colored background or text, be sure you have avoided color combinations that make your pages difficult to read (purple on black, for example). Finally, make certain you have acknowledged all material—graphics as well as text—that you have borrowed from a source.

(6) Posting Your Web Site

Once you have designed a Web site, you will need to upload, or post, it so that others can view it on the Web. Most commonly, Web pages are posted with **ftp** (file transfer protocol) software programs such as Fetch for Macintosh. Recent versions of the most popular Internet browsers contain software for posting pages to the Web. For example, Netscape's Composer comes with the Communicator suite of Web applications and contains a simple built-in ftp client.

To post a Web page, open your program and enter the ftp address of your ISP or host. You will also need a user name and password that you will enter when you have established communication with your host server. Once you have established communication, you can post your Web site almost instantly. (If you have made any mistakes in coding your page, the errors will be apparent as soon as you view the page on the Web.)

14c   MLA Manuscript Guidelines

MLA guidelines are used for papers in the humanities. The following guidelines are based on the *MLA Handbook for Writers of Research Papers* (5th ed.). For an example of a paper that uses MLA manuscript format, **see 9b.**

1. Type your paper with a one-inch margin at the top and bottom and on both sides. Indent the first line of every paragraph, as well as the first line of every item on the Works Cited list, five spaces (or one-half inch). Set off a **long prose quotation** (more than four lines) by indenting ten spaces (or one inch) from the left-hand margin. Double-space your paper throughout.
2. If your instructor does not require a separate title page, use the model on p. 166. Capitalize all important words in the title, but not prepositions, coordinating conjunctions, articles, or the *to* in infinitives, unless

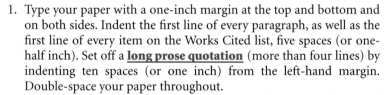

MLA Style Document Formatting (Capital Com. & Tech. College, CT)
  http://webster.commnet.edu/mla/format.htm

248

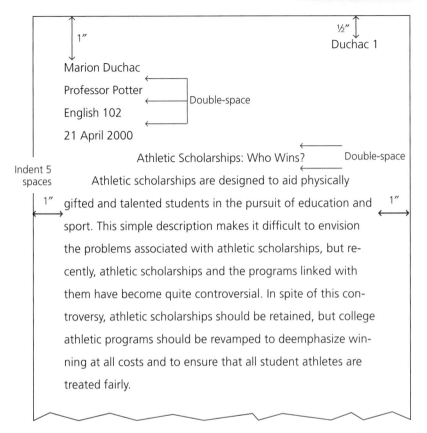

½″
Duchac 1

1″

Marion Duchac

Professor Potter

English 102 ←——— Double-space

21 April 2000

Indent 5 spaces

Athletic Scholarships: Who Wins? Double-space

Athletic scholarships are designed to aid physically

1″ gifted and talented students in the pursuit of education and 1″

sport. This simple description makes it difficult to envision

the problems associated with athletic scholarships, but re-

cently, athletic scholarships and the programs linked with

them have become quite controversial. In spite of this con-

troversy, athletic scholarships should be retained, but college

athletic programs should be revamped to deemphasize win-

ning at all costs and to ensure that all student athletes are

treated fairly.

½″
Williamson 2

1″

½″

1″ The language, manners, and mores of Orwell's world are de- 1″

termined by the state. When the characters in <u>1984</u> are

faced with a decision, they usually. . . .

they begin or end the title. Do not underline the title or enclose it in quotation marks, but do underline words in the title if they would otherwise be underlined (for example, book titles). Never put a period after a title, even if it is a sentence. Double-space between the last line of the title and the first line of your paper. If the title is longer than a single line, double-space and center the second line below the first.

3. If your instructor requires a separate title page, use a format like the one used in the paper in **9b.**

4. Number all pages of your paper consecutively—including the first—in the upper right-hand corner, one-half inch from the top, flush right. (Do not put *p.* before the page numbers, and do not put periods or any other punctuation after them.) Type your name before the page number on every page.

5. The *MLA Handbook* does not mention **headings.** Traditionally, papers in the humanities do not use headings; instead, strong topic sentences or transitional paragraphs introduce ideas. This trend does seem to be changing, however. If you want to use headings, check with your instructor to make sure they are acceptable.

6. Tables and illustrations should be placed as close as possible to the part of the paper in which they are discussed.

See
14a4

    <u>**Tables**</u> should be headed *Table* and given an arabic numeral and a descriptive caption. Type the heading and the descriptive caption flush left on a separate line above the table. Capitalize the heading and the caption as if they were titles. If the table is borrowed from a source, give the full citation below the table beginning at the left-hand margin. Double-space the table's text and the notes.

    Other visuals, such as graphs, diagrams, and photographs, should be labeled *Figure* (abbreviated *Fig.*) and given an arabic number. The label, a descriptive caption, and the full citation are typed below the illustration beginning at the left-hand margin.

7. If you use source material in your paper, follow the MLA documentation style in **9a.**

TYPING YOUR PAPER

Always back up your work. (Make a backup copy every time you finish a typing session so that you have the latest version of your paper.) If your disk crashes or if a file is corrupted, however,

continued on the following page

don't automatically assume that your data is lost. Go to your school's computer center and see if they have a data recovery program such as *Norton Utilities*. These programs do not work in all cases, but frequently they enable you to recover some, if not all, of your work.

14d APA Manuscript Guidelines

APA guidelines are used for papers in the social sciences. The following list is based on the *Publication Manual of the American Psychological Association* (4th ed.). For an example of a paper that uses APA manuscript format, see **10b.**

1. Type your paper with at least a one-inch margin at the top, bottom, and sides of the paper. Do not hyphenate words at the end of a line. Double-space between all lines of the manuscript. (You may use triple- or quadruple-spacing before and after a table.)
2. Indent the first line of every paragraph, as well as the first line of every item on the Reference List, five to seven spaces. Set off quotations of forty or more words in a block format placed five to seven spaces from the left-hand margin. If the quotation is one paragraph or less, do not indent; if it is more than one paragraph, indent the first line of the second and subsequent paragraphs five to seven spaces from the new margin.
3. The title page should follow the model on p. 195.
4. Papers in the social sciences often contain an **abstract,** a short summary of approximately one hundred words. If your instructor requires an abstract, it should appear as a separate numbered page (labeled *Abstract*) after the title page.
5. Number all pages of your paper consecutively. Each page should include the running head as well as the page number in the upper right-hand corner. Begin the text of your paper on a new page. Center the title of the paper at the top of the page; if the title is more than one line, double-space between the lines and center. Skip two spaces and begin typing the text.
6. Major **headings** should be centered and typed with uppercase and lowercase letters. Minor headings should be flush left, typed with uppercase and lowercase letters, and underlined.

See 14a2

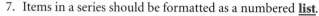

See
14a3

See
14a4

7. Items in a series should be formatted as a numbered **list**.

8. **Tables** (numerical values displayed in columns and rows) should be numbered consecutively in the order in which they are mentioned in the paper (Table 1, Table 2, and so on). Double-space each table and include a brief identifying title (*Table 1. Population Figures for 1995*) directly above it. Begin each table on a separate page after the reference list. Refer to each table by number in the text of your paper—for example, "Table 3 summarizes this study."

   Other types of visuals (charts, graphs, diagrams, and so on) are also numbered consecutively. The label *Figure* and an identifying caption are typed beneath the visual beginning at the left-hand margin.

   APA recommends that tables and figures be placed in an appendix at the end of the paper; however, your instructor may want this material to be included in the body of the paper.

9. If you use source material in your paper, follow the APA documentation style in **10a.**

CHAPTER 15

WRITING FOR THE WORKPLACE

15a Writing Business Letters

Business letters should be brief and to the point, with important information placed early in the letter. Be concise, avoid digressions, and try to sound as natural as possible.

The first paragraph of your letter introduces your subject and mentions any pertinent previous correspondence. The body of your letter presents the facts readers need in order to understand your points. (If your ideas are complicated, present your points in a bulleted or numbered **list**.) Your conclusion should reinforce your message.

See
14a3

BUSINESS LETTER SALUTATIONS

If you are writing to a woman, consult previous correspondence, and use the title she uses. If you do not know her preference, use *Ms.* If you know a person's last name and first initial and do not know whether the person is male or female (or if you do not have a specific person to whom to address your letter), check the company's Web site or call and ask for the full name of the person who should receive your letter. If you are unable to determine the name of the person who will receive your letter, use a neutral form of address—*Dear Editor* or *Dear Personnel Director,* for example. Keep in mind that generic salutations such as *Gentlemen, Dear Sirs,* and *Dear Madam* are both **sexist** and outdated. Whenever possible, use a person's name.

See
28e2

Business Letters: Accentuating the Positive (Purdue)
    http://owl.english.purdue.edu/Files/92.html
Business English Hangman (better-english.com)
    http://www.better-english.com/hangman/hangone.htm
Business English Crosswords (better-english.com)
    http://www.better-english.com/crosswords/test.htm

SAMPLE LETTER—BLOCK FORMAT

Heading | 6732 Wyncote Avenue
Houston, TX 77004
May 3, 1999

Inside address | Mr. William S. Price, Jr., Director
Division of Archives and History
Department of Cultural Resources
109 East Jones Street
Raleigh, NC 27611

Salutation | Dear Mr. Price:

Thank you for sending me the material I requested about pirates in colonial North Carolina.

Body | Both the pamphlets and the bibliography were extremely useful for my research. Without your help, I am sure my paper would not have been so well received.

I have enclosed a copy of my paper, and I would appreciate any comments you may have. Again, thank you for your time and trouble.

Complimentary close | Sincerely yours,

Written signature | *Kevin Wolk*

Typed signature | Kevin Wolk

Copy sent | cc: Dr. N. Provisor, Professor of History

Additional data | Enc.: Research paper

SENDING MESSAGES BY FAX AND E-MAIL

The standards for electronic messages are the same as those for any other form of business correspondence.

Faxes Remember that faxes are often received not by an individual but at a central location, so include a cover sheet that contains the recipient's name and title, the date, the company and department, the fax and telephone numbers, and the total number of pages faxed. In addition, supply your own name and telephone and fax numbers. (It is also a good idea to call ahead to alert the addressee that a fax is coming.)

E-mail Although e-mail can be quite informal, you should treat your e-mail message as if it were a standard written business letter. Include a salutation and a subject line, and be sure to state your purpose and to present your ideas clearly and succinctly. Avoid slang and imprecise diction, and proofread carefully. Also keep in mind that e-mail composed at work is the property of the employer, who has the legal right to access it.

15b Writing Letters of Application and Résumés

When you apply for employment, your primary objective is to obtain an interview. The **letter of application** summarizes your qualifications for a specific position; the **résumé** provides a general overview of your accomplishments.

Writing in the Job Search (Purdue)
   http://owl.english.purdue.edu/writers/by-topic.html#bw
Application Letters: How to Sell Yourself (Purdue)
   http://owl.english.purdue.edu/Files/57.html
Writing Cover Letters (Illinois)
   http://www.english.uiuc.edu/cws/wworkshop/writtech.cover.htm

SAMPLE LETTER OF APPLICATION—
SEMIBLOCK FORMAT

Heading

246 Hillside Drive
Urbana, IL 61801
October 20, 1999
kr237@metropolis.105.com

Inside address

Mr. Maurice Snyder, Personnel Director
Guilford, Fox, and Morris
22 Hamilton Street
Urbana, IL 61822

Salutation

Dear Mr. Snyder:

Body

My college advisor, Dr. Raymond Walsh, has told me that you are interested in hiring a part-time accounting assistant. I believe that my academic background and my work experience qualify me for this position.

I am presently a junior accounting major at the University of Illinois. During the past year, I have taken courses in taxation, trusts, and business law. I am also proficient in *Lotus* and *ClarisWorks.* Last spring, I gained practical accounting experience by working in our department's tax clinic.

Double-⟶
space

After I graduate, I hope to get a master's degree in taxation and then return to the Urbana area. I believe that my experience in taxation as well as my familiarity with the local business community would enable me to contribute to your firm.

Single-⟶
space

I have enclosed a résumé for your examination. I will be available for an interview any time after midterm examinations, which end October 25. I look forward to hearing from you.

Compli-
mentary close

Sincerely yours,

Sandra Kraft

Typed
signature

Sandra Kraft

Additional
data

Enc.: Résumé

256

(1) Letters of Application

Begin your letter of application by identifying the job you are applying for and stating where you heard about it—in a newspaper, in a professional journal, on the Internet, or from your school's job placement service, for example. Be sure to include the date of the advertisement and the exact title of the position. End your introduction with your thesis: a statement of your ability to do the job.

In the body of your letter, provide the information that will convince your reader of your qualifications—for example, relevant courses you have taken and pertinent job experience. Be sure to address any specific points mentioned in the advertisement. Above all, emphasize your strengths, and explain how they relate to the specific job for which you are applying.

Conclude by saying that you have enclosed your résumé. State that you are available for an interview, noting any dates on which you will not be available.

(2) Résumés

A résumé lists relevant information about your education, your job experience, your goals, and your personal interests. When you prepare your résumé, select the information most appropriate for the job you want, emphasizing the accomplishments that differentiate you from other candidates—for example, academic honors or awards.

There is no single correct format for a résumé. You may decide to arrange your résumé in **chronological order,** listing your education and work experience in sequence (beginning with the most recent), or in **emphatic order,** presenting first the material (for example, a particular job) that will be of most interest to an employer. Whatever a résumé's arrangement, it should be brief—one page is sufficient for an undergraduate—easy to read, and clearly and logically organized.

✔ CHECKLIST: COMPONENTS OF A RÉSUMÉ

✔ The **heading** includes your name, school address, home address, telephone number, and e-mail address.

continued on the following page

Action Words for Better Résumés (Purdue)
  http://owl.english.purdue.edu/Files/59.html

continued from the previous page

✔ A statement of your **career objective** (optional), placed at the top of the page, identifies your professional goals.

✔ The **education section** includes the schools you have attended, starting with the most recent one and moving back in time. (After graduation from college, do not list your high school unless you have a compelling reason to do so—for instance, if it is nationally recognized for its academic standards or it has an active alumni network in your field.)

✔ The **summary of work experience** generally starts with your most recent job and moves backward in time.

✔ The **background** or **interests section** lists your most important (or most relevant) special interests and community activities.

✔ The **honors section** lists academic achievements and awards.

✔ The **references section** lists the full names and addresses of at least three references. If your résumé is already one full page long, a line saying that your references will be sent upon request is sufficient.

 ## ELECTRONIC RÉSUMÉS

Increasingly, résumés are posted on electronic bulletin boards or at sites like Monster.com that list résumés for a number of different job categories. The format of an electronic résumé is often similar to the ones described in this section, with two notable exceptions.

First, because of the way employers search a database, keywords are very important in an electronic résumé. Make sure your résumé contains the keywords that employers in your field will want to see—skills that you have and software programs with which you are familiar, for example. In fact, some applicants include a Keyword section at the top of their résumés, before Education and Experience.

Second, many electronic résumés contain words and phrases that are hypertext links to other sites. (These links are highlighted in blue on the résumé.) For example, your name could be a link to your home page, which might include a biographical sketch as

continued on page 261

SAMPLE RÉSUMÉ: CHRONOLOGICAL ORDER

KAREN L. OLSON

SCHOOL
3312 Hamilton St. Apt. 18
Philadelphia, PA 19104
215-382-0831
olsonk@durm.ocs.drexel.edu

HOME
110 Ascot Ct.
Harmony, PA 16037
412-452-2944

EDUCATION

DREXEL UNIVERSITY, Philadelphia, PA 19104
Bachelor of Science in Graphic Design
Anticipated Graduation: June 2000
Cumulative Grade Point Average: 3.2 on a 4.0 scale

COMPUTER SKILLS AND COURSE WORK

HARDWARE
Operate both Macintosh computer and PCs.
SOFTWARE
Adobe Illustrator, Photoshop, and *TypeAlign; QuarkXPress; CorelDRAW; Micrografx Designer*
COURSES
Corporate Identity, Environmental Graphics, Typography, Photography, Painting and Printmaking, Sculpture, Computer Imaging, Art History

EMPLOYMENT EXPERIENCE

UNISYS CORPORATION, Blue Bell, PA 19124
June–September 1999, Cooperative Education
Graphic Designer. Designed interior pages as well as covers for target marketing brochures. Created various logos and spot art designed for use on interoffice memos and departmental publications.

CHARMING SHOPPES, INC., Bensalem, PA 19020
June–December 1998, Cooperative Education
Graphic Designer/Fashion Illustrator. Created graphics for future placement on garments. Did some textile designing. Drew flat illustrations of garments to scale in computer. Prepared presentation boards.

THE TRIANGLE. Drexel University, Philadelphia, PA 19104
January 1999–present
Graphics Editor. Design all display advertisements submitted to Drexel's student newspaper.

DESIGN AND IMAGING STUDIO, Drexel University, Philadelphia, PA 19104
October 1997–June 1999
Monitor. Supervised computer activity in studio. Answered telephone. Assisted other graphic design students in using computer programs.

ACTIVITIES AND AWARDS

The Triangle, Graphics Editor: 1998–present
Kappa Omicron Nu Honor Society, vice president: 1997–present
Dean's List: Spring 1996, fall and winter 1997
Graphics Group, vice president: 1997–present

REFERENCES AND PORTFOLIO

Available upon request.

SAMPLE RÉSUMÉ: EMPHATIC ORDER

Michael D. Fuller

SCHOOL   HOME
27 College Avenue   1203 Hampton Road
University of Maryland   Joppa, MD 21085
College Park, MD 20742   (301) 877-1437
(301) 357-0732
mful532@aol.com

Restaurant Experience

    McDonald's Restaurant, Pikesville, MD. Cook.
    Prepared hamburgers. Acted as assistant manager for two weeks while man-
    ager was on vacation. Supervised employees, helped prepare payroll and
    work schedules. Was named employee of the month. Summer 1998.

    University of Maryland Cafeteria, College Park, MD. Busboy.
    Cleaned tables, set up cafeteria, and prepared hot trays. September
    1999–May 2000.

Other Work Experience

    University of Maryland Library, College Park, MD. Reference assistant.
    Filed, sorted, typed, shelved, and catalogued. Earnings offset college ex-
    penses. September 1998–May 1999.

Education

    University of Maryland, College Park, MD (sophomore).
    Biology major. Expected date of graduation: June 2002.
    Forest Park High School, Baltimore, MD.

Interests

    Member of University Debating Society.
    Tutor in University's Academic Enrichment Program.

References

    Mr. Arthur Sanducci, Manager
    McDonald's Restaurant
    5712 Avery Road
    Pikesville, MD 22513

    Mr. William Czernick, Manager
    Cafeteria
    University of Maryland
    College Park, MD 20742

    Ms. Stephanie Young, Librarian
    Library
    University of Maryland
    College Park, MD 20742

continued from page 258

well as pictures and a short video attachment. Or, a company's name in your Work Experience section could be a link to the company's Web site. Finally, the title of your senior thesis could be a link to a site that contains a copy of the thesis itself. So far, the majority of résumés are still submitted on paper, but electronic résumés are quickly gaining in popularity.

15c   Writing Memos

Unlike letters, memos communicate information *within* a business organization, transmitting brief messages of a paragraph or two or short reports or proposals. Their function is either to convey information or to persuade.

 WRITING MEMOS

In many places of employment, virtually all internal communications—including memos—circulate via e-mail. E-mail should not be an occasion for sloppy, informal writing and does not eliminate the need for careful revising and editing. In general, treat all electronic business communications as if they were hard copy.

SAMPLE MEMO

Opening
component

TO: Ina Ellen, Senior Counselor
FROM: Kim Williams, Student Tutor Supervisor
SUBJECT: Construction of a Tutoring Center
DATE: November 10, 1999

Purpose
statement

This memo proposes the establishment of a tutoring center in the Office of Student Affairs.

BACKGROUND
Under the present system, tutors must work with students at a number of facilities scattered across the university campus. As a result, tutors waste a lot of time running from one facility to another and are often late for appointments.

NEW FACILITY

Body

I propose that we establish a tutoring facility adjacent to the Office of Student Affairs. The two empty classrooms next to the office, presently used for storage of office furniture, would be ideal for this use. We could furnish these offices with the desks and file cabinets already stored in these rooms.

BENEFITS
The benefits of this facility would be the centralizing of the tutoring services and the proximity of the facility to the Office of Student Affairs. The tutoring facility could also use the secretarial services of the Office of Student Affairs.

RECOMMENDATIONS

Conclusion

To implement this project we would need to do the following:

1. Clean up and paint rooms 331 and 333
2. Use folding partitions to divide each room into five single-desk offices
3. Use stored office equipment to furnish the center

I am certain these changes would do much to improve the tutoring service. I look forward to discussing this matter with you in more detail.

Common Sentence Errors

PART 7

SENTENCE ERRORS

❓ FREQUENTLY ASKED QUESTIONS

SENTENCE ERRORS

PART 7

CHAPTER 16

REVISING SENTENCE FRAGMENTS

A **sentence fragment** is an incomplete sentence—a clause or a phrase— that is punctuated as if it were a complete sentence. To determine whether a sentence is incomplete, ask these four questions:

1. Does the word group lack a subject?

   Many astrophysicists now believe that galaxies are distributed in clusters. <u>And even form supercluster complexes.</u>

2. Does the word group lack a verb?

   Three key events defined my generation. <u>The Gulf War, the Oklahoma City bombing, and the Rodney King verdict.</u>

3. Does the word group lack both a subject and a verb?

   Researchers are engaged in a variety of studies. <u>Suggesting a link between alcoholism and heredity.</u> (*Suggesting* is a **verbal,** which cannot serve as a sentence's main verb.)

4. Does the word group consist of a dependent clause alone? (A sentence cannot consist of a single clause that begins with a **subordinating conjunction** or with a **relative pronoun.**)

   > **See 24a2**

   Bishop Desmond Tutu was awarded the 1984 Nobel Peace Prize. <u>Because he struggled to end apartheid.</u>

   The pH meter and the spectrophotometer are two scientific instruments. <u>That changed the chemistry laboratory dramatically.</u>

Sentence Fragments
   http://www.guilford.edu/ASC/grammarland/fragments.html
   http://www.harper.cc.il.us/writ_ctr/fragmnt.htm
   http://www.urich.edu/~writing/wweb/fragment.html

> ✔ **CHECKLIST: REVISING SENTENCE FRAGMENTS**
>
> To revise a sentence fragment, use one or more of the following strategies:
>
> ✔ Supply the missing subject or verb (or both).
> ✔ Attach the fragment to a nearby independent clause.
> ✔ Delete the subordinating conjunction or relative pronoun.

16a   Supplying the Missing Subject or Verb

See
B3.1

When a fragment lacks a subject or a verb or both, you can correct it by supplying the missing words. For example, if the fragment is a **verbal phrase**, you can correct it by substituting a verb for the verbal and adding a subject.

In 1948, India became independent. ~~Divided~~ into the nations of India
— *It was divided* —
and Pakistan.

A familiar trademark can increase a product's sales. ~~Reminding~~ shoppers
— *It reminds* —
the product has a long-standing reputation.

16b   Attaching the Fragment to an Independent Clause

Often, you can correct a fragment by attaching it to a nearby independent clause to create a complete sentence.

(1) Dependent Clause Fragments

A **dependent clause** contains a subject and a verb, but it cannot stand alone as a sentence because it needs an independent clause to complete its meaning. To correct a dependent clause fragment, attach the dependent clause (also called a subordinate clause) to an independent clause to form a **complex sentence**. (You can recognize a dependent clause be-cause it is always introduced by a subordinating conjunction or a relative pronoun.)

See
24a2

although
Property taxes rose sharply,~~Although~~ city services declined.
~~x~~

which
The battery is dead,~~Which~~ means the car won't start.
~~x,~~

🔍 CLOSE UP — REVISING SENTENCE FRAGMENTS: PHRASES

A **phrase** works as part of a sentence, providing information—description, examples, and so on—about other words or word groups in the sentence. However, a phrase cannot stand alone. Many fragments are created when a phrase (for example, a *preposi-tional phrase,* an *appositive,* or a *compound*) is incorrectly punctu-ated as a sentence.

See
B3.1

---

(2) Prepositional Phrase Fragments

A **prepositional phrase** cannot stand alone as a sentence. To correct a prepositional phrase fragment, attach it to the independent clause that contains the word or word group modified by the prepositional phrase.

for
President Johnson did not seek reelection,~~For~~ a number of reasons.
~~x~~

(3) Appositive Fragments

An **appositive**—a noun or noun phrase that identifies or renames an adjacent noun or pronoun—cannot stand alone as a sentence. To correct an appositive fragment, attach the appositive to the independent clause that contains the word or word group the appositive renames.

a
Brian was the star forward of the Blue Devils,~~A~~ team that won nearly
~~x,~~
every game.

Appositives may also be introduced by phrases like *for example,* *namely,* or *such as.* These phrases do not change anything: an appositive still cannot stand alone as a sentence.

such

Fairy tales are full of damsels in distress_x,Such as Rapunzel.

CLOSE UP — REVISING SENTENCE FRAGMENTS: LISTS

See 36a1

When a fragment takes the form of a **list**, add a colon to connect the list to the sentence that introduces it.

Tourists often outnumber residents in four European cities. Venice,

Florence_x:Canterbury, and Bath.

---

(4) Compound Fragments

The last part of a **compound predicate, compound object,** or **compound complement** cannot stand alone as a sentence. To correct this kind of fragment, connect the detached part of the compound to the rest of the sentence.

but

People with dyslexia often have trouble reading_x,But may be very intelligent. (part of compound predicate)

and

They took only a compass and a canteen_x,And some trail mix. (part of compound object)

and

When their supplies ran out, they were surprised_x,And hungry. (part of compound complement)

16c Deleting the Subordinating Conjunction or Relative Pronoun

When a fragment consists of a dependent clause that is punctuated as if it were a complete sentence, you can correct it by attaching it to an adjacent independent clause, as illustrated in **16b.** Alternatively, you can simply delete the subordinating conjunction or relative pronoun.

> City
> Property taxes rose sharply. ~~Although city~~ services declined.

> This
> The battery is dead. ~~Which~~ means the car won't start.

(In the second sentence, the relative pronoun is replaced by *this,* a word that can serve as the sentence's subject.)

Note, however, that deleting the subordinating conjunction or relative pronoun is usually the least desirable way to revise a sentence fragment because it is likely to create two choppy sentences and obscure the connection between them.

CLOSE UP REVISING SENTENCE FRAGMENTS

Sentence fragments are often used in speech and informal writing as well as in journalism, advertising, and creative writing. In most college writing situations, however, sentence fragments are not acceptable. Do not use them without carefully considering their suitability for your audience and purpose.

CHAPTER 17

REVISING COMMA SPLICES AND FUSED SENTENCES

A **run-on sentence** is created when two independent clauses are joined without the necessary punctuation or connective word. A run-on sentence is not just a long sentence—in fact, run-ons can be quite short—but a grammatically incorrect construction. *Comma splices* and *fused sentences* are two kinds of run-on sentences.

A **comma splice** is an error that occurs when two independent clauses are joined with just a comma. A **fused sentence** is an error that occurs when two independent clauses are joined with no punctuation.

COMMA SPLICE: Charles Dickens created the character of Mr. Micawber, he also created Uriah Heep.

FUSED SENTENCE: Charles Dickens created the character of Mr. Micawber he also created Uriah Heep.

To find out if you have created a comma splice or fused sentence, ask yourself these two questions:

1. Have you joined two independent clauses with just a comma? If so, you have created a comma splice.
2. Have you joined two independent clauses with no punctuation? If so, you have created a fused sentence.

> ✔ **CHECKLIST: REVISING COMMA SPLICES AND FUSED SENTENCES**
>
> To revise a comma splice or fused sentence, use one of the following strategies:
>
> ✔ Use a period to separate the clauses.
> ✔ Use a semicolon to separate the clauses.
> ✔ Add an appropriate coordinating conjunction.
> ✔ Subordinate one clause to the other, creating a complex sentence.

17a Revising with Periods

You can revise a comma splice or fused sentence by using a period to separate the independent clauses, creating two separate sentences. This is a good strategy when the clauses are long or when they are not closely related.

In 1894, Frenchman Alfred Dreyfus was falsely convicted of treason, ~~his~~
His

struggle for justice pitted the army against the civil libertarians.

🔍 CLOSE UP COMMA SPLICES AND FUSED SENTENCES

Using a comma to punctuate an interrupted quotation that consists of two complete sentences creates a comma splice. Instead, use a period.

"This is a good course," Eric said, "in fact, I wish I'd taken it
. In

sooner."

17b Revising with Semicolons

You can revise a comma splice or fused sentence by using a **semicolon** to separate two closely related clauses that convey parallel or contrasting information.
See 33a

In pre–World War II western Europe, only a small elite had access to a

university education, this situation changed dramatically after the war.

Run-ons/Comma Splices/Fused Sentences
   http://97.com/pi/writing_center/10.html
   http://www.tmisnet.com/dpec/webpromo/catalog/gmr103.htm
   http://owl.english.purdue.edu/Files/10.html

Chippendale chairs have straight legs; however, Queen Anne chairs have

curved legs.

NOTE: When you use a **transitional word or phrase** (such as *however, therefore,* or *for example*) to connect two independent clauses, the transitional element must be preceded by a semicolon and followed by a comma. If you use a comma alone, you create a comma splice. If you omit punctuation entirely, you create a fused sentence.

17c   Revising with Coordinating Conjunctions

You can revise a comma splice or fused sentence by using an appropriate coordinating conjunction (*and, or, but, nor, for, so, yet*) to create a **compound sentence**. Be sure to add a comma before the coordinating conjunction.

and
Elias Howe invented the sewing machine, Julia Ward Howe was a poet

and social reformer.

17d   Revising with Subordinating Conjunctions or Relative Pronouns

When the ideas in two independent clauses are not of equal importance, revise by using an appropriate subordinating conjunction or relative pronoun to place the less important idea in a dependent clause, creating a **complex sentence**.

because
Stravinsky's ballet *The Rite of Spring* shocked Parisians in 1913, its

rhythms seemed erotic.

who
Lady Mary Wortley Montagu, had suffered from smallpox, herself, ~~she~~

helped spread the practice of inoculation.

CHAPTER 18

REVISING AGREEMENT ERRORS

Agreement is the correspondence between words in number, gender, and person. Subjects and verbs agree in **number** (singular or plural) and **person** (first, second, or third); pronouns and their antecedents agree in number, person, and gender.

See 19a4

18a Understanding Subject-Verb Agreement

See 21b1

Singular subjects have singular verbs, and plural subjects have plural verbs. **Present tense** verbs, except *be* and *have,* add *-s* or *-es* when the subject is third-person singular. Third-person singular subjects include nouns; the personal pronouns *he, she, it,* and *one;* and many indefinite pronouns.

The <u>president</u> <u>has</u> the power to veto congressional legislation.

<u>She</u> frequently <u>cites</u> statistics to support her points.

In every group <u>somebody</u> <u>emerges</u> as a natural leader.

Present tense verbs do not add *-s* or *-es* when the subject is a plural noun, a first-person or second-person pronoun (*I, we, you*), or a third-person plural pronoun (*they*).

<u>Experts</u> <u>recommend</u> that dieters avoid processed meat.

At this stratum, <u>we</u> <u>see</u> rocks dating back ten million years.

<u>They</u> <u>say</u> that some wealthy people default on their student loans.

Subject-Verb Agreement
  http://www.unm.edu/~seceas/sva.htm
Agreement
  http://andromeda.rutgers.edu/~jlynch/Writing/a.html#agreement
Subject-Verb Agreement
  http://www.usca.sc.edu/uscaonlinewr/hos/s-v.html#s-v

In some special situations, subject-verb agreement can be trouble-some.

(1) Words That Come between Subject and Verb

If a modifying phrase comes between subject and verb, the verb should agree with the subject, not with a word in the intervening phrase.

The <u>sound</u> of the drumbeats <u>builds</u> in intensity in *The Emperor Jones.*

The <u>games</u> won by the intramural team <u>are</u> few and far between.

NOTE: When phrases introduced by *along with, as well as, in addition to, including,* and *together with* come between subject and verb, these phrases do not change the subject's number: Heavy <u>rain</u>, along with high winds, <u>causes</u> hazardous driving conditions.

(2) Compound Subjects Joined by *and*

Compound subjects joined by *and* usually take plural verbs.

<u>Air bags and antilock brakes</u> <u>are</u> standard on all new models.

There are, however, two exceptions to this rule. First, compound subjects joined by *and* that stand for a single idea or person are treated as a unit and used with singular verbs.

<u>Rhythm and blues</u> <u>is</u> a forerunner of rock and roll.

Second, when *each* or *every* precedes a compound subject joined by *and,* the subject takes a singular verb.

<u>Every desk and file cabinet</u> <u>was</u> searched before the letter was found.

(3) Compound Subjects Joined by *or*

Compound subjects joined by *or* or by *either . . . or* or *neither . . . nor* may take singular or plural verbs.
If both subjects are singular, use a singular verb; if both subjects are plural, use a plural verb.

<u>Either radiation or chemotherapy</u> <u>is</u> combined with surgery for effective results. (Both *radiation* and *chemotherapy* are singular, so the verb is singular.)

Either radiation treatments or chemotherapy sessions are combined with surgery for effective results. (Both *treatments* and *sessions* are plural, so the verb is plural.)

If one subject is singular and the other is plural, the verb agrees with the subject that is nearer to it.

Either radiation treatments or chemotherapy is combined with surgery for effective results. (Singular verb agrees with *chemotherapy.*)

Either chemotherapy or radiation treatments are combined with surgery for effective results. (Plural verb agrees with *treatments.*)

(4) Indefinite Pronouns

Some **indefinite pronouns**—*both, many, few, several, others*—are always plural and take plural verbs. Most others—*another, anyone, everyone, one, each, either, neither, anything, everything, something, nothing, nobody,* and *somebody*—are singular and take singular verbs.

Anyone is welcome to apply for the scholarship.

Each of the chapters includes a review exercise.

A few indefinite pronouns—*some, all, any, more, most,* and *none*—can be singular or plural, depending on the noun they refer to.

Some of this trouble is to be expected. (*Some* refers to *trouble.*)

Some of the spectators are restless. (*Some* refers to *spectators.*)

(5) Collective Nouns

A **collective noun** names a group of persons or things—for instance, *navy, union, association, band.* When it refers to the group as a unit, a collective noun takes a singular verb; when it refers to the individuals or items that make up the group, it takes a plural verb.

To many people, the royal family symbolizes Great Britain. (The family, as a unit, is the symbol.)

The family all eat at different times. (Each member eats separately.)

When a phrase that names a fixed amount—*three-quarters, twenty dollars, the majority*—is considered as a unit, it takes a singular verb; when it denotes parts of the whole, it takes a plural verb.

Three-quarters of his usual salary <u>is</u> not enough.

Three-quarters of the patients <u>improve</u> dramatically.

CLOSE UP   SUBJECT-VERB AGREEMENT WITH COLLECTIVE NOUNS

The number is always singular, and *a number* is always plural.

The number of voters <u>has</u> declined.

A number of students <u>have</u> missed preregistration.

---

(6) Singular Subjects with Plural Forms

A singular subject takes a singular verb, even if its form is plural.

Statistics <u>deals</u> with the collection and analysis of data.

When such a word has a plural meaning, however, use a plural verb.

The statistics <u>prove</u> him wrong.

CLOSE UP   SUBJECT-VERB AGREEMENT WITH FOREIGN PLURALS

Some nouns retain their Latin plural forms, which do not look like English plural forms. Be particularly careful to use the correct verbs with such words.

criterion is	criteria are
medium is	media are

---

(7) Inverted Subject-Verb Order

Even when the verb comes before the subject (as it does in questions and in sentences beginning with *there is* or *there are*), the subject and verb must agree.

Is either answer correct?

There are currently twelve courts of appeals in the federal system.

(8) Linking Verbs

See
23a

A **linking verb** should agree with its subject, not with the subject complement.

The problem was termites.

Termites were the problem.

(9) Relative Pronouns

See
A2

When you use a **relative pronoun** (*who, which, that,* and so on) to introduce a dependent clause, the verb in that clause agrees with the pronoun's **antecedent,** the word to which the pronoun refers.

The farmer is among the ones who suffer during a grain embargo.

The farmer is the only one who suffers during a grain embargo.

18b Understanding Pronoun-Antecedent Agreement

Singular pronouns—such as *he, him, she, her, it, me, myself,* and *oneself*—should refer to singular antecedents. Plural pronouns—such as *we, us, they, them,* and *their*—should refer to plural antecedents.

(1) Compound Antecedents

In most cases, use a plural pronoun to refer to two or more antecedents connected by *and.*

Mormonism and Christian Science were similar in their beginnings.

However, if a compound antecedent denotes a single unit—one person or thing or idea—use a singular pronoun to refer to the compound antecedent.

In 1904, <u>the husband and father</u> brought <u>his</u> family to America.

Use a singular pronoun when a compound antecedent is preceded by *each* or *every*.

<u>Every programming language and software package</u> has <u>its</u> limitations.

Use a singular pronoun to refer to two or more singular antecedents linked by *or* or *nor*.

<u>Neither Thoreau nor Whitman</u> lived to see <u>his</u> work read widely.

When one part of a compound antecedent is singular and one part is plural, the pronoun agrees with the closer antecedent.

<u>Neither the boy nor his parents</u> had <u>their</u> seatbelts fastened.

(2) Collective Noun Antecedents

If the meaning of a collective noun antecedent is singular (as it will be in most cases), use a singular pronoun. If the meaning is plural, use a plural pronoun.

The teachers' <u>union</u> announced <u>its</u> plan to strike. (The members act as one.)

The <u>team</u> ran on to the field and took <u>their</u> positions. (Each member acts individually.)

(3) Indefinite Pronoun Antecedents

Most **indefinite pronouns**—*each, either, neither, one, anyone,* and the like—are singular and are used with singular pronouns. See A2

<u>Neither</u> of the men had <u>his</u> proposal ready by the deadline.

<u>Each</u> of these neighborhoods has <u>its</u> own traditions and values.

PRONOUN-ANTECEDENT AGREEMENT

In speech and in popular writing, many people use the plural pronouns *they* or *their* with singular indefinite pronouns that refer to people, such as *someone, everyone,* and *nobody.*

Everyone can present their own viewpoint.

In college writing, however, never use a plural pronoun with a singular subject. Instead, you can use both the masculine and the feminine pronoun.

Everyone can present his or her own viewpoint.

Or you can make the sentence's subject plural.

All participants can present their own viewpoints.

The use of *his* alone to refer to a singular indefinite pronoun (Everyone can present *his* own viewpoint) is considered **sexist language**.

See
28e2

CHAPTER 19

REVISING AWKWARD OR CONFUSING SENTENCES

The most common causes of awkward or confusing sentences are *unwarranted shifts, mixed constructions, faulty predication,* and *illogical comparisons.*

19a   Unwarranted Shifts

(1) Shifts in Tense

Verb **tense** in a sentence or in a related group of sentences should not shift without good reason—to indicate changes of time, for example.

See 21b

The Wizard of Oz <u>is</u> a film that has enchanted audiences since it <u>was made</u> in 1939. (acceptable shift from present to past)

Unwarranted shifts can mislead readers and obscure your meaning.

I registered for the course because I thought it sounded interesting. How-
                                                    started
ever, after the first week I ~~start~~ having trouble understanding the lectures.

(unwarranted shift from past to present)

                                                          drive
On the Road is a 1957 novel about friends who ~~drove~~ across the United

States. (unwarranted shift from present to past)

Improving Sentence Clarity (Purdue)
   http://owl.english.purdue.edu/Files/116.html
Consistency in Verb Tense and Pronouns/Point of View; includes self-test
   http://gabiscott.com/bigdog/consistency.htm

See
13b
  NOTE: The present tense is generally used in **writing about literature**.

(2) Shifts in Voice

See
21d
  Unwarranted shifts from active to passive **voice** can be confusing. In the following sentence, for instance, the shift from active (*wrote*) to passive (*was written*) makes it unclear who wrote *The Great Gatsby:*

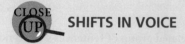

                                                  wrote

F. Scott Fitzgerald wrote *This Side of Paradise*, and later ~~The Great Gatsby.~~

~~was written.~~

CLOSE UP   SHIFTS IN VOICE

  Sometimes a shift from active to passive voice may be necessary to give a sentence proper emphasis.

  Even though consumers protested, the sales tax was increased.

Here the shift from active (*protested*) to passive (*was increased*) keeps the focus on consumer groups and the issue that they protested. To say *the legislature increased the sales tax* would change the emphasis of the sentence.

---

(3) Shifts in Mood

See
21c
  Unnecessary shifts in **mood** can also be confusing. The following sentence shifts from the imperative to the indicative mood:

                                          be

Next, heat the mixture in a test tube, and ~~you should make~~ sure it does

not boil.

(4) Shifts in Person and Number

Person indicates who is speaking (first person—*I, we*), who is spoken to (second person—*you*), and who is spoken about (third person—*he, she, it,* and *they*). Unwarranted shifts between the second and the third person cause most errors.

> you
> When ~~someone~~ look~~s~~ for a car loan, you compare the interest rates of
>
> several banks.

Number indicates one (singular—*novel, it*) or more than one (plural—*novels, they, them*). Singular pronouns should refer to singular **antecedents** and plural pronouns to plural antecedents.

See
18b

> he or she
> If a person does not study regularly, ~~they~~ will have a difficult time passing
>
> Spanish.

(5) Shifts from Direct to Indirect Discourse

Direct discourse reports the exact words of a speaker or writer. It is always enclosed in **quotation marks** and is often accompanied by an identifying tag (*he says, she said*). **Indirect discourse** summarizes the words of a speaker or writer. No quotation marks are used, and the reported words are often introduced with the word *that* or, in the case of questions, with *who, what, why, whether, how,* or *if.*

See
35a

> DIRECT DISCOURSE: My instructor said, "I <u>want</u> your paper by this Friday."
>
> INDIRECT DISCOURSE: My instructor said <u>that he wanted</u> my paper by this Friday.

Statements and questions that shift between indirect and direct discourse are often confusing.

> During the trial, John Brown repeatedly defended his actions and said
>   he was
> that ~~I am~~ not guilty. (shift from indirect to direct discourse)
>   ∧

"Are you   ?"
My mother asked ~~was I ever~~ going to get a job, (question is neither indi-
                                                ∧
rect nor direct discourse)

19b Mixed Constructions

A **mixed construction** is created when a sentence begins with one
grammatical strategy and then abruptly shifts to another.

MIXED: Because she studies every day explains why she gets good
grades.

The sentence above begins with a dependent clause, but an independent
clause does not follow; instead, the dependent clause is illogically used as
the subject of a sentence.

To avoid such errors, be sure you do not use a dependent clause,
prepositional phrase, or independent clause as your sentence's subject.

Because she studies every day, ~~explains why~~ she gets good grades. (depen-

dent clause used as a subject)

                               you can
By calling for information, ~~is the way to~~ learn more about the benefits of

ROTC. (prepositional phrase used as a subject)

Being
~~He was~~ late ~~was what~~ made him miss Act 1. (independent clause used as a

subject)

19c Faulty Predication

Faulty predication occurs when a sentence's predicate does not logically complete its subject.

(1) Incorrect Use of *Be*

Faulty predication is especially common in sentences that contain a
linking verb—a form of the verb *be,* for example—and a subject complement.

caused
Mounting costs and decreasing revenues ~~were~~ the downfall of the hospital.

This sentence incorrectly states that mounting costs and decreasing revenues *were* the downfall of the hospital when, in fact, they were the *reasons* for its downfall. You can correct this problem by providing a subject complement that relates logically to the subject.

(2) *Is When* or *Is Where*

Another kind of faulty predication occurs when a sentence that presents a definition contains a construction like *is where* or *is when*.

the construction of
Taxidermy is ~~where you construct~~ a lifelike representation of an animal

from its preserved skin. (In a definition, *is* must be preceded and followed

by nouns or noun phrases.)

(3) *The Reason . . . Is Because*

A similar type of faulty predication occurs when the phrase *the reason is* precedes *because*. In this situation, *because* (which means "for the reason that") is redundant and can be deleted.

that
The reason we drive is ~~because~~ we are afraid to fly.

19d Incomplete or Illogical Comparisons

A comparison tells how two things are alike or unlike. When you make a comparison, be sure it is **complete** (that readers can tell which two items are being compared) and **logical** (that it equates two comparable items).

than Nina's
My chemistry course is harder. (What two things are being compared?)

dog's
A pig's intelligence is greater than a ~~dog~~. (illogically compares "a pig's intelligence" to "a dog")

REVISING MISPLACED AND DANGLING MODIFIERS

A **modifier** is a word, phrase, or clause that describes or limits another word or word group in a sentence. Normally, a modifier should be placed close to its **headword,** the word or phrase it modifies. **Faulty modification** is the confusing placement of modifiers or the modification of nonexistent words.

20a   Revising Misplaced Modifiers

A **misplaced modifier** is a word or word group whose placement suggests that it modifies one word or phrase when it is intended to modify another.

MISPLACED: Faster than a speeding bullet, the citizens of Metropolis saw Superman flying overhead.

REVISED: The citizens of Metropolis saw Superman flying overhead, faster than a speeding bullet.

(1) Placing Modifying Words Precisely

Limiting modifiers such as *almost, only, even,* and *just* should always immediately precede the words they modify. A different placement changes the meaning of a sentence.

Nick *just* set up camp at the edge of town. (He did it just now.)

Just Nick set up camp at the edge of town. (He did it alone.)

Modifier Placement
    http://webster.commnet.edu/hp/pages/darling/grammar/modifiers.htm

Nick set up camp *just* at the edge of town. (His camp was precisely at the edge.)

When a limiting modifier is placed so that it is not clear whether it modifies a word before it or one after it, it is called a **squinting modifier.**

The life that everyone thought would fulfill her <u>totally</u> bored her.

To correct a squinting modifier, place the modifier so that it clearly modifies its headword.

The life that everyone thought would <u>totally</u> fulfill her bored her. (She was expected to be totally fulfilled.)

The life that everyone thought would fulfill her bored her <u>totally</u>. (She was totally bored.)

(2) Repositioning Misplaced Phrases

Placing a modifying phrase incorrectly can create an unclear, confusing sentence.

Roller-skating along the shore,
⋀Jane watched the boats.~~roller-skating along the shore~~. (can boats roller-

skate?)

Created by a famous artist,
⋀*Venus de Milo* is a statue ~~created by a famous artist~~ with no arms. (Did the

artist have no arms?)

(3) Repositioning Misplaced Dependent Clauses

Dependent clauses that serve as modifiers must be clearly related to their headwords.

, which will benefit everyone,
This diet program⋀will limit the consumption of possible carcinogens,

~~which will benefit everyone~~. (Will carcinogens benefit everyone?)

Misplaced and Dangling Modifiers
  http://www.clearcf.uvic.ca/writersguide/Pages/SentMispMods.html

After they had a glass of wine, the
~~The~~ parents checked to see that the children were sleeping.~~after they had a~~

~~glass of wine.~~ (Did the children drink the wine?)

20b   Revising Intrusive Modifiers

An **intrusive modifier** interrupts a sentence, making it difficult to understand.

Revise when a long modifying phrase comes between an auxiliary verb and a main verb.

Without
~~She had, without~~ giving it a second thought or considering the conse-
she had
quences, planned to reenlist.

Revise when modifiers awkwardly interrupt an infinitive—that is, when modifiers come between the word *to* and the base form of the verb.

defeat his opponent
He hoped to quickly and easily ~~defeat his opponent~~.

20c   Revising Dangling Modifiers

A **dangling modifier** is a word or phrase that cannot logically modify any word or word group in the sentence.

DANGLING: Using this drug, many undesirable side effects are experienced.

Using this drug appears to modify *side effects,* but this interpretation makes no sense. Because its true headword does not appear in the sen-

Dangling Modifiers (U. Vic)
   http://webserver.maclab.comp.uvic.ca/writersguide/Pages/SentDanglMods.
   html

tence, the modifier dangles. One way to correct the dangling modifier is to *create a new subject* by adding a word or word group that it can logically modify.

REVISED: Using this drug, <u>patients</u> experience many undesirable side effects.

Another way to correct the dangling modifier is to *create a dependent clause*.

REVISED: Many undesirable side effects are experienced <u>when this drug is used</u>.

These two options for correcting dangling modifiers are illustrated below.

(1) Creating a New Subject

the technician lifted
<u>Using a pair of forceps,</u>ₐthe skin of the rat's abdomen.~~was~~ lifted. (Modifier

cannot logically modify *skin*.)

Meg found
<u>With fifty pages to read,</u>ₐ*War and Peace* was absorbing. (Modifier cannot

logically modify *War and Peace*.)

DANGLING MODIFIERS AND THE PASSIVE VOICE

Most sentences that include dangling modifiers are in the passive voice and do not indicate a headword. Changing the **passive voice** to **active voice** corrects the dangling modifier by changing the subject of the sentence's main clause to a word that the dangling modifier can logically modify.

See 21d

(2) Creating a Dependent Clause

Before
∧To implement a plus/minus grading system, _was implemented_ ∧all students were polled.

(Modifier cannot logically modify _students._)

Because the magazine had been on
∧On the newsstands only an hour, its sales surprised everyone. (Modifier

cannot logically modify _sales._)

Sentence Grammar

PART 8

SENTENCE
GRAMMAR

❓ FREQUENTLY ASKED QUESTIONS

PART 8

SENTENCE
GRAMMAR

CHAPTER 21

USING VERBS CORRECTLY: FORM, TENSE, MOOD, AND VOICE

21a Verb Forms

Every verb has four **principal parts:** a **base form** (the form of the verb used with *I, we, you,* and *they* in the present tense),* a **present participle** (the *-ing* form of the verb), a **past tense form,** and a **past participle.**

(1) Regular Verbs

A **regular verb** forms both its past tense and its past participle by adding *-d* or *-ed.*

PRINCIPAL PARTS OF REGULAR VERBS

Base Form	Past Tense Form	Past Participle
smile	smiled	smiled
talk	talked	talked
jump	jumped	jumped

---

(2) Irregular Verbs

Irregular verbs do not follow the pattern just discussed. The chart that follows lists the principal parts of the most frequently used irregular verbs. When in doubt about the form of a verb, look up the base form in the dictionary. (If the dictionary lists only the base form, then the verb is regular.)

---

*Note: The verb *be* is so irregular that it is the one exception to this definition; its base form is *be.*

FREQUENTLY USED IRREGULAR VERBS

Base Form	Past Tense Form	Past Participle
arise	arose	arisen
awake	awoke, awaked	awoke, awaked
be	was/were	been
beat	beat	beaten
begin	began	begun
bend	bent	bent
bet	bet, betted	bet
bite	bit	bitten
blow	blew	blown
break	broke	broken
bring	brought	brought
build	built	built
burst	burst	burst
buy	bought	bought
catch	caught	caught
choose	chose	chosen
cling	clung	clung
come	came	come
cost	cost	cost
deal	dealt	dealt
dig	dug	dug
dive	dived, dove	dived
do	did	done
drag	dragged	dragged
draw	drew	drawn
drink	drank	drunk
drive	drove	driven
eat	ate	eaten
fall	fell	fallen

continued on the following page

Regular v. Irregular Verbs (Illinois)
   http://www.english.uiuc.edu/cws/wworkshop/regularverbs.htm
Irregular Verbs (Mercer County (NJ) Community College)
   http://www.mccc.edu/TVC/owl/shea4d.htm

Base Form	Past Tense Form	Past Participle
fight	fought	fought
find	found	found
fly	flew	flown
forget	forgot	forgotten, forgot
freeze	froze	frozen
get	got	gotten
give	gave	given
go	went	gone
grow	grew	grown
hang (execute)	hanged	hanged
hang (suspend)	hung	hung
have	had	had
hear	heard	heard
keep	kept	kept
know	knew	known
lay	laid	laid
lead	led	led
lend	lent	lent
let	let	let
lie (recline)	lay	lain
lie (tell an untruth)	lied	lied
make	made	made
prove	proved	proved, proven
read	read	read
ride	rode	ridden
ring	rang	rung
rise	rose	risen
run	ran	run
say	said	said
see	saw	seen
set (place)	set	set
shake	shook	shaken
shrink	shrank, shrunk	shrunk, shrunken
sing	sang	sung
sink	sank	sunk
sit	sat	sat

continued on the following page

continued from the previous page

Base Form	Past Tense Form	Past Participle
sneak	sneaked	sneaked
speak	spoke	spoken
speed	sped, speeded	sped, speeded
spin	spun	spun
spring	sprang	sprung
stand	stood	stood
steal	stole	stolen
strike	struck	struck, stricken
swear	swore	sworn
swim	swam	swum
swing	swung	swung
take	took	taken
teach	taught	taught
throw	threw	thrown
wake	woke, waked	waked, woken
wear	wore	worn
wring	wrung	wrung
write	wrote	written

CLOSE UP   TROUBLESOME IRREGULAR VERBS: LIE/LAY AND SIT/SET

Lie means "to recline" and does not take an object ("He likes to *lie* on the floor"); *lay* means "to place" or "to put" and does take an object ("He wants to *lay* a rug on the floor"):

Base Form	Past Tense Form	Past Participle
lie	lay	lain
lay	laid	laid

continued on the following page

Sit means "to assume a seated position" and does not take an object ("She wants to *sit* on the table"); *set* means "to place" or "to put" and usually takes an object ("She wants to *set* a vase on the table"):

Base Form	Past Tense Form	Past Participle
sit	sat	sat
set	set	set

21b Tense

Tense is the form that a verb takes to indicate when an action occurred or when a condition existed.

ENGLISH VERB TENSES

Simple Tenses

> Present (I *finish*, she or he *finishes*)
> Past (I *finished*)
> Future (I *will finish*)

Perfect Tenses

> Present perfect (I *have finished*, she or he *has finished*)
> Past perfect (I *had finished*)
> Future perfect (I *will have finished*)

Progressive Tenses

> Present progressive (I *am finishing*, she or he *is finishing*)
> Past progressive (I *was finishing*)
> Future progressive (I *will be finishing*)
> Present perfect progressive (I *have been finishing*)
> Past perfect progressive (I *had been finishing*)
> Future perfect progressive (I *will have been finishing*)

---

(1) Using the Simple Tenses

The **simple tenses** include *present, past,* and *future.*

The **present tense** usually indicates an action taking place at the time it is expressed in speech or writing or an action that occurs regularly.

I <u>see</u> your point. (an action taking place when it is expressed)

He <u>wears</u> wool in the winter. (an action that occurs regularly)

CLOSE UP · SPECIAL USES OF THE PRESENT TENSE

The present tense has four special uses.

TO INDICATE FUTURE TIME: The grades <u>arrive</u> next Thursday.

TO STATE A GENERALLY HELD BELIEF: Studying <u>pays</u> off.

TO STATE A SCIENTIFIC TRUTH: An object at rest <u>tends</u> to stay at rest.

TO DISCUSS A LITERARY WORK: *Family Installments* <u>tells</u> the story of a Puerto Rican family.

The **past tense** indicates that an action has already taken place.

John Glenn <u>orbited</u> the earth three times on February 20, 1962. (an action completed in the past)

As a young man, Mark Twain <u>traveled</u> through the Southwest. (an action that recurred in the past but did not extend into the present)

The **future tense** indicates that an action will or is likely to take place.

Halley's Comet <u>will reappear</u> in 2061. (a future action that will definitely occur)

The land boom in Nevada <u>will</u> probably <u>continue</u>. (a future action that is likely to occur)

Verb tense (U. Ottawa)
   http://www.uottawa.ca/academic/arts/writcent/hypergrammar/usetense.html
English Verb Tenses (Illinois)
   http://deil.lang.uiuc.edu/class.pages/Structure1/tenses.html

(2) Using the Perfect Tenses

The **perfect tenses** designate actions that were or will be completed before other actions or conditions. The perfect tenses are formed with the appropriate tense form of the auxiliary verb *have* plus the past participle.

The **present perfect** tense can indicate two types of continuing action beginning in the past.

Dr. Kim <u>has finished</u> studying the effects of BHA on rats. (an action that began in the past and is finished at the present time)

My mother <u>has invested</u> her money wisely. (an action that began in the past and extends into the present)

The **past perfect** tense indicates an action occurring before a certain time in the past.

By 1946 engineers <u>had built</u> the first electronic digital computer.

The **future perfect** tense indicates that an action will be finished by a certain future time.

By Tuesday the transit authority <u>will have run</u> out of money.

(3) Using the Progressive Tenses

The **progressive tenses** express continuing action. They are formed with the appropriate tense of the verb *be* plus the present participle.

The **present progressive** tense indicates that something is happening at the time it is expressed in speech or writing.

The volcano <u>is erupting</u>, and lava <u>is flowing</u> toward the town.

The **past progressive** tense indicates two kinds of past action.

Roderick Usher's actions <u>were becoming</u> increasingly bizarre. (a continuing action in the past)

Verb Tense Review Quiz (D. Oliver)
   http://www.pacificnet.net/~sperling/quiz/vtr.html
Verb Tense Consistency (Emory U.)
   http://www.emory.edu/ENGLISH/WC/verbconsist.html

The French revolutionary Marat was stabbed to death while he <u>was bathing</u>. (an action occurring at the same time in the past as another action)

The **future progressive** tense indicates a continuing action in the future.

The treasury secretary <u>will be</u> carefully <u>monitoring</u> the money supply.

The **present perfect progressive** tense indicates action continuing from the past into the present and possibly into the future.

Rescuers <u>have been working</u> around the clock.

The **past perfect progressive** tense indicates that a past action went on until another one occurred.

Before President Kennedy was assassinated, he <u>had been working</u> on civil rights legislation.

The **future perfect progressive** tense indicates that an action will continue until a certain future time.

By eleven o'clock we <u>will have been driving</u> for seven hours.

(4) Using Verb Tenses in a Sentence

Verb tenses sometimes shift within a sentence.

The debate <u>was</u> not impressive, but the election <u>will determine</u> the winner.

When a **verb** appears in a dependent clause, its tense depends on the tense of the main verb in the independent clause. When the main verb is in the past tense, the verb in the dependent clause is usually in the past or past perfect tense. When the main verb is in the past perfect tense, the verb in the dependent clause is usually in the past tense. (When the main verb in the independent clause is in any tense except the past or past perfect, the verb in the dependent clause may be in any tense needed for meaning.)

Main Verb	*Verb in Dependent Clause*
George Hepplewhite <u>was</u> (past) an English cabinetmaker	who <u>designed</u> (past) distinctive chair backs.

The battle <u>had ended</u> (past perfect)	by the time reinforcements <u>arrived</u>. (past)

When an **infinitive** appears in a verbal phrase, the tense it expresses depends on the tense of the sentence's main verb. The *present infinitive* (*to* plus the base form of the verb) indicates an action happening at the same time as or later than the main verb. The *perfect infinitive* (*to have* plus the past participle) indicates action happening earlier than the main verb.

Main Verb	*Infinitive*
I <u>went</u>	<u>to see</u> the Rangers play last week. (The going and seeing occurred at the same time.)
I <u>want</u>	<u>to see</u> the Rangers play tomorrow. (Wanting occurs in the present, and seeing will occur in the future.)
I would <u>like</u>	<u>to have seen</u> the Rangers play. (Liking occurs in the present, and seeing would have occurred in the past.)

When a **participle** appears in a verbal phrase, its tense depends on the tense of the sentence's main verb. The *present participle* indicates action happening at the same time as the action of the main verb. The *past participle* or the *present perfect participle* indicates action occurring before the action of the main verb.

Participle	*Main Verb*
<u>Addressing</u> the 1896 Democratic Convention,	William Jennings Bryan <u>delivered</u> his Cross of Gold speech. (The addressing and the delivery occurred at the same time.)
<u>Having written</u> her term paper,	Camille <u>studied</u> for her history final. (The writing occurred before the studying.)

21c Mood

Mood is the form a verb takes to indicate whether a writer is making a statement, asking a question, giving a command, or expressing a wish or a contrary-to-fact statement. The three moods in English are the *indicative,* the *imperative,* and the *subjunctive.*

The **indicative** mood expresses an opinion, states a fact, or asks a question: Jackie Robinson <u>had</u> an impact on professional baseball.

The **imperative** mood is used in commands and direct requests. Usually the imperative includes only the base form of the verb without a subject: <u>Use</u> a dictionary.

(1) Forming the Subjunctive Mood

The **subjunctive** mood causes the greatest difficulty for writers. The **present subjunctive** uses the base form of the verb, regardless of the subject. The **past subjunctive** has the same form as the past tense of the verb. (The auxiliary verb *be,* however, takes the form *were* regardless of the number or person of the subject.)

Dr. Gorman suggested that I <u>study</u> the Cambrian Period. (present subjunctive)

I wish I <u>were</u> going to Europe. (past subjunctive)

(2) Using the Subjunctive Mood

Use the present subjunctive in *that* clauses after words such as *ask, suggest, require, recommend,* and *demand.*

The report recommended that juveniles <u>be</u> given mandatory counseling.

Captain Ahab insisted that his crew <u>hunt</u> the white whale.

 Use the past subjunctive in **conditional statements** (statements beginning with *if* that are contrary to fact, including statements that express a wish).

If John <u>were</u> here, he could see Marsha. (John is not here.)

The father acted as if he <u>were</u> having the baby. (The father couldn't be having the baby.)

I wish I <u>were</u> more organized. (expresses a wish)

CLOSE UP   CONDITIONAL STATEMENTS

If an *if* clause expresses a condition that is possible, use the indicative mood, not the subjunctive.

continued on the following page

If a peace treaty <u>is</u> signed, the world will be safer. (A peace treaty is possible.)

21d Voice

Voice is the form that a verb takes to indicate whether its subject acts or is acted upon. When the subject of a verb does something—that is, acts—the verb is in the **active voice.** When the subject of a verb receives the action—that is, is acted upon—the verb is in the **passive voice.**

ACTIVE VOICE: Hart Crane <u>wrote</u> *The Bridge.*

PASSIVE VOICE: *The Bridge* <u>was written</u> by Hart Crane.

 **VOICE**

Because the active voice emphasizes the doer of an action, it is usually briefer, clearer, and more **<u>emphatic</u>** than the passive voice. Whenever possible, use active voice in your college writing.

See 25e

303

CHAPTER 22

USING PRONOUNS CORRECTLY

22a Understanding Pronoun Case

Pronouns change **case** to indicate their function in a sentence. English has three cases: *subjective, objective,* and *possessive.*

PRONOUN CASE FORMS

Subjective

| I | he, she | it | we | you | they | who | whoever |

Objective

| me | him, her | it | us | you | them | whom | whomever |

Possessive

| my | his, her | its | our | your | their | whose | |
| (mine) | (hers) | | (ours) | (yours) | (theirs) | | |

---

(1) Subjective Case

A pronoun takes the **subjective case** in the following situations:

SUBJECT OF A VERB: <u>I</u> bought a new mountain bike.

SUBJECT COMPLEMENT: It was <u>he</u> for whom the men were looking.

Using Pronouns Clearly
    http://owl.english.purdue.edu/Files/79.html
Pronouns and Names (M. Browning)
    http://www.princeton.edu/~browning/binding.html
Pronoun Types and Common Mistakes (Emory U.)
    http://www.emory.edu/ENGLISH/WC/pronounref.html

APPOSITIVE IDENTIFYING SUBJECT: Both scientists, <u>Oppenheimer and he</u>, worked on the atomic bomb.

(2) Objective Case

A pronoun takes the **objective case** in these situations:

DIRECT OBJECT: Our sociology teacher likes Adam and <u>me</u>.

INDIRECT OBJECT: The plumber's bill gave <u>him</u> quite a shock.

OBJECT OF A PREPOSITION: Between <u>us</u> we own ten shares of stock.

APPOSITIVE IDENTIFYING AN OBJECT: Rachel discussed both authors, <u>Hannah Arendt and her</u>.

CLOSE UP — PRONOUN CASE IN COMPOUND CONSTRUCTIONS

I is not necessarily more appropriate than *me*. In compound constructions like the following, *me* is correct.

Just between you and <u>me</u> [not *I*], I think we're going to have a quiz. (*Me* is the object of the preposition *between*.)

---

(3) Possessive Case

A pronoun takes the **possessive case** when it indicates ownership (*our* car, *your* book). Remember to use the possessive, not the objective, case before a **gerund**.

> See A3

Napoleon approved of <u>their</u> [not *them*] ruling Naples. (*Ruling* is a gerund.)

22b Determining Pronoun Case in Special Situations

(1) Implied Comparisons with *Than* or *As*

When a sentence containing an implied comparison ends with a pronoun, your meaning dictates your choice of pronoun.

Darcy likes John more than <u>I</u>. (more than I like John)

Darcy likes John more than <u>me</u>. (more than she likes me)

(2) *Who* and *Whom*

The case of the pronouns *who* and *whom* depends on their function *within their own clause.* When a pronoun serves as the subject of its clause, use *who* or *whoever;* when it functions as an object, use *whom* or *whomever.*

The Salvation Army gives food and shelter to <u>whoever</u> is in need. (*Whoever* is the subject of the dependent clause *whoever is in need.*)

I wonder <u>whom</u> jazz musician Miles Davis influenced. (*Whom* is the object of *influenced* in the dependent clause *whom jazz musician Miles Davis influenced.*)

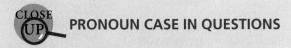

PRONOUN CASE IN QUESTIONS

To determine the case of *who* at the beginning of a question, use a personal pronoun to answer the question. The case of *who* should be the same as the case of the personal pronoun.

<u>Who</u> wrote *The Age of Innocence?* <u>She</u> wrote it. (subject)

<u>Whom</u> do you support for mayor? I support <u>her</u>. (object)

(3) Appositives

An **appositive** is a noun or noun phrase that identifies or renames an adjacent noun or pronoun. The case of a pronoun in an appositive depends on the function of the word it describes.

We heard two Motown recording artists, Smokey Robinson and <u>him</u>. (*Recording artists* is the object of the verb *heard,* so the pronoun in the appositive *Smokey Robinson and him* takes the objective case.)

Two Motown recording artists, Smokey Robinson and <u>he</u>, recorded for Motown Records. (*Recording artists* is the subject of the sentence, so the pronoun in the appositive *Smokey Robinson and he* takes the subjective case.)

(4) *We* and *Us* before a Noun

When a first-person plural pronoun directly precedes a noun, the case of the pronoun depends on the way the noun functions in the sentence.

<u>We</u> women must stick together. (*Women* is the subject of the sentence, so the pronoun *we* must be in the subjective case.)

Teachers make learning easy for <u>us</u> students. (*Students* is the object of the preposition *for,* so the pronoun *us* must be in the objective case.)

22c   Revising Pronoun Reference Errors

An **antecedent** is the word or word group to which a pronoun refers. The connection between a pronoun and its antecedent should always be clear.

(1) Ambiguous Antecedent

Sometimes a pronoun—for example, *this, that, which,* or *it*—could refer to more than one antecedent in the sentence. In such cases, substitute a noun for the pronoun to eliminate the ambiguity.

The accountant took out his calculator and completed the tax return.
Then, he put ~~it~~ _{the calculator} into his briefcase.

Sometimes a pronoun does not seem to refer to any specific antecedent. In such cases, supply a noun to clarify the reference.

Some one-celled organisms contain chlorophyll yet are considered animals. This ᴧ_{paradox} illustrates the difficulty of classifying single-celled organisms.

(2) Remote Antecedent

The farther a pronoun is from its antecedent, the more difficult it is for readers to make a connection between them.

During the mid-1800s, many Czechs began to immigrate to America. By

1860, about 23,000 Czechs had left their country. By 1900, 13,000 Czech

America's
immigrants were coming to ~~its~~ shores each year.

(3) Nonexistent Antecedent

Sometimes a pronoun refers to a nonexistent antecedent.

Our township has decided to build a computer lab in the elementary

teachers
school because ~~they~~ feel that fourth graders should begin using computers.
         ˄

CLOSE UP   **PRONOUN REFERENCE**

Expressions such as "*It* says in the paper" and "*They* said on the
news" refer to unidentified antecedents and are not acceptable in
college writing. Substitute the appropriate noun for the unclear
pronoun: "*The article* in the paper says. . . ." and "In his commen-
tary, *Ted Koppel* observes. . . ."

---

(4) *Who, Which,* and *That*

In general, *who* refers to people or to animals that have names. *Which*
and *that* refer to objects, events, or unnamed animals and sometimes to
groups of people.

David Henry Hwang, <u>who</u> wrote the Tony Award–winning play *M.
Butterfly,* also wrote *Family Devotions* and *FOB.*

The spotted owl, <u>which</u> lives in old growth forests, is in danger of ex-
tinction.

Houses <u>that</u> are built today are usually more energy efficient than
those built twenty years ago.

CHAPTER 23

USING ADJECTIVES AND ADVERBS CORRECTLY

?   **Adjectives** modify nouns and pronouns. **Adverbs** modify verbs; adjectives; other adverbs; or entire phrases, clauses, or sentences.

The *function* of a word, not its form, determines whether it is classified as an adjective or as an adverb. Many adverbs (such as *immediately* and *hopelessly*) end in *-ly,* but others (such as *almost* and *very*) do not. Moreover, some words that end in *-ly* (such as *lively*) are adjectives.

23a   Using Adjectives

See B2   Be sure to use an adjective, not an adverb, as a subject complement. A **subject complement** is a word that follows a linking verb and modifies the sentence's subject, not its verb. (A **linking verb** does not show physical or emotional action. *Seem, appear, believe, become, grow, turn, remain, prove, look, sound, smell, taste, feel,* and the forms of the verb *be* are or can be used as linking verbs.)

> Michelle seemed <u>brave</u>. (*Seemed* shows no action and is therefore a linking verb. Because *brave* is a subject complement that modifies the noun *Michelle,* it takes the adjective form.)

> Michelle smiled <u>bravely</u>. (*Smiled* shows action, so it is not a linking verb. *Bravely* modifies *smiled,* so it takes the adverb form.)

Adjectives
    http://webster.commnet.edu/HP/pages/darling/grammar/adjectives/htm
Adjectives (Bowling Green)
    http://www.bgsu.edu/departments/writing-lab/uses_of_adjectives.html

Sometimes the same verb can function as either a linking verb or an action verb. Compare these two sentences.

He looked <u>hungry</u>. (*Hungry* modifies the subject.)

He looked <u>hungrily</u> at the sandwich. (*Hungrily* modifies the verb.)

23b   Using Adverbs

Be sure to use an adverb, not an adjective, to modify verbs; adjectives; other adverbs; or entire phrases, clauses, or sentences.

        very well
Most students did ~~great~~ on the midterm.

                   ly
My parents dress a lot more conservative‸than my friends do.

CLOSE UP   USING ADJECTIVES AND ADVERBS

In informal speech, adjective forms such as *good, bad, sure, real, slow, quick,* and *loud* are often used to modify verbs, adjectives, and adverbs. Avoid these informal modifiers in college writing.

           really well
The program ran ~~real good~~ the first time we tried it, but the new
           badly
system performed ~~bad~~.

23c   Using Comparative and Superlative Forms

COMPARATIVE AND SUPERLATIVE FORMS

Form	*Function*	*Example*
Positive	Describes a quality; indicates no comparisons	big

continued on the following page

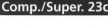
Form	Function	Example
Comparative	Indicates comparisons between *two* qualities (greater or lesser)	bigger
Superlative	Indicates comparisons among *three or more* qualities (greatest or least)	biggest

NOTE: Some adverbs, particularly those indicating time, place, and degree (*almost, very, here, yesterday, immediately*), do not have comparative or superlative forms.

(1) Comparative Forms

To form the comparative, all one-syllable adjectives and many two-syllable adjectives (particularly those that end in *-y, -ly, -le, -er,* and *-ow*) add *-er:* slow<u>er</u>, funni<u>er</u>. (Note that a final *y* becomes *i* before *-er* is added.)

Other two-syllable adjectives and all long adjectives form the comparative with *more:* <u>more</u> famous, <u>more</u> incredible.

Adverbs ending in *-ly* also form the comparative with *more:* <u>more</u> slowly. Other adverbs use the *-er* ending to form the comparative: soon<u>er</u>.

All adjectives and adverbs indicate a lesser degree with *less:* <u>less</u> lovely, <u>less</u> slowly.

(2) Superlative Forms

Adjectives that form the comparative with *-er* add *-est* to form the superlative: nic<u>est</u>, funni<u>est</u>. Adjectives that indicate the comparative with *more* use *most* to indicate the superlative: <u>most</u> famous, <u>most</u> challenging.

The majority of adverbs use *most* to indicate the superlative: <u>most</u> quickly. Others use the *-est* ending: soon<u>est</u>.

All adjectives and adverbs use *least* to indicate the least degree: <u>least</u> interesting, <u>least</u> willingly.

Adverbs
  http://webster.commnet.edu/HP/pages/darling/grammar/adverbs.htm
Adverbs (Bowling Green)
  http://www.bgsu.edu/departments/writing-lab/uses_of_adverbs.html

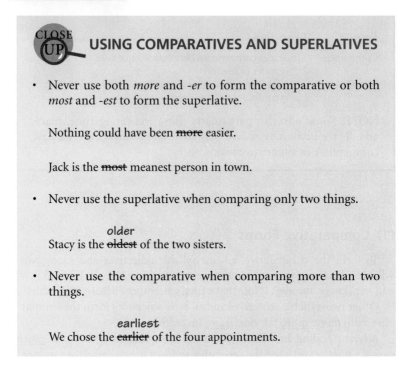

USING COMPARATIVES AND SUPERLATIVES

- Never use both *more* and *-er* to form the comparative or both *most* and *-est* to form the superlative.

Nothing could have been ~~more~~ easier.

Jack is the ~~most~~ meanest person in town.

- Never use the superlative when comparing only two things.

        older
Stacy is the ~~oldest~~ of the two sisters.

- Never use the comparative when comparing more than two things.

        earliest
We chose the ~~earlier~~ of the four appointments.

(3) Irregular Comparatives and Superlatives

Some adjectives and adverbs have irregular comparative and superlative forms. Instead of adding a word or an ending to the positive form, they use different words to indicate the comparative and the superlative.

IRREGULAR COMPARATIVES AND SUPERLATIVES			
	Positive	*Comparative*	*Superlative*
Adjectives:	good	better	best
	bad	worse	worst
	a little	less	least
	many, some, much	more	most
Adverbs:	well	better	best
	badly	worse	worst

23d Avoiding Illogical Comparisons

Many adjectives and adverbs can logically exist only in the positive degree. For example, words like *perfect, unique, excellent, impossible,* and *dead* cannot have comparative or superlative forms.

> I read ~~the most~~ ^{an} excellent story.

I read ~~the most~~ **an** excellent story.

The vase in her collection was ~~very~~ unique.

These words can, however, be modified by words that suggest approaching the absolute state—*nearly* or *almost,* for example.

He revised until his draft was <u>almost perfect</u>.

23e Avoiding Double Negatives

Be careful not to create a **double negative** by using a negative modifier (such as *never, no,* or *not*) with another negative word, such as *nearly, hardly, none,* or *nothing.* Remember that many contractions include the negative *not.*

See C3.5

Old dogs cannot learn ~~no~~ new tricks.

The instructor doesn't give ~~no~~ partial credit.

Sentence Style

SENTENCE STYLE

PART 9

CHAPTER 24

WRITING VARIED SENTENCES

Varying the way you construct your sentences can help make your writing lively and interesting. This strategy can also help you place proper emphasis on the most important ideas in your sentences.

24a Using Compound, Complex, and Compound-Complex Sentences

Paragraphs that mix simple, compound, and complex sentences are generally more interesting and easier to follow than those that do not.

(1) Compound Sentences

A **compound sentence** is created when two or more independent clauses are joined with *coordinating conjunctions, transitional words and phrases, correlative conjunctions, semicolons,* or *colons.*

Coordinating Conjunctions
The pianist made several mistakes, <u>but</u> the concert was still a success.

NOTE: Use a comma before a coordinating conjunction—a*nd, or, nor, but, for, so,* and *yet*—that joins two **<u>independent clauses</u>**.

See
32a

Simple and Complex Sentences (Texas)
  http://ccwf.cc.utexas.edu/~lhoffman/CSD368K.lecture.ComplexSen.html
Common Problems in Sentence Construction (Grammar Central)
  http://www.teleport.com/~awyatt/homework/grammar/less11.html
Elementary Rules of Composition from Strunk's *Elements of Style*
  http://www.bartleby.com/141/strunk.html#III
Sentence Craft (L. Behrens, UCSB)
  http://writing.ucsb.edu/faculty/behrens/index

Transitional Words and Phrases
Aerobic exercise can help lower blood pressure; <u>however</u>, those with high blood pressure should still limit salt intake.

The saxophone does not belong to the brass family; <u>in fact</u>, it is a member of the woodwind family.

NOTE: Use a semicolon—not a comma—before a transitional word or phrase that joins two independent clauses. Frequently used **transitional words and phrases** include conjunctive adverbs like *consequently, finally, still,* and *thus* as well as expressions like *for example, in fact, on the other hand,* and *for instance.*

Correlative Conjunctions
Diana <u>not only</u> passed the exam, <u>but</u> she <u>also</u> received the highest grade in the class.

<u>Either</u> he left his coat in his locker, <u>or</u> he left it on the bus.

Semicolons
Alaska is the largest state; Rhode Island is the smallest.

Colons
He got his orders: he was to leave for France on Sunday.

(2) Complex Sentences

A **complex sentence** consists of one independent clause and at least one dependent clause. A **subordinating conjunction** or **relative pronoun** links the independent and dependent clauses and indicates the relationship between them.

                    (dependent clause)   (independent clause)
[After the town was evacuated], [the hurricane began].

        (independent clause)   (dependent clause)
[Officials watched the storm], [which threatened to destroy the town].

Grammar Central's Achieving Sentence Variety
    http://www.teleport.com/~awyatt/homework/grammar/less9.html
Sentence Variety (Rhodes College)
    http://www.rhodes.edu/kamhi/center/gram/variety.html
Varying Sentence Patterns (RPI)
    http://www.rpi.edu/dept/llc/writecenter/web/text/prose1.html#6

Sometimes a dependent clause may be embedded within an independent clause.

(dependent clause)
Town officials, [who were very concerned], watched the storm.

FREQUENTLY USED SUBORDINATING CONJUNCTIONS

after	before	until
although	if	when
as	once	whenever
as if	since	where
as though	that	wherever
because	unless	while

RELATIVE PRONOUNS

that	whatever	who (whose, whom)
what	which	whoever (whomever)

---

(3) Compound-Complex Sentences

A **compound-complex sentence** consists of two or more independent clauses and at least one dependent clause.

(dependent clause)
[When small foreign imports began dominating the U.S.

(independent clause)
automobile industry], [consumers were very responsive],

(independent clause)
but [American autoworkers were dismayed].

24b Varying Sentence Length

(1) Combining Choppy Simple Sentences

Strings of short simple sentences can be tedious—and sometimes hard to follow, as the following paragraph illustrates:

John Peter Zenger was a newspaper editor. He waged and won an important battle for freedom of the press in America. He criticized the policies of the British governor. He was charged with criminal libel as a result. Zenger's lawyers were disbarred by the governor. Andrew Hamilton defended him. Hamilton convinced the jury that Zenger's criticisms were true. Therefore, the statements were not libelous.

❓ You can revise such choppy sentences by using *coordination, subordination,* or *embedding* to combine them with adjacent sentences.

Coordination pairs similar elements—words, phrases, or clauses—giving equal weight to each.

Two choppy sentences linked with *and,* creating compound sentence

John Peter Zenger was a newspaper editor. He waged and won an important battle for freedom of the press in America. <u>He criticized the policies of the British governor, and as a result, he was charged with criminal libel.</u> Zenger's lawyers were disbarred by the governor. Andrew Hamilton defended him. Hamilton convinced the jury that Zenger's criticisms were true. Therefore, the statements were not libelous.

Subordination places the more important idea in an independent clause and the less important idea in a dependent clause.

Simple sentences become dependent clauses, creating complex sentences

<u>John Peter Zenger was a newspaper editor who waged and won an important battle for freedom of the press in America.</u> He criticized the policies of the British governor, and as a result, he was charged with criminal libel. <u>When Zenger's lawyers were disbarred by the governor, Andrew Hamilton defended him.</u> Hamilton convinced the jury that Zenger's criticisms were true. Therefore, the statements were not libelous.

Embedding is the working of additional words and phrases into sentences.

The sentence *Hamilton convinced the jury . . .* becomes the phrase *convincing the jury*

John Peter Zenger was a newspaper editor who waged and won an important battle for freedom of the press in America. He criticized the policies of the British governor, and as a result, he was charged with criminal libel. <u>When Zenger's lawyers were disbarred by the governor, Andrew Hamilton defended him, convincing the jury that Zenger's criticisms were true.</u> Therefore, the statements were not libelous.

This final revision of the original string of choppy sentences uses coordination, subordination, and embedding to vary sentence length but retains the final short simple sentence for emphasis.

(2) Following a Long Sentence with a Short One

Another way to add interest with sentences of varying lengths is to follow one or more long sentences with a short one. This shifting of gears also places emphasis on the short sentence.

> Over the years, vitamin boosters say, a misconception has grown that as long as there are no signs or symptoms of say, scurvy, then we have all of the vitamin C we need. Although we know how much of a particular vitamin or mineral will prevent clinical disease, we have practically no information on how much is necessary for peak health. <u>In short, we know how sick is sick, but we don't know how well is well.</u>
>
> (*Philadelphia Magazine*)

24c   Breaking Up Strings of Compound Sentences

An unbroken series of compound sentences can be dull. Moreover, when you connect clauses only with coordinating conjunctions, you do not indicate exactly how ideas are related or which is most important.

ALL COMPOUND SENTENCES: A volcano that is erupting is considered *active*, <u>but</u> one that may erupt is designated *dormant,* <u>and</u> one that has not erupted for a long time is called *extinct*. Most active volcanoes are located in "The Ring of Fire," a belt that circles the Pacific Ocean, <u>and</u> they can be extremely destructive. Italy's Vesuvius erupted in AD 79, <u>and</u> it destroyed the town of Pompeii. In 1883 Krakatau, located between the Indonesian islands of Java and Sumatra, erupted, <u>and</u> it caused a tidal wave, <u>and</u> more than 36,000 people were killed. Martinique's Mont Pelée erupted in 1902, and its lava <u>and</u> ash killed 30,000 people, and this completely wiped out the town of St. Pierre.

VARIED SENTENCES: A volcano that is erupting is considered *active*. [**simple sentence**] One that may erupt is designated *dormant,* and one that has not erupted for a long time is called *extinct*. [**compound sentence**] Most active volcanoes are located in "The Ring of Fire," a belt that circles the Pacific Ocean. [**simple sentence with modifier**] Active volcanoes can be extremely destructive. [**simple sentence**] Erupting in AD 79, Italy's Vesuvius destroyed the town of Pompeii. [**simple sentence with modifier**] When Krakatau, located between the Indonesian islands of Java and Sumatra, erupted in 1883, it caused a tidal wave that killed 36,000 people. [**compound-complex sentence with modifier**] The eruption of Martinique's Mont Pelée in 1902 produced lava and ash that killed 30,000 people, completely wiping out the town of St. Pierre. [**complex sentence with modifier**]

24d Varying Sentence Types

See B4.2

To achieve sentence variety, mix <u>**declarative**</u> sentences (statements) with occasional <u>**imperative**</u> sentences (commands or requests) and **rhetorical questions** (questions that readers are not expected to answer).

Local television newscasts seem to be delivering less and less news. Although we tune in to be updated on local, national, and world events, only about 30 percent of most newscasts is devoted to news. The remaining time is spent on feature stories, advertising, weather, sports, and casual conversation between anchors. Given this focus on "soft" material, what options do those of us wishing to find out what happened in the world have? [**rhetorical question**] Critics of local television have a few suggestions. First, write to your local station's management voicing your concern; then, try to get others to sign a petition. [**imperatives**] If changes are not made, you can turn off your television and read the newspaper.

Other options for varying sentence types include mixing simple, compound, and complex sentences (**see 24a**); mixing cumulative and periodic sentences (**see 25b**); and using balanced sentences where appropriate (**see 25c**).

24e Varying Sentence Openings

?

Rather than beginning every sentence with the subject, try beginning with modifying *words, phrases,* or *clauses.*

Words

<u>Proud</u> and <u>relieved</u>, they watched their daughter receive her diploma. (adjectives)

<u>Hungrily</u>, he devoured his lunch. (adverb)

322

Phrases

For better or worse, credit cards are now widely available to college students. (prepositional phrase)

Located on the west coast of Great Britain, Wales is part of the United Kingdom. (participial phrase)

His interest widening, Picasso designed ballet sets and illustrated books. (absolute phrase)

Clauses

After Woodrow Wilson was incapacitated by a stroke, his wife unofficially performed many presidential duties. (adverb clause)

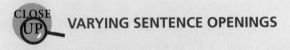

VARYING SENTENCE OPENINGS

If you begin a sentence with a coordinating conjunction, be sure that you have not created a fragment by incorrectly punctuating a **compound predicate**, **compound object**, and **compound complement** as a sentence.

See 16b4

24f Varying Standard Word Order

(1) Inverting Word Order

You can vary standard subject-verb-object (or subject-verb-complement) word order by placing the complement or direct object *before* the verb instead of in its conventional position or by placing the verb *before* the subject instead of after it.

(object)   (verb)

A cheery smile he had for everyone.

(subject)

(complement)

Especially useful was the book's index.

(verb)   (subject)

These strategies are useful because they draw attention to the word or word group that appears in an unexpected place—but overuse of inverted word order can be distracting, so use it in moderation.

(2) Separating Subject from Verb

You can place words or phrases between the subject and verb—but be sure the word group is not so long that it obscures the connection between subject and verb or create an **agreement** error.

(subject)   (verb)

Many <u>states</u>, hoping to reduce needless fatalities, <u>require</u> that children ride in government-approved child safety seats.

CHAPTER 25

WRITING EMPHATIC SENTENCES

In speaking, we emphasize certain ideas and deemphasize others with intonation and gesture; in writing, we convey emphasis through the selection and arrangement of words.

25a Conveying Emphasis through Word Order

Readers tend to focus on the *beginning* and *end* of a sentence, expecting to find key information there.

(1) Beginning with Important Ideas

Placing key ideas at the beginning of a sentence stresses their importance. The unedited version of the following sentence places emphasis on the study, not on those who conducted it or those who participated in it. Editing focuses attention on the researcher, not on the study.

~~In a landmark study of alcoholism,~~ Dr. George Vaillant of Harvard,ᴧ ^, in a landmark study of alcoholism,^ followed two hundred Harvard graduates and four hundred inner-city, working-class men from the Boston area.

CLOSE UP   WRITING EMPHATIC SENTENCES

Because sentence beginnings are so important, empty opening phrases like *there is* or *there are* generally weaken a sentence.

continued on the following page

Placement of Emphatic Words
    http://www.rpi.edu/dept/llc/writecenter/web/text/prose1.html#4
From Strunk's *Elements of Style*
    http://www.bartelby.com/141/strunk.html#18

continued from the previous page

MIT places
~~There is~~ heavy emphasis ~~placed~~ on the development of computa-

tional skills. ~~at MIT.~~

(2) Ending with Important Ideas

Placing key elements at the end of a sentence is another way to convey their importance.

Using a Colon or a Dash   A colon or a dash can add emphasis by isolating an important word or phrase at the end of a sentence.

Beth had always dreamed of owning one special car: a 1953 Corvette.

The elderly need a good deal of special attention—and they deserve that attention.

 ADDING EMPHASIS TO SENTENCES

See 2b2

When they are placed at the end of a sentence, conjunctive adverbs or other transitional expressions lose their power to indicate the relationship between ideas. Place **transitional words and phrases** earlier in the sentence, where they can serve this purpose and also add emphasis.

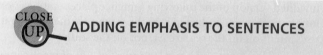

however,
Smokers do have rights;they should not try to impose their habit

on others; ~~however.~~

Using Climactic Word Order   **Climactic word order** is the arrangement of a series of items from the least to the most important. When you use climactic word order, the momentum of the sentence places emphasis on the idea at the end.

The nation's most prominent orchestras all boast large annual budgets, locations in important cities, and extremely talented musicians and conductors. (*Talented musicians* is the most important idea.)

(3) Experimenting with Word Order

In English sentences, the most common order is subject-verb-object (or subject-verb-complement). When you depart from this expected word order, you call attention to the word, phrase, or clause you have relocated—or even to the entire sentence.

More modest and less inventive than Turner's paintings are John Constable's landscapes.

Here the writer calls special attention to the modifying phrase *more modest and less inventive than Turner's paintings* by **inverting word order**, placing the complement and the verb before the subject.

See
24f1

25b Conveying Emphasis through Sentence Structure

(1) Using Cumulative Sentences

A **cumulative sentence** begins with an independent clause followed by additional words, phrases, or clauses that expand or develop it.

She holds me in strong arms, arms that have chopped cotton, dismembered trees, scattered corn for chickens, cradled infants, shaken the daylights out of half-grown upstart teenagers.

(Rebecca Hill, *Blue Rise*)

Because it presents its main idea first, a cumulative sentence tends to be clear and straightforward. When you want to communicate an idea in a direct manner, a cumulative sentence is the appropriate choice.

NOTE: Most English sentences are cumulative.

(2) Using Periodic Sentences

A **periodic sentence** ends with the main idea. It moves from supporting details, expressed in modifying phrases and dependent clauses, to the main idea, placed in the independent clause.

Unlike World Wars I and II, which ended decisively with the unconditional surrender of U.S. enemies, the war in Vietnam did not end when American troops withdrew.

In some periodic sentences the modifying phrase or dependent clause comes between subject and predicate.

Columbus, after several discouraging and unsuccessful voyages, finally reached America.

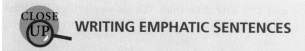

WRITING EMPHATIC SENTENCES

Periodic sentences are generally more emphatic than cumulative sentences, but the most emphatic sentence is not always the best choice. Because the periodic structure forces readers to wait—or even to search—for the delayed main idea, periodic sentences tend not to be as straightforward as cumulative ones.

25c Conveying Emphasis through Parallelism and Balance

See 27a

By reinforcing the correspondence between grammatical elements, **parallelism** helps writers convey information clearly, quickly, and emphatically.

We seek an individual <u>who is</u> a self-starter, <u>who owns</u> a late-model automobile, and <u>who is</u> willing to work evenings. (classified advertisement)

<u>Do not pass</u> go; <u>do not collect</u> $200. (instructions)

The Faust legend is central <u>in Benét's *The Devil and Daniel Webster*</u>, <u>in Goethe's *Faust*</u>, and <u>in Marlowe's *Dr. Faustus*</u>. (examination answer)

A **balanced sentence** is neatly divided between two parallel structures—for example, two independent clauses in a compound sentence. The symmetrical structure of a balanced sentence highlights correspondences or contrasts between clauses.

In the fifties, the electronic miracle was the television; in the eighties, the electronic miracle was the computer.

Alive, the elephant was worth at least a hundred pounds; dead, he would only be worth the value of his tusks, five pounds, possibly.
(George Orwell, "Shooting an Elephant")

25d Conveying Emphasis through Repetition

<u>Unnecessary repetition</u> makes sentences dull and monotonous as well as wordy.

He had a good arm and <u>also</u> could field well, and he was <u>also</u> a fast runner.

Effective repetition, however, can place emphasis on key words or ideas. For example, you can repeat a word or word group in a parallel series.

They decided to begin again: <u>to begin</u> hoping, <u>to begin</u> trying to change, <u>to begin</u> working toward a goal.

Even repeating a key word or phrase just once can add emphasis.

During those years when I was just learning to speak, my mother and father addressed me only <u>in Spanish</u>; <u>in Spanish</u> I learned to reply.
(Richard Rodriguez, *Aria: A Memoir of a Bilingual Childhood*)

25e Conveying Emphasis through Active Voice

<u>Active voice</u> verbs are generally more emphatic—and more concise—than **passive voice** verbs.

PASSIVE: The prediction that oil prices will rise is now being made by economists.

ACTIVE: Economists are now predicting that oil prices will rise.

329

The passive voice tends to focus your readers' attention on the action or on its receiver rather than on who is performing it. The receiver of the action is the subject of a passive sentence, so the actor fades into the background (*by economists*) or is omitted (*the prediction . . . is now being made*).

Sometimes, of course, you want to stress the action rather than the actor. If so, it makes sense to use the passive voice. You also use the passive voice when the identity of the person performing the action is irrelevant or unknown: *The course was canceled.* For this reason the passive voice is frequently used in scientific and technical writing: *The beaker was filled with a saline solution.*

CHAPTER 26

WRITING CONCISE SENTENCES

A sentence is not concise simply because it is short; a concise sentence contains only the words necessary to make its point.

26a Eliminating Nonessential Words

A good way to find out which words are essential in a sentence is to underline the key words. Then, look carefully at the remaining words so you can see which are unnecessary and delete them.

> It seems to me that it doesn't make sense to allow any <u>bail</u> to be <u>granted</u> to <u>anyone</u> who has ever been <u>convicted</u> of a <u>violent crime</u>.

The underlining shows you immediately that none of the words in the long introductory phrase are essential. The following revision includes just the words necessary to convey the key ideas:

> Bail should not be granted to anyone who has ever been convicted of a violent crime.

Whenever possible, delete nonessential words—*deadwood, utility words,* and *circumlocution*—from your writing.

(1) Deleting Deadwood

Deadwood refers to unnecessary phrases that take up space and add nothing to meaning.

Writing Concise Sentences
   http://webster.commnet.edu/hp/pages/darling/grammar/concise.htm
Eliminating "Word Clutter"
   http://www2.rscc.cc.tn.us/~jordan_jj/OWL/Clutter.html
Eliminating Wordiness (Texas)
   http://uwc.fac.utexas.edu/stu/handouts/wordines.html

Many
~~There were many~~ factors ~~that~~ influenced his decision to become a priest.

The two plots are ~~both~~ similar in ~~the way~~ that they trace the characters' increasing rage.

Shoppers ~~who are~~ looking for bargains often go to outlets.

an exhausting
They played a̱ racquetball game ~~that was exhausting~~.

This
~~In this~~ article ~~it~~ discusses lead poisoning.

is
The only truly tragic character in *Hamlet* ~~would have to be~~ Ophelia.

Deadwood also includes unnecessary statements of opinion, such as *I feel, it seems to me,* and *in my opinion.*

The
~~In my opinion, the~~ characters seem undeveloped.

This
~~As far as I'm concerned, this~~ course looks interesting.

(2) Deleting or Replacing Utility Words

Utility words contribute nothing to a sentence. Utility words include nouns with imprecise meanings (*factor, situation, type, aspect,* and so on); adjectives so general that they are almost meaningless (*good, bad, important*); and common adverbs denoting degree (*basically, very, definitely*).

Registration
~~The registration situation~~ was disorganized.

an
The scholarship offered Fran ~~a good~~ opportunity to study Spanish.

It was ~~actually~~ a worthwhile book, but I didn't ~~completely~~ finish it.

(3) Avoiding Circumlocution

Taking a roundabout way to say something (using ten words when five will do) is called **circumlocution.** Instead of complicated phrases and constructions, use short, concrete, specific words and phrases, and come right to the point.

~~It is not unlikely that the~~ The trend toward smaller cars will probably continue.

Joel was in the army ~~during the same time that~~ while I was in college.

REVISING WORDY PHRASES

A wordy phrase can almost always be replaced by a more concise, more direct term.

Wordy	*Concise*
at the present time	now
at this point in time	now
for the purpose of	for
due to the fact that	because
on account of the fact that	because
until such time as	until
in the event that	if
by means of	by
in the vicinity of	near
have the ability to	be able to

26b   Eliminating Unnecessary Repetition

See 25d

Repetition can make your writing more **emphatic**, but unnecessary repetition and redundant word groups can obscure your meaning. Correct unnecessary repetition by using one of the following strategies.

(1) Deleting Repeated Words

The childhood disease chicken pox occasionally leads to dangerous com-
plications, such as ~~the disease known as~~ Reye's syndrome.

(2) Substituting a Pronoun

Fictional detective Miss Marple has solved many crimes. *The Murder at*
the Vicarage was one of ~~Miss Marple's~~ her most challenging cases.

(3) Creating Appositives

Red Barber, ~~was~~ a sportscaster, ~~He~~ was known for his colorful expressions.

(4) Creating Compounds

In 1964, Ted Briggs was discharged from the Air Force. ~~He then~~ got a job
with Maxwell Data Processing. ~~He~~ married Susan, and Thompson ~~that same~~
~~year.~~

(5) Creating Complex Sentences

Americans value freedom of speech, which ~~Freedom of speech~~ is guaranteed by
the First Amendment.

❓ 26c Tightening Rambling Sentences

The combination of nonessential words, unnecessary repetition, and
complicated syntax creates **rambling sentences.** Revising rambling sentences frequently requires extensive editing.

(1) Eliminating Excessive Coordination

When you string a series of clauses together with coordinating conjunctions, you create a rambling, unfocused compound sentence. To revise such

sentences, first identify the main idea or ideas, and then subordinate the supporting details.

WORDY: Benjamin Franklin was the son of a candlemaker, but he later apprenticed as a printer, and this experience led to his buying *The Pennsylvania Gazette,* and he managed this periodical with great success.

CONCISE: Benjamin Franklin, the son of a candlemaker, later apprenticed as a printer, an experience that led to his buying *The Pennsylvania Gazette,* which he managed with great success.

(2) Eliminating Adjective Clauses

A series of **adjective clauses** is also likely to produce a rambling sentence. To revise, substitute concise modifying words or phrases for the adjective clauses.

See
B3.2

WORDY: *Moby Dick,* <u>which is a novel about a white whale,</u> was written by Herman Melville, <u>who was friendly with Nathanial Hawthorne,</u> <u>who urged him to revise the first draft.</u>

CONCISE: *Moby Dick,* a novel about a white whale, was written by Herman Melville, who revised the first draft at the urging of his friend Nathaniel Hawthorne.

(3) Eliminating Passive Constructions

Excessive use of the **passive voice** can make sentences ramble. Correct this problem by changing passive to active voice.

See
21d

WORDY: "Buy American" rallies <u>are being organized by</u> concerned Americans who hope that jobs <u>can be saved by</u> such gatherings.

CONCISE: Concerned Americans <u>are organizing</u> "Buy American" rallies, hoping that such gatherings <u>can save</u> jobs.

(4) Eliminating Wordy Prepositional Phrases

Substitute adjectives or adverbs for wordy **prepositional phrases**.

See
B3.1

        dangerous   exciting
The trip was ~~one of danger~~ but also ~~one of excitement~~.

          confidently   authoritatively
He spoke ~~in a confident manner~~ and ~~with a lot of authority~~.

(5) Eliminating Wordy Noun Constructions

Substitute strong verbs for wordy **noun phrases**.

                decided
We ~~made the decision~~ to postpone the meeting until ~~the appearance of~~
                      appear
all the board members‸

CHAPTER 27

USING PARALLELISM

Parallelism is the use of matching words, phrases, clauses, or sentence structures to express equivalent ideas. Effective parallelism adds unity, balance, and force to your writing.

27a Using Parallelism Effectively

Parallelism highlights the correspondence between *items in a series,* *paired items,* and elements in *lists* and *outlines.*

(1) With Items in a Series

Eat, drink, and be merry.

Baby food consumption, toy production, and marijuana use are likely to decline as the U.S. population grows older.

Three factors influenced his decision to seek new employment: his desire to relocate, his need for greater responsibility, and his dissatisfaction with his current job.

NOTE: For information on punctuating items in a series, see **32b** and **33b.**

(2) With Paired Items

The thank-you note was short but sweet.

Roosevelt represented the United States, and Churchill represented Great Britain.

Parallelism (U.Vic)
  http://www.clearcf.uvic.ca/writersguide/Pages/SentParallel.html
Parallel Structure (Bellevue (WA) C.C.)
  http://www.bcc.ctc.edu/writinglab/Parallel.html
Parallelism (Illinois)
  http://www.english.uiuc.edu/cws/wworkshop/parallel.htm

Ask not what your country can do for you; ask what you can do for your country.

(John F. Kennedy, inaugural address)

Paired elements linked by **correlative conjunctions** (such as *not only/but also, both/and, either/or, neither/nor,* and *whether/or*) should be parallel.

The design team paid close attention not only <u>to color</u> but also <u>to texture</u>.

Either <u>repeat physics</u> or <u>take calculus</u>.

Parallelism also highlights the contrast between paired elements linked by *than* or *as.*

Richard Wright and James Baldwin chose <u>to live in Paris</u> rather than <u>to remain in the United States</u>.

Success is as much <u>a matter of hard work</u> as <u>a matter of luck</u>.

(3) In Lists and Outlines

Elements in a list should be parallel.

The Irish potato famine had four major causes:
1. The establishment of the landlord-tenant system
2. The failure of the potato crop
3. The reluctance of England to offer adequate financial assistance
4. The passage of the Corn Laws

See
1c5

Elements in an **outline** should also be parallel.

27b   Revising Faulty Parallelism

?

When elements that have the same function in a sentence are not presented in parallel terms, the sentence is flawed by **faulty parallelism.**

FAULTY PARALLELISM: Many people in developing countries suffer because the countries lack sufficient housing to accommodate them, sufficient food to feed them, and their health-care facilities are inadequate.

Because the three reasons in the previous sentence are presented in a series, readers expect them to be expressed in parallel terms. The first two elements satisfy this expectation.

> sufficient housing to accommodate them . . .
>
> sufficient food to feed them . . .

The third item in the series, however, breaks this pattern.

> their health-care facilities are inadequate.

To create a clear, emphatic sentence, all three elements should be presented in parallel terms.

> Many people in developing countries suffer because the countries lack <u>sufficient housing to accommodate them</u>, <u>sufficient food to feed them</u>, and <u>sufficient health-care facilities to serve them</u>.

(1) Using Parallel Elements

To create parallelism, match nouns with nouns, verbs with verbs, and phrases or clauses with similarly constructed phrases or clauses.

> Popular exercises for men and women include aerobic dancing, weight
> lifting
> ~~lifters~~, and jogging.

> having
> I look forward to hearing from you and to ~~have~~ an opportunity to tell you
> more about myself.

(2) Repeating Signals of Parallelism

Although the use of similar grammatical structures may sometimes be enough to convey parallelism, sentences are often clearer if other key words are also parallel. In the following sentence, repeating the preposition *by* makes it clear that *not* applies only to the first phrase.

> Computerization has helped industry by not allowing labor costs to sky-
> by   by
> rocket,increasing the speed of production, and,improving efficiency.

Using Words Effectively

❓ FREQUENTLY ASKED QUESTIONS

USING WORDS EFFECTIVELY

PART 10

CHAPTER 28

CHOOSING WORDS

28a Choosing an Appropriate Level of Diction

Diction, which comes from the Latin word for *say,* means the choice and use of words. Different audiences and situations call for different levels of diction.

(1) Formal Diction

Formal diction is grammatically correct and uses words familiar to an academic audience. A writer of formal diction often maintains emotional distance from the audience by using the impersonal *one* rather than the more personal *I* and *you.* In addition, the tone of the writing—as determined by word choice, sentence structure, and choice of subject—is dignified and objective.

> We learn to perceive in the sense that we learn to respond to things in particular ways because of the contingencies of which they are a part. We may perceive the sun, for example, simply because it is an extremely powerful stimulus, but it has been a permanent part of the environment of the species throughout its evolution, and more specific behavior with respect to it could have been selected by contingencies of survival (as it has been in many other species).
>
> (B.F. Skinner, *Beyond Freedom and Dignity*)

(2) Informal Diction

Informal diction is the language that people use in everyday conversation. You should use informal diction in your college writing only to imitate speech or dialect or to give a paper a conversational tone.

Roget's Thesaurus
  http://www.thesaurus.com/
dictionary.com's list of online dictionaries
  http://www.dictionary.com/general/

Colloquial Diction   **Colloquial diction** is the language of everyday speech. Contractions—*isn't, I'm*—are typical colloquialisms, as are **clipped forms**—*phone* for *telephone, TV* for *television, dorm* for *dormitory.* Other colloquialisms include placeholders like *kind of* and utility words like *nice* for *acceptable, funny* for *odd,* and *great* for almost anything. Colloquial English also includes verb forms like *get across* for *communicate, come up with* for *find,* and *check out* for *investigate.*

Slang   **Slang** is a vivid and forceful use of language that packs a rhetorical punch. It is often restricted to a single group of people—urban teenagers, rock musicians, or computer users, for example. Slang words are extremely informal. Words like *uptight, groovy,* and *hippie* emerged in the 1960s. During the 1970s, technology, music, politics, and feminism influenced slang, giving us words like *hacker, disco, stonewalling,* and *macho.* The 1980s contributed expressions like *sound bite, yuppie,* and *chocoholic;* slang in the 1990s included expressions such as *wonk, hip-hop, downsize,* and *flame.*

Regionalisms   **Regionalisms** are words, expressions, and idiomatic forms that are used in particular geographical areas but may not be understood by a general audience. In eastern Tennessee, for example, a paper bag is a *poke,* and empty soda bottles are *dope bottles.* In Lancaster, Pennsylvania, which has a large Amish population, it is not unusual to hear an elderly person saying *darest* for *dare not* or *daresome* for *adventurous.* And New Yorkers stand *on line* for a movie, whereas people in most other parts of the country stand *in line.*

Nonstandard Diction   **Nonstandard diction** refers to words and expressions not generally considered a part of standard English—words like *ain't, nohow, anywheres, nowheres, hisself,* and *theirselves.*

No absolute rules distinguish standard from nonstandard usage. In fact, some linguists reject the idea of nonstandard usage altogether, arguing that this designation serves only to relegate both the language and those who use it to second-class status.

❓ (3) College Writing

The level of diction appropriate for college writing depends on your assignment and your audience. A personal-experience essay calls for a somewhat informal style, but a research paper, an examination, or a report calls for more formal diction. In general, most college writing falls somewhere between formal and informal English, using a conversational tone but maintaining grammatical correctness and using a specialized vocabulary when the situation requires it. (This level of diction is used in this book.)

28b   Choosing the Right Word   ❓

Choosing the right word to use in a particular context is very important. If you use the wrong word—or even *almost* the right one—you run the risk of misrepresenting your ideas.

(1) Denotation and Connotation

A word's **denotation** is its explicit dictionary meaning, what it stands for without any emotional associations. A word's **connotations** are the emotional, social, and political associations it has in addition to its denotative meaning.

Word	Denotation	Connotation
politician	someone who holds a political office	opportunist; wheeler-dealer

Words can have similar but not identical denotations, and this can cause confusion. For example, you may say *molecule* when you mean *atom* or *compound* when you mean *mixture.*

Selecting a word with the appropriate connotation can be a challenge. For example, the word *skinny* has negative connotations, whereas *thin* is neutral, and *slender* is positive. And *mentally ill, insane, neurotic, crazy, psychopathic,* and *emotionally disturbed* have different emotional, social, and political connotations that affect the way people respond. If you use terms without considering their connotations, you run the risk of undercutting your credibility, to say nothing of confusing and possibly angering your readers.

(2) Euphemisms

A **euphemism** is a term used in place of a blunt or harsh term that describes a subject society considers offensive or distasteful. College writing is no place for euphemisms. Say what you mean—*pregnant,* not *expecting; died,* not *passed away;* and *strike,* not *work stoppage.*

(3) Specific and General Words

Specific words refer to particular persons, items, or events; **general** words denote an entire class or group. *Queen Elizabeth II,* for example, is more specific than *monarch; jeans* is more specific than *clothing;* and *Jeep* is more specific than *vehicle.* You can use general words to describe entire classes of items, but you must use specific words to clarify such generalizations.

(4) Abstract and Concrete Words

Abstract words—*beauty, truth, justice,* and so on—refer to ideas, qualities, or conditions that cannot be perceived by the senses. **Concrete** words name things that readers can *see, hear, taste, smell,* or *touch.* As with general and specific words, whether a word is abstract or concrete is relative. The more concrete your words and phrases, the more vivid the image you evoke in the reader.

USING CONCRETE WORDS

See
26a2

Take particular care to avoid abstract terms such as *nice, great,* and *terrific* that say nothing and could be used in almost any sentence. These **utility words** convey only enthusiasm, not precise meanings. Replace them with more specific words.

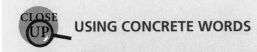

The book was ~~good~~ a complex and suspensefully plotted mystery.

28c Avoiding Unoriginal Language

(1) Jargon

Jargon, the specialized or technical vocabulary of a trade, profession, or academic discipline, is useful for communicating in the field in which it was developed. Outside that field, however, it is often confusing.

ORIGINAL: The patient had an acute myocardial infarction.

TRANSLATION: The patient had a heart attack.

When you write, avoid jargon and use a vocabulary that is appropriate for your audience and purpose.

(2) Neologisms

Neologisms are newly coined words that are not part of standard English. New situations call for new words, and frequently such words become a part of the language—*e-mail, voice mail, fax,* and *online,* for example. Others, however, are never accepted. If you are not sure whether to use a term, look it up in a current college **dictionary**. If it is not there, you probably should not use it.

See
Ch 29

(3) Avoiding Pretentious Diction

Good writing is clear writing, and pompous or flowery language is no substitute for clarity. Revise to eliminate **pretentious diction,** inappropriately elevated and wordy language.

>   asleep   thought   hiking
> As I fell ~~into slumber~~, I ~~cogitated~~ about my day ~~ambling~~ through ~~the~~
>
> ~~splendor of~~ the Appalachian Mountains.

(4) Clichés

Clichés are trite expressions that have lost their impact because they have been so overused. Familiar sayings like "rush to judgment" and "what goes around comes around," for example, do little to enhance your writing.

The purpose of college writing is always to convey information clearly; clichés do just the opposite. Take the time to think of fresh expressions.

Avoiding Clichés
   http://www.urich.edu/~writing/wweb/cliche.html
Cliché Finder
   http://www.westegg.com/cliche/

28d   Using Figures of Speech

Writers often go beyond the literal meanings of words to achieve special effects through **figures of speech.** Although you should not overuse figures of speech, do not be afraid to use them when you think they will help you communicate your ideas to your readers.

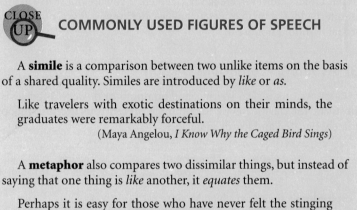

CLOSE UP   COMMONLY USED FIGURES OF SPEECH

A **simile** is a comparison between two unlike items on the basis of a shared quality. Similes are introduced by *like* or *as.*

> Like travelers with exotic destinations on their minds, the graduates were remarkably forceful.
> (Maya Angelou, *I Know Why the Caged Bird Sings*)

A **metaphor** also compares two dissimilar things, but instead of saying that one thing is *like* another, it *equates* them.

> Perhaps it is easy for those who have never felt the stinging darts of segregation to say, "Wait."
> (Martin Luther King, Jr., "Letter from Birmingham Jail")

An **analogy** explains an unfamiliar concept or thing by comparing it to a more familiar one.

> According to Robert Frost, writing free verse is like playing tennis without a net.

Personification gives an idea or inanimate object human attributes, feelings, or powers. We use personification every day in expressions such as *The engine died* or *The wind roared.*

NOTE: A **dead metaphor** (or **simile**) is a figure of speech that has been overused. As a result, it has become a pat, meaningless expression that evokes no particular visual image. Examples include *happy as a clam, free as a bird,* and *Herculean efforts.* As you write, avoid overused figures of speech; instead, try to use expressions that call up vivid images in a reader's mind.

28e   Avoiding Biased Language

(1)   Offensive Labels

When referring to a racial, ethnic, or religious group, use words with neutral connotations or words that the group itself uses in *formal* speech or writing.

Also, avoid potentially offensive labels relating to age (*brat, codger*), social class or geography (*beaner, redneck, hillbilly*), occupation (*shrink, shyster*), marital status (*old maid*), physical ability, or sexual orientation.

(2) Sexist Language

Sexist language entails much more than the use of derogatory words such as *hunk, chick,* and *bimbo.* Assuming that some professions are exclusive to one gender—for instance, that *nurse* denotes only women and that *doctor* denotes only men—is also sexist. So is the use of job titles such as *postman* for *letter carrier, fireman* for *firefighter,* and *stewardess* for *flight attendant.*

Sexist language also occurs when a writer fails to apply the same terminology to both men and women. For example, refer to two scientists with PhDs not as Dr. Sagan and Mrs. Yallow, but as Dr. Sagan and Dr. Yallow. Refer to two writers as James and Wharton, or Henry James and Edith Wharton, not James and Mrs. Wharton.

In your writing, always use *women*—not *girls, gals,* or *ladies*—when referring to adult females. Use *Ms.* as the form of address when a woman's marital status is unknown or irrelevant. (If the woman you are addressing refers to herself as *Mrs.* or *Miss,* however, use the form of address she prefers.) Finally, avoid using the generic *he* or *him* when your subject could be either male or female. Use the third-person plural or the phrase *he or she* (not *he/she*).

SEXIST: Before boarding, each passenger should make certain that <u>he</u> has <u>his</u> ticket.

REVISED: Before boarding, <u>passengers</u> should make certain that <u>they</u> have <u>their</u> tickets.

REVISED: Before boarding, each <u>passenger</u> should make certain that <u>he or she</u> has a ticket.

Remember, however, not to overuse *his or her* or *he or she* constructions, which can make your writing repetitious and wordy.

349

AVOIDING SEXIST LANGUAGE

When trying to avoid sexist use of *he* and *him*, be careful not to use *they* or *their* to refer to a singular antecedent.

> Drivers
> ~~Any driver~~ caught speeding should have their driving privileges
>
> suspended.

✔ ELIMINATING SEXIST LANGUAGE

SEXIST USAGE	POSSIBLE REVISIONS
Mankind	People, human beings
Man's accomplishments	Human accomplishments
Man-made	Synthetic
Female engineer (lawyer, accountant, etc.), male model	Engineer, (lawyer, accountant, etc.), model
Policeman/woman	Police officer
Salesman/woman/girl	Salesperson/representative
Businessman/woman	Businessperson, executive
Everyone should complete his application by Tuesday.	Everyone should complete his or her application by Tuesday.
	All students should complete their applications by Tuesday.

Avoiding Sexist or "Gender-biased" Language (Harvard U.)
http://www.fas.harvard.edu/~wricntr/gender.html

CHAPTER 29

USING A DICTIONARY

Every writer should own a dictionary. The most widely used type of  dictionary is a one-volume **desk dictionary** or **college dictionary.**

To fit a lot of information into a small space, dictionaries use a system of symbols, abbreviations, and typefaces. Each dictionary uses a slightly different system, so consult the preface of your dictionary to determine how its system operates.

A labeled entry from *The American Heritage College Dictionary* appears below.

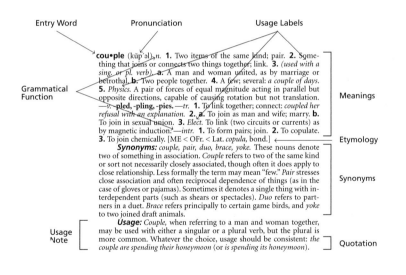

Webster's Dictionary Online
  http://www.m-w.com/dictionary.htm
How Does a Word Get Into the Dictionary?
  http://www.m-w.com/about/wordin.htm
D. Wilton's Etymology Page
  http://www.wilton.net/etyma1.htm

Entry Word, Pronunciation Guide, and Part-of-Speech Label   The **entry word,** which appears in boldface at the beginning of the entry, gives the spelling of a word and indicates how the word is divided into syllables.

> **col • or** *n.* Also chiefly British **col • our**

The **pronunciation guide** appears in parentheses or between slashes after the main entry. Dictionaries use symbols to represent sounds, and an explanation of these symbols usually appears at the bottom of each page or across the bottom of facing pages throughout the alphabetical listing.

Abbreviations called **part-of-speech labels** indicate parts of speech and grammatical forms.

If a verb is **<u>regular</u>**, the entry provides only the base form of the verb. If a verb is **<u>irregular</u>**, the part-of-speech label indicates the irregular principal parts of the verb.

> **with • draw** . . . *v.* -drew, -drawn, -drawing

In addition, the label indicates whether a verb is transitive (*tr.*), intransitive (*intr.*), or both.

Part-of-speech labels also indicate the plural form of irregular nouns. (When the plural form is regular, it is not shown.)

> **child** . . . *n. pl.* chil · dren

Finally, part-of-speech labels indicate the **<u>comparative</u>** and **<u>superlative</u>** forms of both regular and irregular adjectives and adverbs.

Etymology   The **etymology** of a word—its history, its evolution over the years—appears in brackets either before or after the list of meanings.

Meanings   Some dictionaries give the most common meaning first and then list less common ones. Others begin with the oldest meaning and move to the most current ones. Check the preface of your dictionary to find out how its entries are arranged.

Synonyms and Antonyms   A dictionary entry often lists synonyms (and occasionally antonyms) in addition to definitions. **Synonyms** are words that have similar meanings, such as *well* and *healthy*. **Antonyms** are words that have opposite meanings, such as *courage* and *cowardice*.

USING A THESAURUS

When you consult a print or online **thesaurus,** a list of synonyms and antonyms, remember that no two words have exactly the same meanings. Use synonyms carefully, checking your dictionary to make sure the connotation of the synonym is very close to that of the original word.

Idioms   Dictionary entries often show how certain words are used in set expressions called **idioms.** The meaning of such phrases cannot always be determined from the words alone. For example, what are we to make of the expressions "catch a cold" and "take a walk"?

Dictionaries also indicate the idiomatic use of **prepositions**. For example, we do not say that we *abide with* a decision; we say *abide by*.

See
C5

Usage Labels   Dictionaries use **usage labels** to indicate in what contexts words are acceptable. Among these labels are *nonstandard* (in wide use but not considered standard usage); *informal/colloquial* (part of the language of conversation and acceptable in informal writing); *slang* (appropriate only in extremely informal situations); *dialect/regional* (limited to a certain geographical region); *obsolete* (no longer in use); *archaic/rare* (once common but now seldom used); and *poetic* (common only in poetry).

ELECTRONIC DICTIONARIES

Electronic dictionaries include the same amount of information that one-volume desk dictionaries have. Electronic dictionaries come in two forms—CD-ROM and online. Typically, you have to download a CD-ROM dictionary onto your hard drive before you can use it with your word processing program. To use an online dictionary, you have to log on to a Web site such as http://www.m-w.com/dictionary.htm.

Idioms
   http://www.pacificnet.net/~sperling/idioms/

CHAPTER 30

A GLOSSARY OF USAGE

This glossary of usage lists words and phrases that are often troublesome for writers.

a, an   Use *a* before words that begin with consonants and words with initial vowels that sound like consonants: *a* person, *a* historical document, *a* one-horse carriage, *a* uniform. Use *an* before words that begin with vowels and *a* that begin with a silent *h: an* artist, *an* honest person.

accept, except   *Accept* is a verb that means "to receive"; *except* as a preposition or conjunction means "other than" and as a verb means "to leave out": The auditors will *accept* all your claims *except* the last two. Some businesses are *excepted* from the regulation.

advice, advise   *Advice* is a noun meaning "opinion or information offered"; *advise* is a verb that means "to offer advice to": The broker *advised* her client to take his attorney's *advice*.

affect, effect   *Affect* is a verb meaning "to influence"; *effect* can be a verb or a noun—as a verb it means "to bring about," and as a noun it means "result": We know how the drug *affects* patients immediately, but little is known of its long-term *effects*. The arbitrator tried to *effect* a settlement between the parties.

all ready, already   *All ready* means "completely prepared"; *Already* means "by or before this or that time": I was *all ready* to help, but it was *already* too late.

all right, alright   Although the use of *alright* is increasing, current usage calls for *all right*.

Words or Expressions Commonly Misused (Strunk's *Element's of Style*)
   http://www.bartleby.com/141/strunk3.html
A Word A Day (wordsmith.org): new word defined, with examples, each day.
   http://www.wordsmith.org/words/today.html
Paul Brians' Common Errors in English (Usage)
   http://www.wsu.edu/~brians/errors/errors.html

allusion, illusion An *allusion* is a reference or hint; an *illusion* is something that is not what it seems: The poem makes an *allusion* to the Pandora myth. The shadows created an optical *illusion*.

a lot *A lot* is always two words.

among, between *Among* refers to groups of more than two things; *between* refers to just two things: The three parties agreed *among* themselves to settle the case. There will be a brief intermission *between* the two acts. Note that *amongst* is British, not American, usage.

amount, number *Amount* refers to a quantity that cannot be counted; *number* refers to things that can be counted: Even a small *amount* of caffeine can be harmful. Seeing their commander fall, a large *number* of troops ran to his aid.

an, a See **a, an.**

and/or In business or technical writing, use *and/or* when either or both of the items it connects can apply. In college writing, however, avoid the use of *and/or.*

as ... as ... In such constructions, *as* signals a comparison; therefore, you must always use the second *as: East of Eden* is *as* long *as* if not longer than *The Grapes of Wrath.*

as, like *As* can be used as a conjunction (to introduce a complete clause) or as a preposition; *like* should be used as a preposition only: In *The Scarlet Letter* Hawthorne uses imagery *as* (not *like*) he does in his other works. After classes, Fred works *as* a manager of a fast-food restaurant. Writers *like* Carl Sandburg appear once in a generation.

at, to Many people use the prepositions *at* and *to* after *where* in conversation: *Where* are you working *at? Where* are you going *to?* This is redundant and should not be used in college writing.

awhile, a while *Awhile* is an adverb; *a while,* which consists of an article and a noun, is used as the object of a preposition: Before we continue, we will rest *awhile.* (modifies the verb *rest*); Before we continue, we will rest for *a while.* (object of the preposition *for*)

bad, badly *Bad* is an adjective, and *badly* is an adverb: The school board decided that *Huckleberry Finn* was a *bad* book. American automobile makers did not do *badly* this year. After verbs that refer to any of the senses or after any other linking verb, use the adjective form: He looked *bad.* He felt *bad.* It seemed *bad.*

being as, being that These awkward phrases add unnecessary words and weaken your writing. Use *because* instead.

beside, besides   *Beside* is a preposition meaning "next to"; *besides* can be either a preposition meaning "except" or "other than" or an adverb meaning "as well": *Beside* the tower was a wall that ran the length of the city. *Besides* its industrial uses, laser technology has many other applications. Edison invented not only the lightbulb but the phonograph *besides*.

between, among   See **among, between.**

bring, take   *Bring* means to transport from a farther place to a nearer place; *take* means to carry or convey from a nearer place to a farther one: *Bring* me a souvenir from your trip. *Take* this message to the general and wait for a reply.

can, may   *Can* denotes ability, and *may* indicates permission: If you *can* play, you *may* use my piano.

capital, capitol   *Capital* refers to a city that is an official seat of government; *capitol* refers to a building in which a legislature meets: Washington, DC, is the *capital* of the United States. When we were there, we visited the *Capitol* building.

center around   This imprecise phrase is acceptable in speech and informal writing but not in college writing. Use *center on* instead.

cite, site   *Cite* is a verb meaning "to quote as an authority or example"; *site* is a noun meaning "a place or setting": Jeff *cited* five sources in his research paper. The builder cleared the *site* for the new bank.

climactic, climatic   *Climactic* means "of or related to a climax"; *climatic* means "of or related to climate": The *climactic* moment of the movie occured unexpectedly. If scientists are correct, the *climatic* conditions of Earth are changing.

coarse, course   *Coarse* is an adjective meaning "inferior" or "having a rough, uneven texture"; *course* is a noun meaning "a route or path," "an area on which a sport is played," or "a unit of study": *Coarse* sandpaper is used to smooth the surface. The *course* of true love never runs smoothly. Last semester I had to drop a *course*.

compare to, compare with   *Compare to* means "to liken" or "to represent as similar"; *compare with* means "to examine in order to find ways in which two things are similar or different": Shall I *compare* you *to* a summer's day? Jane *compared* the paintings of Cézanne *with* those of Magritte.

complement, compliment   *Complement* means "to complete or add to"; *compliment* means "to give praise": A double-blind study would *complement* their preliminary research. My instructor *complimented* me on my improvement.

conscious, conscience   *Conscious* is an adjective meaning "having one's mental faculties awake"; *conscience* is a noun that means the moral sense of right and wrong: The patient will remain *conscious* during the procedure. His *conscience* would not allow him to lie.

continual, continuous   *Continual* means "recurring at intervals"; *continuous* refers to an action that occurs without interruption: A pulsar is a star that emits a *continual* stream of electromagnetic radiation. (It emits radiation at regular intervals.) A small battery allows the watch to run *continuously* for five years. (It runs without stopping.)

could of, should of, would of   The contractions *could've, should've,* and *would've* are often misspelled as the nonstandard constructions *could of, should of,* and *would of.* Use *could have, should have,* and *would have* in college writing.

council, counsel   A *council* is "a body of people who serve in a legislative or advisory capacity"; *counsel* means "to offer advice or guidance": The city *council* argued about the proposed ban on smoking. The judge *counseled* the couple to settle their differences.

couple of   *Couple* means "a pair," but *couple of* is often used colloquially to mean "several" or "a few." In your college writing, specify "four points" or "two examples" rather than using "a couple of."

criterion, criteria   *Criteria,* from the Greek, is the plural of *criterion,* meaning "standard for judgment": Of all the *criteria* for hiring graduating seniors, class rank is the most important *criterion.*   ❓

data   *Data* is the plural of the Latin *datum,* meaning "fact." In everyday speech and writing, *data* is used for both singular and plural. In college writing, use *data* only for the plural: The *data* discussed in this section *are* summarized in Appendix A.

different from, different than   *Different than* is widely used in American speech. In college writing, use *different from.*

discreet, discrete   *Discreet* means "careful or prudent"; *discrete* means "separate or individually distinct": Because Madame Bovary was not *discreet,* her reputation suffered. Atoms can be broken into hundreds of *discrete* particles.

disinterested, uninterested   *Disinterested* means "objective" or "capable of making an impartial judgment"; *uninterested* means "indifferent or unconcerned": The American judicial system depends on *disinterested* jurors. Finding no treasure, Hernando de Soto was *uninterested* in going farther.

don't, doesn't   *Don't* is the contraction of *do not*; *doesn't* is the contraction of *does not*. Do not confuse the two: My dog *doesn't* (not *don't*) like to walk in the rain.

effect, affect   See **affect, effect.**

e.g.   *E.g.* is an abbreviation for the Latin *exempli gratia,* meaning "for example" or "for instance." In college writing, do not use *e.g.* Instead, use its English equivalent.

emigrate from, immigrate to   To *emigrate* is "to leave one's country and settle in another"; to *immigrate* is "to come to another country and reside there." The noun forms of these words are *emigrant* and *immigrant*: My great-grandfather *emigrated from* Warsaw along with many other *emigrants* from Poland. Many people *immigrate* to the United States for economic reasons, but such *immigrants* still face great challenges.

eminent, imminent   *Eminent* is an adjective meaning "standing above others" or "prominent"; *imminent* means "about to occur": Oliver Wendell Holmes, Jr., was an *eminent* jurist. In ancient times, a comet signaled *imminent* disaster.

enthused   *Enthused,* a colloquial form of *enthusiastic,* should not be used in college writing.

etc.   *Etc.,* the abbreviation of *et cetera,* means "and the rest." Do not use it in your college writing. Instead, say "and so on" —or, better yet, specify exactly what *etc.* stands for.

everyday, every day   *Everyday* is an adjective that means "ordinary" or "commonplace"; *every day* means "occurring daily": In the Gettysburg Address, Lincoln used *everyday* language. She exercises almost *every day.*

everyone, every one   *Everyone* is an indefinite pronoun meaning "every person"; *every one* means "every individual or thing in a particular group": *Everyone* seems happier in the spring. *Every one* of the packages had been opened.

except, accept   See **accept, except.**

explicit, implicit   *Explicit* means "expressed or stated directly"; *implicit* means "implied" or "expressed or stated indirectly": The director *explicitly* warned the actors to be on time for rehearsals. Her *implicit* message was that lateness would not be tolerated.

farther, further   *Farther* designates distance; *further* designates degree: I have traveled *farther* from home than any of my relatives. Critics charge that welfare subsidies encourage *further* dependence.

fewer, less   Use *fewer* with nouns that can be counted: *fewer* books, *fewer* people, *fewer* dollars. Use *less* with quantities that cannot be counted: *less* pain, *less* power, *less* enthusiasm.

firstly (secondly, thirdly, . . .)   Archaic forms meaning "in the first . . . second . . . third place." Use *first, second, third.*

further, farther   See **farther, further.**

good, well   *Good* is an adjective, never an adverb: She is a *good* swimmer. *Well* can function as an adverb or as an adjective. As an adverb, it means "in a good manner": She swam *well* (not *good*) in the meet. *Well* is used as an adjective with verbs that denote a state of being or feeling. Here *well* can mean "in good health": I feel *well*.

got to   *Got to* is not acceptable in college writing. To indicate obligation, use *have to, has to,* or *must.*

hanged, hung   Both *hanged* and *hung* are past participles of *hang*. *Hanged* is used to refer to executions; *hung* is used to mean "suspended": Billy Budd was *hanged* for killing the master-at-arms. The stockings were *hung* by the chimney with care.

he, she   Traditionally *he* has been used in the generic sense to refer to both males and females. To acknowledge the equality of the sexes, however, avoid the generic *he*. Use plural pronouns whenever possible. See **28e.2.**

hopefully   The adverb *hopefully*, meaning "in a hopeful manner," should modify a verb, an adjective, or another adverb. Do not use *hopefully* as a sentence modifier meaning "it is hoped." Rather than "*Hopefully*, scientists will soon discover a cure for AIDS," write "Scientists *hope* they will soon discover a cure for AIDS."

i.e.   *I.e.* is an abbreviation for the Latin *id est*, meaning "that is." In college writing, do not use *i.e.* Instead, use its English equivalent.

if, whether   When asking indirect questions or expressing doubt, use *whether:* He asked *whether* (not *if*) the flight would be delayed. The flight attendant was not sure *whether* (not *if*) it would be delayed.

illusion, allusion   See **allusion, illusion.**

immigrate to, emigrate from   See **emigrate from, immigrate to.**

implicit, explicit   See **explicit, implicit.**

imply, infer   *Imply* means "to hint" or "to suggest"; *infer* means "to conclude from": Mark Antony *implied* that the conspirators had murdered Caesar. The crowd *inferred* his meaning and called for justice.

infer, imply   See **imply, infer.**

inside of, outside of   *Of* is unnecessary when *inside* and *outside* are used as prepositions. *Inside of* is colloquial in references to time: He waited *inside* (not *inside of*) the coffee shop. He could run a mile in *under* (not *inside of*) eight minutes.

irregardless, regardless   *Irregardless* is a nonstandard version of *regardless*. Use *regardless* instead.

is when, is where   These constructions are faulty when they appear in definitions: A playoff *is* an additional game played to establish the winner of a tie. (not "A playoff *is when* an additional game is played. . . . ")

its, it's   *Its* is a possessive pronoun; *it's* is a contraction of *it is*: *It's* no secret that the bank is out to protect *its* assets.

kind of, sort of   *Kind of* and *sort of* to mean "rather" or "somewhat" are colloquial and should not appear in college writing: It is well known that Napoleon was *rather* (not *kind of*) short.

lay, lie   See **lie, lay.**

leave, let   *Leave* means "to go away from" or "to let remain"; *let* means "to allow" or "to permit": *Let* (not *leave*) me give you a hand.

less, fewer   See **fewer, less.**

let, leave   See **leave, let.**

lie, lay   *Lie* is an intransitive verb (one that does not take an object) meaning "to recline." Its principal forms are *lie, lay, lain, lying*: Each afternoon she would *lie* in the sun and listen to the surf. *As I Lay Dying* is a novel by William Faulkner. By 1871, Troy had *lain* undisturbed for two thousand years. The painting shows a nude *lying* on a couch. *Lay* is a transitive verb (one that takes an object) meaning "to put" or "to place." Its principal forms are *lay, laid, laid, laying*: The Federalist Papers *lay* the foundation for American conservatism. In October 1781, the British *laid* down their arms and surrendered. He had *laid* his money on the counter before leaving. We watched the stonemasons *laying* a wall.

like, as   See **as, like.**

loose, lose   *Loose* is an adjective meaning "not rigidly fastened or securely attached"; *lose* is a verb meaning "to misplace": The marble facing of the building became *loose* and fell to the sidewalk. After only two drinks, most people *lose* their ability to judge distance.

lots, lots of, a lot of   These words are colloquial substitutes for *many, much,* or *a great deal of*. Avoid their use in college writing: The students had many (not *lots of* or *a lot of*) options for essay topics.

man   Like the generic pronoun *he, man* has been used in English to denote members of both sexes. This usage is being replaced by *human beings, people,* or similar terms that do not specify gender. See **28e.2.**

may, can   See **can, may.**

may be, maybe   *May be* is a verb phrase; *maybe* is an adverb meaning "perhaps": She *may be* the smartest student in the class. *Maybe* her experience has given her an advantage.

media, medium   *Medium,* meaning a "means of conveying or broadcasting something," is singular; *media* is the plural form and requires a plural verb: The *media* have distorted the issue.

might have, might of   *Might of* is a nonstandard spelling of the contraction of *might have* (*might've*). Use *might have* in college writing.

number, amount   See **amount, number.**

OK, O.K., okay   All three spellings are acceptable, but this term should be avoided in college writing. Replace it with a more specific word or words: The instructor's lecture was *adequate* (not *okay*), if uninspiring.

outside of, inside of   See **inside of, outside of.**

passed, past   *Passed* is the past tense of the verb *pass; past* means "belonging to a former time" or "no longer current": The car must have been going eighty miles per hour when it *passed* us. In the envelope was a bill marked *past* due.

percent, percentage   *Percent* indicates a part of a hundred when a specific number is referred to: "*10 percent* of his salary." *Percentage* is used when no specific number is referred to: "a *percentage* of next year's receipts." In technical and business writing, it is permissible to use the % sign after percentages you are comparing. Write out the word *percent* in college writing.

phenomenon, phenomena   A *phenomenon* is a single observable fact or event. It can also refer to a rare or significant occurrence. *Phenomena* is the plural form and requires a plural verb: Many supposedly paranormal *phenomena* are easily explained.

plus   As a preposition, *plus* means "in addition to." Avoid using *plus* as a substitute for *and:* Include the principal, *plus* the interest, in your calculations. Your quote was too high; moreover (not *plus*), it was inaccurate.

precede, proceed   *Precede* means "to go or come before"; *proceed* means "to go forward in an orderly way": Robert Frost's *North of Boston* was *preceded* by an earlier volume. In 1532, Francisco Pizarro landed at Tumbes and *proceeded* south.

principal, principle   As a noun, *principal* means "a sum of money (minus interest) invested or lent" or "a person in the leading position"; as an adjective it means "most important." A *principle* is a rule of conduct or a basic truth: He wanted to reduce the *principal* of the loan. The *principal* of the high school is a talented administrator. Women are the *principal* wage earners in many American households. The Constitution embodies certain fundamental *principles.*

quote, quotation   *Quote* is a verb. *Quotation* is a noun. In college writing, do not use *quote* as a shortened form of *quotation*: He included several *quotations* (not *quotes*) from experts.

raise, rise   *Raise* is a transitive verb, and *rise* is an intransitive verb—that is, *raise* takes an object, and *rise* does not: My grandparents *raised* a large family. The sun will *rise* at 6:12 this morning.

real, really   *Real* means "genuine" or "authentic"; *really* means "actually." In your college writing, do not use *real* as an adjective meaning "very."

reason is that, reason is because   *Reason* should be used with *that* and not with *because*, which is redundant: The *reason* he left *is that* (not *is because*) you insulted him.

regardless, irregardless   See **irregardless, regardless.**

respectably, respectfully, respectively   *Respectably* means "worthy of respect"; *respectfully* means "giving honor or deference"; *respectively* means "in the order given": He skated quite *respectably* at his first Olympics. The seminar taught us to treat others *respectfully.* The first- and second-place winners were Tai and Kim, *respectively.*

rise, raise   See **raise, rise.**

set, sit   *Set* means "to put down" or "to lay." Its principal forms are *set* and *setting*: After rocking the baby to sleep, he *set* her down carefully in her crib. After *setting* her down, he took a nap. *Sit* means "to assume a sitting position." Its principal forms are *sit, sat,* and *sitting*: Many children *sit* in front of the television five to six hours a day. The dog *sat* by the fire. We were *sitting* in the airport when the flight was cancelled.

shall, will   *Will* has all but replaced *shall* to express all future action.

should of   See **could of, should of, would of.**

since   Do not use *since* for *because* if there is any chance of confusion. In the sentence "*Since* President Nixon traveled to China, trade between China and the United States has increased," *since* could mean either "from the time that" or "because." To be clear, use *because.*

sit, set See **set, sit.**

so Avoid using *so* alone as a vague intensifier meaning "very" or "extremely." Follow *so* with *that* and a clause that describes the result: She was *so* pleased with their work *that* she took them out to lunch.

sometime, sometimes, some time *Sometime* means "at some time in the future"; *sometimes* means "now and then"; *some time* means "a period of time": The president will address Congress *sometime* next week. All automobiles, no matter how reliable, *sometimes* need repairs. It has been *some time* since I read that book.

sort of, kind of See **kind of, sort of.**

stationary, stationery *Stationary* means "staying in one place"; *stationery* means "materials for writing" or "letter paper": The communications satellite appears to be *stationary* in the sky. The secretaries supply departmental offices with *stationery.*

supposed to, used to *Supposed to* and *used to* are often misspelled. Both verbs require the final *d* to indicate past tense.

take, bring See **bring, take.**

than, then *Than* is a conjunction used to indicate a comparison; *then* is an adverb indicating time: The new shopping center is bigger *than* the old one. He did his research; *then* he wrote a report.

that, which, who Use *that* or *which* when referring to a thing; use *who* when referring to a person: It was a speech *that* inspired many. The movie, *which* was a huge success, failed to impress her. Anyone *who* (not *that*) takes the course will benefit.

their, there, they're *Their* is a possessive pronoun; *there* indicates place and is also used in the expressions *there is* and *there are; they're* is a contraction of *they are:* Watson and Crick did *their* DNA work at Cambridge University. I love New York, but I wouldn't want to live *there. There* is nothing we can do to resurrect an extinct species. When *they're* well treated, ferrets make excellent pets.

themselves; theirselves, theirself *Theirselves* and *theirself* are nonstandard variants of *themselves.*

then, than See **than, then.**

till, until, 'til *Till* and *until* have the same meaning, and both are acceptable. *Until* is preferred in college writing. *'Til,* a contraction of *until,* should be avoided.

to, at See **at, to.**

to, too, two *To* is a preposition that indicates direction; *too* is an adverb that means "also" or "more than is needed"; *two* expresses the number 2: Last year we flew from New York *to* California. "Tippecanoe and Tyler, *too*" was William Henry Harrison's campaign slogan. The plot was *too* complicated for the average reader. Just north of *Two* Rivers, Wisconsin, is a petrified forest.

try to, try and *Try and* is the colloquial equivalent of the more formal *try to:* He decided to *try to* (not *try and*) do better. In college writing, use *try to.*

-type Deleting this empty suffix eliminates clutter and clarifies meaning: Found in the wreckage was an *incendiary* (not *incendiary-type*) device.

uninterested, disinterested See **disinterested, uninterested.**

unique Because *unique* means "the only one," not "remarkable" or "unusual," never use constructions like "the most unique" or "very unique."

until See **till, until, 'til.**

used to See **supposed to, used to.**

utilize In most cases, replace *utilize* with *use* (*utilize* often sounds pretentious).

wait for, wait on To *wait for* means "to defer action until something occurs." To *wait on* means "to act as a waiter": I am *waiting for* (not *on*) dinner.

weather, whether *Weather* is a noun meaning "the state of the atmosphere"; *whether* is a conjunction used to introduce an alternative: The *weather* outside is frightful, but the fire inside is delightful. It is doubtful *whether* we will be able to ski tomorrow.

well, good See **good, well.**

were, we're *Were* is a verb; *we're* is the contraction of *we are:* The Trojans *were* asleep when the Greeks attacked. We must act now if *we're* going to succeed.

whether, if See **if, whether.**

which, who, that See **that, which, who.**

who, whom When a pronoun serves as the subject of its clause, use *who* or *whoever;* when it functions in a clause as an object, use *whom* or *whomever:* Sarah, *who* is studying ancient civilizations, would like to visit Greece. Sarah, *whom* I met in France, wants me to travel to

Greece with her. To determine which to use at the beginning of a question, use a personal pronoun to answer the question: *Who* tried to call me? *He* called. (subject); *Whom* do you want for the job? I want *her.* (object)

who's, whose   *Who's* means "who is"; *whose* indicates possession: *Who's* going to take calculus? The writer *whose* book was in the window was autographing copies.

will, shall   See **shall, will.**

would of   See **could of, should of, would of.**

your, you're   *Your* indicates possession, and *you're* is the contraction of *you are:* You can improve *your* stamina by jogging two miles a day. *You're* certain to be the winner.

Understanding Punctuation

CHAPTER 31

USING END PUNCTUATION

31a Using Periods

(1) Ending a Sentence

Periods signal the end of a statement, a mild command or polite request, or an indirect question.

Something is rotten in Denmark. (statement)

Be sure to have the oil checked before you start out. (mild command)

When the bell rings, please exit in an orderly fashion. (polite request)

They wondered whether the water was safe to drink. (indirect question)

(2) Marking an Abbreviation

Periods also appear in most abbreviations.

Mr. Spock	Aug.	Dr. Who
9 p.m.	etc.	221 B Baker St.

If an abbreviation ends the sentence, do not add another period: He promised to be there at 6 a.m.

However, do add a question mark if the sentence is a question: Did he arrive at 6 p.m.?

If the abbreviation appears *within* a sentence, use normal punctuation after the period.

He promised to be there at 6 p.m., but he forgot.

NASA's Guide to Punctuation
   http://stipo.larc.nasa.gov/sp7084/sp7084ch3.html
Punctuation Guide (Purdue)
   http://owl.english.purdue.edu/Files/16.html

ABBREVIATIONS WITHOUT PERIODS

Abbreviations composed of all capital letters do not usually require periods unless they stand for initials of people's names (E.B. White).

MD   RN   BC

Familiar abbreviations of the names of corporation or government agencies and abbreviations of scientific and technical terms do not require periods.

CD-ROM   NYU   DNA   EPA   HBO

Acronyms—new words formed from the initial letters or first few letters of a series of words—do not include periods.

modem   op-ed   scuba   radar
OSHA   AIDS   NAFTA   CAT scan

Clipped forms (commonly accepted shortened forms of words, such as *gym, dorm, math,* and *fax*) do not use periods.

(3) Marking Divisions in Dramatic, Poetic, and Biblical References

Periods separate act, scene, and line numbers in plays; book and line numbers in long poems; and chapter and verse numbers in biblical references. (Do not space between the periods and the elements they separate.)

DRAMATIC REFERENCE: *Hamlet* 2.2.1–5

POETIC REFERENCE: *Paradise Lost* 7.163–67

BIBLICAL REFERENCE: *Judges* 4.14

(4) Marking Divisions in Electronic Addresses

Periods, along with other punctuation marks (such as slashes and colons), are frequently used in electronic addresses (URLs).

mckay@smu.edu

http://www.nwu.org/nwu

NOTE: When you type an electronic address, do not end it with a period or add spaces after periods within the address.

31b   Using Question Marks

(1) Marking the End of a Direct Question

Use a question mark to signal the end of a direct question.

Who was that masked man?

"Is this a silver bullet?" they asked. (declarative sentence opening with a direct question)

Did he say where he came from? Who his companion was? Where they were headed? (series of direct questions with each question asked separately)

Use a pair of dashes or a pair of parentheses around a direct question within a declarative sentence.

Someone—a disgruntled office seeker?—is sabotaging the campaign.

Part of the shipment (three dozen cases?) was delayed.

(2) Marking Questionable Dates and Numbers

Use a question mark in parentheses to indicate that a date or number is uncertain.

Aristophanes, the Greek playwright, was born in 448 (?) BC and died in 380 (?) BC.

(3) Editing Misused Question Marks

Use a period, not a question mark, with an indirect question.

The personnel officer asked whether he knew how to type?.

Do not use a question mark to convey sarcasm. Instead, suggest your attitude through word choice.

not very
I refused his generous (?) offer.

31c   Using Exclamation Points

An exclamation point is used to signal the end of an emotional or emphatic statement, an emphatic interjection, or a forceful command.

Remember the Maine!

"No! Don't leave!" he cried.

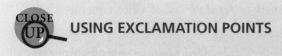

USING EXCLAMATION POINTS

Except for recording dialogue, exclamation points are almost never appropriate in college writing. Even in informal writing, use exclamation points sparingly.

CHAPTER 32

USING COMMAS

32a Setting Off Independent Clauses

Use a comma when you form a compound sentence by linking two independent clauses with a **coordinating conjunction** or a pair of **correlative conjunctions**.

See
A7

The House approved the bill, <u>but</u> the Senate rejected it.

<u>Either</u> the hard drive is full, <u>or</u> the modem is too slow.

NOTE: You may omit the comma if two clauses connected by a coordinating conjunction are very short.

Seek and ye shall find.   Love it or leave it.

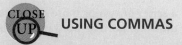 **USING COMMAS**

Use a **semicolon**—not a comma—to separate two independent clauses linked by a coordinating conjunction when at least one of the clauses already contains a comma or when the clauses are especially complex.

See
Ch. 33

32b Setting Off Items in a Series

Use commas between items in a series of three or more coordinate elements (words, phrases, or clauses).

Almost Everything You Need to Know about Commas
   http://cavern.uark.edu/~qwrtcntr/handouts/commas.html
Comma Splice
   http://www.vetl.uh.edu/sefh/writing/punct6.html

Chipmunk, *raccoon*, and *Mugwump* are Native American words.

You may pay <u>by check</u>, <u>with a credit card</u>, or <u>in cash</u>.

<u>Brazilians speak Portuguese</u>, <u>Colombians speak Spanish</u>, and <u>Haitians speak French and Creole</u>.

? NOTE: To avoid ambiguity, always use a comma before the coordinating conjunction that separates the last two items in a series.

The party was made special by the company, the light from the hundreds

of twinkling candles⌃and the enormous piñata.

Do not use a comma to introduce or to close a series.

Three important criteria are⸝fat content, salt content, and taste.

The provinces Quebec, Ontario, and Alberta⸝are in Canada.

 NOTE: If a phrase or clause in a **series** already contains commas, separate the items with semicolons.

Use a comma between items in a series of two or more **coordinate adjectives**—adjectives that modify the same word or word group—unless they are joined by a conjunction.

She brushed her <u>long</u>, <u>shining</u> hair.

The baby was <u>tired</u> and <u>cranky</u> and <u>wet</u>.

✔ CHECKLIST: PUNCTUATING ADJECTIVES IN A SERIES

   ✔ If you can reverse the order of the adjectives or insert *and* between the adjectives without changing the meaning, the adjectives are coordinate, and you should use a comma.

   She brushed her long, shining hair.

   She brushed her shining, long hair.

   She brushed her long [and] shining hair.

continued on the following page

✔ If you cannot reverse the order of the adjectives or insert *and,* the adjectives are not coordinate, and you should not use a comma.

Ten red balloons fell from the ceiling.

Red ten balloons fell from the ceiling.

Ten [and] red balloons fell from the ceiling.

NOTE: Numbers—such as *ten*—are not coordinate with other adjectives.

32c   Setting Off Introductory Elements   ❓

(1) Dependent Clauses

An introductory dependent clause is generally set off from the rest of the sentence by a comma.

> Although the CIA used to call undercover agents *penetration agents*, they now routinely refer to them as *moles.*

If the dependent clause is short, you may omit the comma—*provided the sentence will be clear without it.*

> When I exercise I drink plenty of water.

NOTE: Do not use a comma to set off a dependent clause at the *end* of a sentence.

(2) Verbal and Prepositional Phrases

Introductory verbal and prepositional phrases are usually set off by commas.

> Thinking that this might be his last chance, Scott struggled toward the Pole. (participial phrase)

> To write well, one must read a lot. (infinitive phrase)

> During the Depression, movie attendance rose. (prepositional phrase)

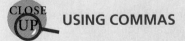 **USING COMMAS**

Verbal phrases that serve as subjects are *not* set off by commas.

<u>Laughing out loud</u> can release tension. (gerund phrase)

<u>To know him</u> is to love him. (infinitive phrase)

If the introductory phrase is short and no ambiguity is possible, you may omit the comma.

<u>After the exam</u> I took a four-hour nap.

(3) Transitional Words and Phrases

When a transitional word or phrase begins a sentence, it is usually set off with a comma.

<u>However</u>, any plan that is enacted must be fair.

<u>In other words</u>, we cannot act hastily.

32d   Setting Off Nonessential Material

Use commas to set off nonessential material whether it appears at the beginning, in the middle, or at the end of a sentence.

(1) Nonrestrictive Modifiers

Restrictive modifiers, which supply information essential to the meaning of the word or word group they modify, are *not* set off from it by commas. **Nonrestrictive modifiers,** which supply information not essential to the meaning of the word or word group they modify, *are* set off by commas.

Compare these two sentences:

Actors who have inflated egos are often insecure.

Actors, who have inflated egos, are often insecure.

In the first sentence, *who have inflated egos* is **restrictive.** The sentence indicates that only those actors with inflated egos—not all actors—are insecure.

In the second sentence, the modifying phrase *who have inflated egos* is **nonrestrictive.** The sentence indicates that *all* actors—not just those with inflated egos—are insecure.

As the following examples illustrate, commas set off only nonrestrictive modifiers—those that supply nonessential information—never restrictive modifiers, which supply essential information.

Adjective Clauses
RESTRICTIVE: Speaking in public is something <u>that most people fear.</u>

NONRESTRICTIVE: He ran for the bus, <u>which was late as usual.</u>

Prepositional Phrases
RESTRICTIVE: The man <u>with the gun</u> demanded their money.

NONRESTRICTIVE: The clerk, with a nod, dismissed me.

Verbal Phrases
RESTRICTIVE: The candidates <u>running for mayor</u> have agreed to a debate.

NONRESTRICTIVE: The marathoner, <u>running his fastest,</u> beat his previous record.

Appositives:
RESTRICTIVE: The film *Citizen Kane* made Orson Welles famous.

NONRESTRICTIVE: *Citizen Kane,* <u>Orson Welles's first film,</u> made him famous.

✔ CHECKLIST: RESTRICTIVE AND NONRESTRICTIVE MODIFIERS

To determine whether a modifier is restrictive or nonrestrictive, ask these questions:

✔ Is the modifier essential to the meaning of the noun it modifies (*The man with the gun,* not just any man)? If so, it is restrictive and does not take commas.

continued on the following page

continued from the previous page

✔ Is the modifier introduced by *that* (*something that most people fear*)? If so, it is restrictive. *That* cannot introduce a nonrestrictive clause.

✔ Can you delete the relative pronoun without causing ambiguity or confusion (*something [that] most people fear*)? If so, the clause is restrictive.

✔ Is the appositive more specific than the noun that precedes it (*the film* Citizen Kane)? If so, it is restrictive.

CLOSE UP   **USING COMMAS WITH *THAT* AND *WHICH***

That introduces only restrictive clauses.

I bought a used car <u>that</u> cost $2,000.

Which introduces both restrictive and nonrestrictive clauses.

RESTRICTIVE: I bought a used car <u>which</u> cost $2,000.

NONRESTRICTIVE: The used car I bought, <u>which</u> cost $2,000, broke down after a week.

Many writers, however, prefer to use *which* only to introduce nonrestrictive clauses.

(2) Transitional Words and Phrases

See 2b2

Transitional words and phrases—which include conjunctive adverbs like *however, therefore, thus,* and *nevertheless* as well as expressions like *for example* and *on the other hand*—qualify, clarify, and make connections. However, they are not essential to meaning. For this reason, they are always set off by commas when they interrupt or come at the end of a clause.

The Outward Bound program, <u>for example</u>, is extremely safe.

Some things were easier after school started. Other things were a lot harder, <u>however</u>.

NOTE: A **<u>transitional word or phrase</u>** is also usually set off by a comma when it occurs at the beginning of a clause.

See 32c3

CLOSE UP   TRANSITIONAL WORDS AND PHRASES

When a transitional word or phrase joins two independent clauses, it must be preceded by a semicolon and followed by a comma.

Laughter is the best medicine; <u>of course</u>, penicillin also comes in handy sometimes.

(3) Contradictory Phrases and Absolute Phrases

A phrase that expresses contrast is usually set off by commas.

This medicine is taken after meals, <u>never on an empty stomach</u>.

Mark McGwire, <u>not Sammy Sosa</u>, was the first to break Roger Maris's record.

An **absolute phrase,** which usually consists of a noun and a participle, is always set off by commas from the sentence it modifies.

<u>His fear increasing</u>, he waited to enter the haunted house.

Many soldiers were lost in Southeast Asia, <u>their bodies never recovered</u>.

(4) Miscellaneous Nonessential Material

Other nonessential material usually set off by commas includes tag questions, names in direct address, mild interjections, and *yes* and *no*.

This is your first day on the job, <u>isn't it</u>?

I wonder, <u>Mr. Honeywell</u>, whether Mr. Albright deserves a raise.

<u>Well</u>, it's about time.

<u>Yes</u>, we have no bananas.

32e   Using Commas in Other Conventional Contexts

❓ (1) With Direct Quotations

In most cases, use commas to set off a direct quotation from the **identifying tag** (*he said, she answered,* and so on).

Emerson said₉ "I greet you at the beginning of a great career."

"I greet you at the beginning of a great career₉" Emerson said.

"I greet you₉" Emerson said₉ "at the beginning of a great career."

When the identifying tag comes between two complete sentences, however, the tag is introduced by a comma but followed by a period.

"Winning isn't everything₉" Vince Lombardi said. "It's the only thing."

If the first sentence of an interrupted quotation ends with a question mark or exclamation point, do not use commas.

"Should we hold the front page?" she asked. "It's a slow news day."

"Hold the front page!" he cried. "It's a slow news day."

(2) With Titles or Degrees Following a Name

Hamlet₉ Prince of Denmark₉ is Shakespeare's most famous character.

Michael Crichton₉ MD₉ wrote *Jurassic Park.*

(3) In Addresses and Dates

Her address is 600 West End Avenue₉ New York₉ NY 10024.

On August 30₉ 1983₉ the space shuttle *Challenger* was launched.

When a date or address falls within a sentence, a comma follows the last element. No comma separates the street number from the street or the state name from the zip code.

NOTE: When only the month and year are given, no commas are used (August 1983).

32f Using Commas to Prevent Misreading

In some cases, you must use a comma to avoid ambiguity. Consider the following sentence:

Those who can, sprint the final lap.

Without the comma, *can* appears to be an auxiliary verb ("Those who can sprint. . . ."), and the sentence seems incomplete. The comma tells readers to pause, preventing confusion.

Also use a comma to acknowledge the omission of a repeated word, usually a verb, and to separate words repeated consecutively.

Pam carried the box; Tim, the suitcase.

Everything bad that could have happened, happened.

32g Editing Misused Commas

Do not use commas in the following situations.

(1) To Set Off Restrictive Modifiers

Commas are used to set off **nonrestrictive modifiers** only. Do not use commas to set off restrictive elements.

See
32d1

The film, *Malcolm X,* was directed by Spike Lee.

They planned a picnic, in the park.

(2) Between Inseparable Grammatical Constructions

Do not place a comma between grammatical elements that cannot be logically separated: a subject and its predicate, a verb and its complement or direct object, a preposition and its object, or an adjective and the word or phrase it modifies.

A woman with dark red hair, opened the door. (comma incorrectly

placed between subject and predicate)

Louis Braille developed, an alphabet of raised dots for the blind. (comma incorrectly placed between verb and object)

They relaxed somewhat during, the last part of the obstacle course. (comma incorrectly placed between preposition and object)

Wind-dispersed weeds include the well-known and plentiful, dandelions, milkweed, and thistle. (comma incorrectly placed between adjective and words it modifies)

(3) Between a Verb and an Indirect Quotation or Question

Do not use commas between verbs and indirect quotations or questions.

General Douglas MacArthur vowed, that he would return. (comma incorrectly placed between verb and indirect quotation)

The landlord asked, if we would sign a two-year lease. (comma incorrectly placed between verb and indirect question)

(4) In Compounds That Are Not Independent Clauses

Do not use commas between two elements of a compound subject, predicate, object, or complement.

During the 1400s plagues, and pestilence were common. (compound subject)

Many women thirty-five and older are returning to college, and tend to be good students. (compound predicate)

Mattel has marketed a lab coat/ and an astronaut suit for its Barbie doll. (compound object)

People buy bottled water because it is pure/ and fashionable. (compound complement)

(5) Before a Dependent Clause at the End of a Sentence

A comma is not generally used before a dependent clause that falls at the end of a sentence.

Jane Addams founded Hull House/ because she wanted to help Chicago's poor.

CHAPTER 33

USING SEMICOLONS

The **semicolon** is used only between items of equal grammatical rank: two independent clauses, two phrases, and so on.

33a   Separating Independent Clauses

Use a semicolon between closely related independent clauses that convey parallel or contrasting information but are not joined by a coordinating conjunction.

> Paul Revere's *The Boston Massacre* is traditional American protest art; Edward Hick's paintings are socially conscious art with a religious strain.

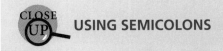

CLOSE UP   USING SEMICOLONS

See Ch. 17

Using only a comma or no punctuation at all between independent clauses creates a **comma splice** or **fused sentence**.

Use a semicolon between two independent clauses when the second clause is introduced by a transitional word or phrase.

> Thomas Jefferson brought two hundred vanilla beans and a recipe for vanilla ice cream back from France; thus, he gave America its all-time favorite ice cream flavor.

Semicolons (U. of Wisc)
   http://www.wisc.edu/writing/Handbook/main.html
Using Semicolons (U. Richmond)
   http://www.urich.edu/~writing/wweb/semicolon.html

33b Separating Items in a Series

Use semicolons between items in a series when one or more of these items include commas.

Three papers are posted on the bulletin board outside the building: a description of the exams; a list of appeal procedures for students who fail; and an employment ad from an automobile factory, addressed specifically to candidates whose appeals are turned down.

(Andrea Lee, *Russian Journal*)

As ballooning became established, a series of firsts ensued: The first balloonist in the United States was 13-year-old Edward Warren, 1784; the first woman aeronaut was a Madame Thible who, depending on your source, either recited poetry or sang as she lifted off; the first airmail letter, written by Ben Franklin's grandson, was carried by balloon; and the first bird's-eye photograph of Paris was taken by a balloon.

(Elaine B. Steiner, *Games*)

Laramie, Wyoming; Wyoming, Delaware; and Delaware, Ohio, were three of the places they visited.

33c Editing Misused Semicolons

Do not use semicolons in the following situations.

(1) Between a Phrase and a Clause

Increasing rapidly,̸ computer crime poses a challenge for government, financial, and military agencies.

(2) Between a Dependent and an Independent Clause

Because drugs can now suppress the body's immune reaction,̸ fewer organ transplants are rejected.

(3) To Introduce a List

Use a colon, not a semicolon, to introduce a **list**.

The evening news is a battleground for the four major television networks: CBS, NBC, ABC, and Fox.

(4) To Introduce a Quotation

Do not use a semicolon to introduce a **quotation**.

Marie Antoinette may not have said, "Let them eat cake."

CHAPTER 34

USING APOSTROPHES

Use an apostrophe to form the possessive case, to indicate omissions in contractions, and to form certain plurals.

34a Forming the Possessive Case

The possessive case indicates ownership. In English, the possessive case of nouns and indefinite pronouns is indicated either with a phrase that includes the word *of* (the hands *of* the clock) or with an apostrophe and, in most cases, an *s* (the clock's hands).

(1) Singular Nouns and Indefinite Pronouns

To form the possessive case of singular nouns and indefinite pronouns, add *'s.*

"The Monk's Tale" is one of Chaucer's *Canterbury Tales.*

When we would arrive was anyone's guess.

(2) Singular Nouns Ending in *-s*   ❓

To form the possessive case of singular nouns that end in *-s,* add *'s* in most cases.

Reading Henry James's *The Ambassadors* was not Maris's idea of fun.

NOTE: With some singular nouns that end in *-s,* pronouncing the possessive ending as a separate syllable can sound awkward; in such cases, it is acceptable to use just an apostrophe: Crispus Attucks' death, Aristophanes' *Lysistrata.*

Apostrophe (U. of Arkansas)
    http://cavern.uark.edu/~qwrtcntr/handouts/apostro.html

(3) Plural nouns

To form the possessive case of regular plural nouns (those that end in -*s* or -*es*), add only an apostrophe.

Employees received two weeks' severance pay and three months' medical benefits.

The Lopezes' three children are triplets.

To form the possessive case of nouns that have irregular plurals, add '*s*.

The Children's Hour is a play by Lillian Hellman.

(4) Compound Nouns or Groups of Words

To form the possessive case of compound words or of groups of words, add '*s* to the last word.

the secretary of state's resignation   someone else's responsibility

(5) Two or More Items

To indicate individual ownership of two or more items, add '*s* to each item.

Ernest Hemingway's and Gertrude Stein's writing styles have some similarities.

To indicate joint ownership, add -'*s* only to the last item.

We studied Lewis and Clark's expedition.

CLOSE UP   APOSTROPHES WITH PLURAL NOUNS AND PERSONAL PRONOUNS

Do not use apostrophes with plural nouns that are not possessive.

The Thompson's are out.

continued on the following page

The Lopez's have three children. (es)

Down vest's are warm.

Do not use apostrophes to form the possessive case of personal pronouns.

This ticket must be your's or her's.

The doll had lost it's right eye.

NOTE: Be careful not to confuse **contractions** with the possessive forms of personal pronouns.

See 34b1

Contraction	*Possessive Form*
Who's on first?	Whose book is this?
They're playing our song.	Their team is winning.
It's raining.	Its paws were muddy.
You're a real pal.	Your résumé is very impressive.

?

34b Indicating Omissions in Contractions

(1) Omitted Letters

Apostrophes replace omitted letters in contractions that combine a pronoun and a verb (*he* + *will* = *he'll*) or the elements of a verb phrase (*do* + *not* = *don't*).

FREQUENTLY USED CONTRACTIONS

it's (it is)	let's (let us)
we've (we have)	isn't (is not)
who's (who is)	you'd (you would)

continued on the following page

continued from the previous page

> they're (they are)   wouldn't (would not)
> we'll (we will)   don't (do not)
> I'm (I am)   won't (will not)

NOTE: Contractions are generally not used in college writing.

(2) Omitted Numbers

In informal writing, an apostrophe may also be used to represent the century in a year: Class of ʼ03, the ʼ60s.

34c   Forming Plurals

In a few special situations, add *'s* to form plurals.

FORMING PLURALS WITH APOSTROPHES

Plurals of Letters
> The Italian language has no *j*'s or *k*'s.

Plurals of Words Referred to as Words
> The supervisor would accept no *if*'s, *and*'s, or *but*'s.

NOTE: **Elements spoken of as themselves** (letters, numerals, or words) are set in italic type; the plural ending, however, is not.

See
39c

CHAPTER 35

USING QUOTATION MARKS

Use quotation marks to set off brief quotations, dialogue, titles, and words used in special ways. Do not use quotation marks with long passages of prose or poetry.

35a Setting Off Quotations

When you quote a word, phrase, or brief passage from someone else's speech or writing, enclose the quoted material in a pair of quotation marks.

> Gloria Steinem observed, "We are becoming the men we once hoped to marry."

> In an essay about advertising in women's magazines, Gloria Steinem wrote, "When *Ms.* began, we didn't even consider *not* taking ads."

Special rules govern the punctuation of a quotation when it is used **?** with an **identifying tag,** a phrase (such as *he said*) that identifies the speaker or writer.

Punctuation guidelines for various situations are outlined below.

(1) Identifying Tag in the Middle of a Quoted Passage

Use a pair of commas to set off an identifying tag that interrupts a quoted passage.

> "In the future," pop artist Andy Warhol once said, "everyone will be world famous for fifteen minutes."

If the identifying tag follows a completed sentence but the quoted passage continues, use a period after the tag, and begin the new sentence with a capital letter and quotation marks.

> "Be careful," Erin warned. "Reptiles can be tricky."

Gallery of Misused Quotation Marks
  http://www.juvalamu.com/qmarks/
Quotation Marks Exercises
  http://owl.english.purdue.edu/Files/15.html

(2) Identifying Tag at the Beginning of a Quoted Passage

Use a comma after an identifying tag that introduces quoted speech or writing.

The Raven repeated, "Nevermore."

Use a **colon** instead of a comma before a quotation if the identifying tag is a complete sentence.

She gave her final answer: "No."

(3) Identifying Tag at the End of a Quoted Passage

Use a comma to separate a quotation from an identifying tag that follows it.

"Be careful out there," the sergeant warned.

If the quotation ends with a question mark or an exclamation point, use that punctuation mark instead of the comma. In this situation, the tag begins with a lowercase letter even though it follows end punctuation.

"Is Ankara the capital of Turkey?" she asked.
"Oh, boy!" he cried.

NOTE: Commas and periods are always placed *inside* quotation marks. For information on placement of other punctuation marks with quotation marks, **see 35e.**

35b Setting Off Dialogue, Long Prose Passages, and Poetry

(1) Dialogue

When you record dialogue, enclose the quoted words in quotation marks. Begin a new paragraph each time a new speaker is introduced.

"Sharp on time as usual," Davis said with his habitual guilty grin.

"My watch is always a little fast," Castle said, apologizing for the criticism which he had not expressed. "An anxiety complex, I suppose."

(Graham Greene, *The Human Factor*)

(2) Long Prose Passages

When you quote a short prose passage, set it off in quotation marks.

Galsworthy describes Aunt Juley as "prostrated by the blow" (329).

However, do not enclose a **long prose passage** (a passage of more than four lines) in quotation marks. Instead, set it off by indenting the entire passage one inch (or ten spaces) from the left-hand margin. Double-space above and below the quoted passage, and double-space between lines within it. Introduce the passage with a colon.

The following portrait of Aunt Juley illustrates several of the devices Galsworthy uses throughout The Forsyte Saga, such as a journalistic detachment that is almost cruel in its scrutiny, a subtle sense of the grotesque, and an ironic stance:

> Aunt Juley stayed in her room, prostrated by the blow. Her face, discoloured by tears, was divided into compartments by the little ridges of pouting flesh which had swollen with emotion. [. . .] At fixed intervals she went to her drawer, and took from beneath the lavender bags a fresh pocket-handkerchief. Her warm heart could not bear the thought that Ann was lying there so cold. (329)

Many similar portraits of characters appear throughout the novel.

LONG PROSE PASSAGES

When you quote a long prose passage that is a single paragraph, do not indent the first line. When quoting two or more paragraphs, however, indent the first line of each paragraph (including the first) three additional spaces. If the first sentence of the passage does not begin a paragraph in the source, do not indent—but do indent the first line of each subsequent paragraph. If the passage you are quoting includes material set in quotation marks, keep the quotation marks.

NOTE: With long prose passages, parenthetical documentation is placed one space *after* the end punctuation. (With short prose passages, parenthetical documentation goes *before* the end punctuation.)

(3) Poetry

One line of poetry is treated like a short prose passage—enclosed in quotation marks and run into the text. Two or three lines of poetry, separated by **slashes,** are also run into the text.

Alexander Pope writes, "True Ease in Writing comes from Art, not Chance, / As those move easiest who have learned to dance."

See
35b2

More than three lines of poetry should be set off like a **long prose passage**. For special emphasis, fewer lines may also be set off in this manner. Punctuation, spelling, capitalization, and indentation are reproduced *exactly.*

Wilfred Owen, a poet who was killed in action in World War I, expressed the horrors of war with vivid imagery:

> Bent double, like old beggars under sacks.
>
> Knock-kneed, coughing like hags, we cursed through sludge.
>
> Till on the haunting flares we turned our backs
>
> And towards our distant rest began to trudge. (1–4)

35c Setting Off Titles

<u>Titles</u> of short works and titles of parts of long works are enclosed in quotation marks. Other titles are italicized.

See 39a

NOTE: *MLA* style recommends underlining to indicate italics.

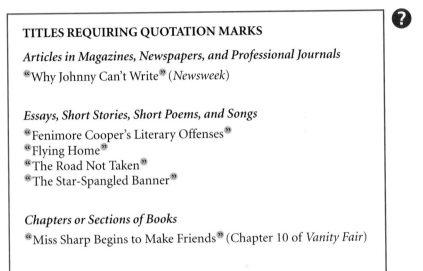

TITLES REQUIRING QUOTATION MARKS

Articles in Magazines, Newspapers, and Professional Journals
"Why Johnny Can't Write" (*Newsweek*)

Essays, Short Stories, Short Poems, and Songs
"Fenimore Cooper's Literary Offenses"
"Flying Home"
"The Road Not Taken"
"The Star-Spangled Banner"

Chapters or Sections of Books
"Miss Sharp Begins to Make Friends" (Chapter 10 of *Vanity Fair*)

Episodes of Radio or Television Series
"Lucy Goes to the Hospital" (*I Love Lucy*)

35d Setting Off Words Used in Special Ways

A word used in a special or unusual way is enclosed in quotation marks.

It was clear that adults approved of children who were "readers," but it was not at all clear why this was so.
(Annie Dillard, *New York Times Magazine*)

A **coinage**—an invented word—also takes quotation marks.

After the twins were born, the minivan became a "babymobile."

35e   Using Quotation Marks with Other Punctuation

?   Quotation marks come *after* the comma or period at the end of a quotation.

> Many, like Frost, think about "the road not taken," but not many have taken "the one less traveled by."

Quotation marks come *before* a semicolon or colon at the end of a quotation.

> Students who do not pass the test receive "certificates of completion"; those who pass are awarded diplomas.

> Taxpayers were pleased with the first of the candidate's promised "sweeping new reforms": a balanced budget.

If a question mark, exclamation point, or dash is part of the quotation, place the quotation marks *after* the punctuation.

> "Who's there?" she demanded.

> "Stop!" he cried.

> "Should we leave now, or—" Vicki paused, unable to continue.

If a question mark, exclamation point, or dash is *not* part of the quotation, place the quotation marks *before* the punctuation.

> Did you finish reading "The Black Cat"?

> Whatever you do, don't yell "Uncle"!

> The first story—Updike's "A & P"—provoked discussion.

? 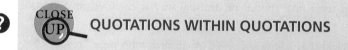 **QUOTATIONS WITHIN QUOTATIONS**

Use *single* quotation marks to enclose a quotation within a quotation.

continued on the following page

Claire noted, "Liberace always said, 'I cried all the way to the bank.'"

Also use single quotation marks within a quotation to indicate a title that would normally be enclosed in double quotation marks.

I think what she said was, "Play it, Sam. Play 'As Time Goes By.'"

Use double quotation marks around quotations or titles within a **long prose passage**.

See 35b2

35f Editing Misused Quotation Marks

Do not use quotation marks in the following situations.

(1) To Set Off Indirect Quotations

Quotation marks should not be used to set off **indirect quotations** (someone else's written or spoken words that are not quoted exactly).

Freud wondered ~~"~~what a woman wanted~~?"~~

(2) To Set Off Slang or Technical Terms

Do not use quotation marks to set off slang or technical terms.

Dawn is ~~"~~into~~"~~ running.

~~"~~Biofeedback~~"~~ is sometimes used to treat migraines.

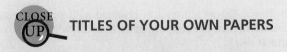

TITLES OF YOUR OWN PAPERS

Do not use quotation marks to set off the title on the title page or the first page of your own papers. See **14b.**

CHAPTER 36

USING OTHER PUNCTUATION MARKS

36a Using Colons

The **colon** is a strong punctuation mark that points readers ahead to the rest of the sentence. When a colon introduces a list or series, explanatory material, or a quotation, it must be preceded by a complete sentence.

(1) Introducing Lists or Series

Colons set off lists or series, including those introduced by phrases like *the following* or *as follows.*

Waiting tables requires three skills: memory, speed, and balance.

(2) Introducing Explanatory Material

Colons often introduce material that explains, exemplifies, or summarizes. Frequently this material is presented in the form of an **appositive,** a word group that identifies or renames an adjacent noun or pronoun.

Diego Rivera painted a controversial mural: the one commissioned for Rockefeller Center in the 1930s.

She had one dream: to play professional basketball.

Sometimes a colon separates two independent clauses, the second illustrating or clarifying the first.

A *U.S. News & World Report* survey has revealed a surprising fact: Americans spend more time at shopping malls than anywhere else except at home and at work.

Punctuation Marks (other than commas)
  http://webster.commnet.edu/hp/pages/darling/grammar/marks.htm

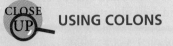

USING COLONS

When a complete sentence follows a colon, it may begin with either a capital or a lowercase letter. However, if it is a quotation, the first word is always capitalized (unless it was not capitalized in the source).

(3) Introducing Quotations

A **quotation** of more than four lines is always introduced by a colon. In addition, a colon is used before a short quotation when it is introduced by a complete independent clause.

See
35b2

?

With dignity, Bartleby repeated the words again● "I prefer not to."

OTHER CONVENTIONAL USES OF COLONS

To Separate Titles from Subtitles
Family Installments●: Memories of Growing Up Hispanic

To Separate Minutes from Hours
6●15 a.m.

After Salutations in **Business Letters**
Dear Dr. Evans●

See
15a

(4) Editing Misused Colons

Colons are not used after expressions such as *namely, for example, such as,* or *that is.*

The Eye Institute treats patients with a wide variety of conditions, such

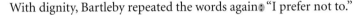

as: myopia, glaucoma, and cataracts.

Colons should not be placed between verbs and their objects or complements, or between prepositions and their objects.

James Michener wrote/ *Hawaii, Centennial, Space,* and *Poland.*

Hitler's armies marched through/ the Netherlands, Belgium, and France.

36b Using Dashes

(1) Setting Off Nonessential Material

Like commas, **dashes** can set off **nonessential material**, but unlike commas, dashes tend to call attention to the material they set off. Indicate a dash with two unspaced hyphens (unless your word processing program has a dash function).

Explanations, qualifications, examples, definitions, and appositives may be set off by dashes for emphasis or clarity.

Neither of the boys—both nine-year-olds—had any history of violence.

Too many parents learn the dangers of swimming pools the hard way—after their toddler has drowned.

(2) Introducing a Summary

A dash is used to introduce a statement that summarizes a list or series before it.

"Study hard," "Respect your elders," "Don't talk with your mouth full"—Sharon had often heard her parents say these things.

(3) Indicating an Interruption

In dialogue, a dash may mark a hesitation or an unfinished thought.

"I think—no, I know—this is the worst day of my life," Julie sighed.

(4) Editing Overused Dashes

Because too many dashes can make a passage seem disorganized and out of control, they should not be overused.

Registration was a nightmare, ~~most~~ **Most** of the courses I wanted to take—

geology and conversational Spanish, for instance—met at inconvenient

times—or were closed by the time I tried to sign up for them.

36c Using Parentheses

(1) Setting Off Nonessential Material

Parentheses enclose material that is relatively unimportant in a sentence—for example, material that expands, clarifies, illustrates, or supplements.

In some European countries (notably Sweden and France), high-quality day care is offered at little or no cost to parents.

When a complete sentence set off by parentheses falls within another sentence, it should not begin with a capital letter or end with a period.

The area is so cold (temperatures average in the low twenties) that it is virtually uninhabitable.

If the parenthetical sentence does *not* fall within another sentence, however, it must begin with a capital letter and end with appropriate punctuation.

(2) Using Parentheses in Other Situations

Parentheses are used around letters and numbers that identify points on a list, dates, cross-references, and documentation.

All reports must include the following components: (1) an opening summary, (2) a background statement, and (3) a list of conclusions.

Russia defeated Sweden in the Great Northern War (1700–1721).

Other scholars also make this point (see p. 54).

One critic has called the novel "puerile" (Arvin 72).

36d   Using Brackets

(1) Setting Off Comments within Quotations

Brackets within quotations tell readers that the enclosed words are yours and not those of your source. You can bracket an explanation, a clarification, a correction, or an opinion.

"Even at Princeton he [F. Scott Fitzgerald] felt like an outsider."

If a quotation contains an error, indicate that the error is not yours by following the error with the italicized Latin word *sic* ("thus") in brackets.

"The octopuss [*sic*] is a cephalopod mollusk with eight arms."

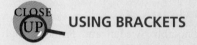

USING BRACKETS

Use brackets to indicate changes that enable you to fit a **quotation** smoothly into your sentence. If you use ellipses to indicate omitted words, enclose the ellipses in brackets.

(2) Using Brackets in Place of Parentheses within Parentheses

Use brackets instead of parentheses that fall within parentheses.

In her study of American education (*The Troubled Crusade* [New York: Basic, 1963]), Diane Ravitch addresses issues like educational reforms and campus unrest.

36e   Using Slashes

(1) Separating One Option from Another

The either/or fallacy is a common error in logic.

Writer/director Spike Lee will speak at the film festival.

Notice that in this case there is no space before or after the slash.

(2) Separating Lines of Poetry Run into the Text

The poet James Schevill writes, "I study my defects ⫽ And learn how to perfect them."

In this case, leave a space both before and after the slash.

36f Using Ellipses

(1) Indicating an Omission in Quoted Prose

Use an **ellipsis**—three *spaced* periods—to indicate that you have omitted words or entire sentences from a prose quotation. Enclose the ellipses in brackets.

> ORIGINAL: "When I was a young man, being anxious to distinguish myself, I was perpetually starting new propositions. But I soon gave this over; for I found that generally what was new was false." (Samuel Johnson)
>
> WITH OMISSIONS: "When I was a young man, [...] I was perpetually starting new propositions. But I soon [...] found that generally what was new was false."

NOTE: When you delete words immediately after an internal punctuation mark (such as a comma), you retain the punctuation before the ellipsis.

When you delete words *at the beginning of a sentence within a quoted passage,* retain the previous sentence's punctuation, followed by an ellipsis.

> In her final paragraph, Jaynes poses—and answers—her central question: "What is power? [...] the option not only of saying *no* but also of saying *yes.*"

When you delete words *at the end of a sentence of a quoted passage,* retain the sentence's period or other end punctuation, followed by an ellipsis.

> According to humorist Dave Barry, "from outer space Europe appears to be shaped like a large ketchup stain. [...]"

Similarly, if you omit *one or more complete sentences from a quoted passage,* retain the previous sentence's end punctuation, followed by an ellipsis.

NOTE: Never begin a quotation with an ellipsis. Use an ellipsis only if you delete words in the middle or at the end of a quoted passage.

CLOSE UP USING ELLIPSES

If a quotation ending with an ellipsis is followed by parenthetical documentation, the final punctuation *follows* the documentation.

As Jarman argues, "Compromise was impossible [. . .]" (161).

(2) Indicating an Omission in Quoted Poetry

When you omit one or more lines of poetry, use a complete line of spaced periods.

ORIGINAL:
> *Stitch! Stitch! Stitch!*
> *In poverty, hunger, and dirt,*
> *And still with a voice of dolorous pitch,*
> *Would that its tone could reach the Rich,*
> *She sang this "Song of the Shirt!"*

> (Thomas Hood)

WITH OMISSION:
> *Stitch! Stitch! Stitch!*
> *In poverty, hunger, and dirt,*
> [. . . . .]
> *She sang this "Song of the Shirt!"*

PART 12

Understanding Spelling and Mechanics

PART 12

SPELLING &
MECHANICS

? FREQUENTLY ASKED QUESTIONS

PART 12

SPELLING &
MECHANICS

CHAPTER 37

SPELLING

Most people can spell even difficult words "almost" correctly; usually only a letter or two are wrong. For this reason, memorizing a few rules and their exceptions and learning the correct spelling of the most commonly misspelled words can make a big difference.

37a Understanding Spelling and Pronunciation

Sound alone does not necessarily indicate a word's spelling in English, and the inconsistency between sound and spelling creates a number of problems. Because pronunciation provides no clues to spelling, you must memorize the spellings of many words and use a **dictionary** or spell checker regularly.

See
Ch. 29

(1) Vowels in Unstressed Positions

Many unstressed vowels sound exactly alike when we say them. For instance, it is hard to tell from pronunciation alone that the *i* in *terrible* is not an *a*. In addition, the unstressed vowels *a, e,* and *i* are impossible to distinguish in the suffixes *-able* and *-ible, -ance* and *-ence,* and *-ant* and *-ent.*

comfort<u>able</u>   brilli<u>ance</u>   serv<u>ant</u>
compat<u>ible</u>   excell<u>ence</u>   independ<u>ent</u>

Words Commonly Misspelled (from Strunk's *Elements of Style*)
　　http://www.bartleby.com/141/strunk4.html
Spelling Test and Tips
　　http://www.sentex.net/~mmcadams/spelling.html
Spelling Tips
　　http://owl.english.purdue.edu/Files/Spelling.html
American vs. British Spelling
　　http://www.geocities.com/Athens/Atlantis/2284/

(2) Silent Letters

Some English words contain silent letters, such as the *b* in *climb* and the *t* in *mortgage*.

aisle	depot	pneumonia
climb	knight	silhouette
condemn	mortgage	sovereign

(3) Words That Are Often Pronounced Carelessly

Most of us pronounce words rather carelessly in everyday speech. Consequently, when spelling, we may leave out, add, or transpose letters. The following words are often misspelled because they are pronounced incorrectly:

candidate	library	recognize
environment	lightning	specific
February	nuclear	supposed to
government	perform	surprise
hundred	quantity	used to

(4) American and British Spellings

Some words are spelled one way in the United States and another way in Great Britain and the Commonwealth nations.

American	*British*
color	colour
defense	defence
judgment	judgement
theater	theatre
traveled	travelled

(5) Homophones

Homophones are words—such as *accept* and *except*—that are pronounced alike but spelled differently.

accept	to receive
except	other than
affect	to have an influence on (*verb*)
effect	result (*noun*); to cause (*verb*)
its	possessive of *it*
it's	contraction of *it is*

principal   most important (*adjective*); head of a school (*noun*)
principle   a basic truth; rule of conduct

For a full list of these and other homophones, along with their meanings and sentences illustrating their use, consult **Chapter 30,** "A Glossary of Usage."

CLOSE UP SPELLING: ONE WORD OR TWO?

Some words may be written as one word or two, depending on meaning.

any way vs. anyway
The early pioneers made the trip west *any way* they could.
It began to rain, but the game continued *anyway.*

every day vs. everyday
Every day brings new opportunities.
John thought of his birthday as an *everyday* event.

Other words are frequently misspelled because people are not sure whether they are one word or two.

One Word	Two Words
already	a lot
cannot	all right
classroom	even though
overweight	no one

Consult a dictionary if you have any doubts about whether a word is written as one word or two.

RUNNING A SPELL CHECK

If you use a spell checker, remember that spell checkers will not identify a word that is spelled correctly but used incorrectly—*then*

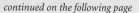

continued on the following page

continued from the previous page

for *than* or *its* for *it's,* for example—or a typo that creates another word, such as *form* for *from.* For this reason you still need to proofread your papers, even after you have run a spell check.

37b   Learning Spelling Rules

Memorizing a few reliable rules can help you overcome problems caused by the general inconsistency between pronunciation and spelling.

(1) The *ie/ei* Combinations

The old rule still stands: Use *i* before *e* except after *c* or when pronounced *ay,* as in *neighbor.*

I BEFORE *E:*   belief, chief, niece, friend

EI AFTER *C:*   ceiling, deceit, receive

EI PRONOUNCED *AY:*   weigh, freight, eight

Exceptions: *either, neither, foreign, leisure, weird,* and *seize.* In addition, if the *ie* combination is not pronounced as a unit, the rule does not apply: *atheist, science.*

(2) Doubling Final Consonants

The only words that double their consonants before a suffix that begins with a vowel (such as *-ed* or *-ing*) are those that pass all three of the following tests:

1. They have one syllable or are stressed on the last syllable.
2. They contain only one vowel in the last syllable.
3. They end in a single consonant.

The word *tap* satisfies all three conditions: it has only one syllable, it contains only one vowel (*a*), and it ends in a single consonant (*p*). Therefore, the final consonant doubles before a suffix beginning with a vowel (*tapped, tapping*). The word *relent* meets two of the conditions (it is stressed on the last syllable, and it has one vowel in the last syllable), but it does not end in a single consonant. Therefore, its final consonant is not doubled (*relented, relenting*).

(3) Silent *e* before a Suffix

When a suffix that starts with a consonant is added to a word ending in a silent *e*, the *e* is generally kept: *hope/hopeful; lame/lamely; bore/boredom.* **Exceptions:** *argument, truly, ninth, judgment,* and *acknowledgment.*

When a suffix that starts with a vowel is added to a word ending in a silent *e*, the *e* is generally dropped: *hope/hoping; trace/traced; grieve/grievance; love/lovable.* **Exceptions:** *changeable, noticeable,* and *courageous.*

(4) *Y* before a Suffix

When a word ends in a consonant plus *y*, the *y* generally changes to an *i* when a suffix is added (beauty + ful = beautiful). The *y* is retained, however, when the suffix -*ing* is added (tally + ing = tallying) and in some one-syllable words (dry + ness = dryness).

When a word ends in a vowel plus *y*, the *y* is retained (joy + ful = joyful; employ + er = employer). **Exception:** day + ly = daily.

(5) *Seed* Endings

Endings with the sound *seed* are nearly always spelled *cede*, as in *precede, intercede, concede,* and so on. The only exceptions are *supersede, exceed, proceed,* and *succeed.*

(6) -*Able,* -*Ible*

If the root of a word is itself an independent word, the suffix -*able* is most commonly used. If the root of a word is not an independent word, the suffix -*ible* is most often used.

*comfort*able	*compat*ible
*agree*able	*incred*ible
*dry*able	*plaus*ible

(7) Plurals

Most nouns form plurals by adding *s: savage/savages, tortilla/tortillas, boat/boats.* There are, however, a number of exceptions.

Words Ending in -f *or* -fe   Some words ending in -*f* or -*fe* form plurals by changing the *f* to *v* and adding *es* or *s: life/lives, self/selves.* Others add just *s: belief/beliefs, safe/safes*. Words ending in -*ff* take *s* to form plurals: *tariff/tariffs*.

Words Ending in -y   Most words that end in a consonant followed by *y* form plurals by changing the *y* to *i* and adding *es: baby/babies.* **Exceptions:** proper nouns such as *Kennedys* (never *Kennedies*).

Words that end in a vowel followed by a *y* form plurals by adding *s: monkey/monkeys.*

Words Ending in -o   Words that end in a vowel followed by *o* form the plural by adding *s: radio/radios, stereo/stereos, zoo/zoos.* Most words that end in a consonant followed by *o* add *es* to form the plural: *tomato/tomatoes, hero/heroes.* **Exceptions:** *silo/silos, piano/pianos, memo/memos, soprano/sopranos.*

Words Ending in -s, -ss, -sh, -ch, -x, *and* -z   These words form plurals by adding *es: Jones/Joneses, mass/masses, rash/rashes, lunch/lunches, box/boxes, buzz/buzzes.*

NOTE: Some one-syllable words that end in -*s* or -*z* double their final consonants when forming plurals: *quiz/quizzes.*

Compound Nouns   **Compound nouns**—nouns formed from two or more words—usually conform to the rules governing the last word in the compound construction: *welfare state/welfare states; snowball/snowballs.* However, where the first element of the compound noun is more important than the others, the plural is formed with the first element: *sister-in-law/sisters-in-law, attorney general/attorneys general.*

Foreign Plurals   Some words, especially those borrowed from Latin or Greek, keep their foreign plurals.

Singular	*Plural*
basis	bases
criterion	criteria
datum	data
larva	larvae
medium	media
memorandum	memoranda
stimulus	stimuli

SPELLING AN UNFAMILIAR WORD

Most spell checkers have a "guess" function that enables you to look up a word even if you do not know how to spell it. You select the word in question and the computer lists the word or words to which you might be referring.

CHAPTER 38

CAPITALIZATION

38a Capitalizing the First Word of a Sentence

Capitalize the first word of a sentence, including a sentence of quoted speech or writing.

As Shakespeare wrote, "Who steals my purse steals trash."

Do not capitalize a sentence set off within another sentence by dashes or parentheses.

Finding the store closed—it was a holiday—they went home.

The candidates are Frank Lester and Jane Lester (they are not related).

See 36a2 Capitalization is optional when a complete sentence is introduced by a **colon**.

CLOSE UP **USING CAPITAL LETTERS IN POETRY**

Remember that the first word of a line of poetry is generally capitalized. If the poet uses a lowercase letter to begin a line, however, follow that style when you quote the line.

Using Capitals
   http://www.clearcf.uvic.ca/writersguide/Pages/Capitals.html
Steve Tripp's Capitalization Page + Exercises
   http://www.u-aizu.ac.jp/~tripp/cap.html

38b   Capitalizing Proper Nouns

Proper nouns—the names of specific persons, places, or things—are capitalized, and so are adjectives formed from proper nouns.

(1) Specific People's Names

Eleanor Roosevelt   Elvis Presley

Capitalize a title when it precedes a person's name or is used instead of the name. (Senator Barbara Boxer, Dad). Titles that *follow* names or those that refer to the general position, not the particular person who holds it, are usually not capitalized (Barbara Boxer, the senator from California).

You may, however, capitalize titles that indicate very high-ranking positions even when they are used alone or when they follow a name: the Pope; William Jefferson Clinton, President of the United States. A title denoting a family relationship is never capitalized when it follows an article or a possessive pronoun (a dad, his mom).

Capitalize titles or abbreviations of academic degrees, even when they follow a name: Dr. Benjamin Spock, Benjamin Spock, MD.

(2) Names of Particular Things

the *Titanic*   the World Series

the Brooklyn Bridge   Mount Rushmore

(3) Places and Geographical Regions

Saturn   the Straits of Magellan

Budapest   the Western Hemisphere

Capitalize *north, east, south,* and *west* when they denote particular geographical regions, but not when they designate directions.

There are more tornadoes in Kansas than in the East. (*East* refers to a specific region.)

Turn west at Broad Street and continue north to Market. (*West* and *north* refer to directions, not specific regions.)

(4) Days of the Week, Months, and Holidays

Saturday   Rosh Hashanah

January   Cinco de Mayo

(5) Historical Periods, Events, Documents, and Names of Legal Cases

the Reformation   the Treaty of Versailles

the Battle of Gettysburg   *Brown v. Board of Education*

(6) Philosophic, Literary, and Artistic Movements

Naturalism   Neoclassicism

Romanticism   Expressionism

(7) Races, Ethnic Groups, Nationalities, and Languages

African American   Korean

Latino/Latina   Dutch

? NOTE: When the words *black* and *white* refer to races, they have traditionally not been capitalized. Current usage is divided on whether to capitalize *black*.

(8) Religions and Their Followers; Sacred Books and Figures

Jews   the Talmud   Buddha

Islam   God   the Scriptures

(9) Specific Organizations

the New York Yankees   the American Bar Association

the Democratic Party   the Anti-Defamation League

(10) Businesses, Government Agencies, and Other Institutions

Congress   Lincoln High School

the Environmental Protection Agency   the University of Maryland

(11) Brand Names and Words Formed from Them

Coke   Astroturf   Rollerblades

NOTE: Brand names that over long use have become synonymous with the product—for example, *nylon* and *aspirin*—are no longer capitalized. (Consult a dictionary to determine whether or not to capitalize a familiar brand name.)

(12) Specific Academic Courses

Sociology 201   English 101

NOTE: Do not capitalize a general subject area (sociology, zoology) unless it is the name of a language (French).

(13) Adjectives Formed from Proper Nouns

Keynesian economics   Elizabethan era

Freudian slip   Shakespearean sonnet

When words derived from proper nouns have lost their specialized meanings, do not capitalize them: *china bowl, french fries.*

38c   Capitalizing Important Words in Titles ❓

In general, capitalize all words in titles with the exception of articles (*a, an,* and *the*), prepositions, coordinating conjunctions, and the *to* in infinitives. If an article, preposition, or coordinating conjunction is the *first* or *last* word in the title, however, do capitalize it.

The Declaration of Independence   *A Man and a Woman*

Across the River and into the Trees   *What Friends Are For*

38d   Capitalizing the Pronoun *I*, the Interjection *O*, and Other Single Letters in Special Constructions

Always capitalize the pronoun *I*, even if it is part of a contraction (*I'm, I'll, I've*).

Always capitalize the interjection *O*.

Give us peace in our time, <u>O</u> Lord.

However, capitalize the interjection *oh* only when it begins a sentence.
     Many other single letters are capitalized in certain usages. Check your
dictionary to determine whether to use a capital letter.

an A in history   vitamin B

D day   C major

38e   Editing Misused Capitals

Do not use capital letters for emphasis or as an attention-getting device. If you are not certain whether a word should be capitalized, consult
your dictionary.

 (1) Seasons

Do not capitalize the names of the seasons—summer, fall, winter,
spring—unless they are strongly personified, as in *Old Man Winter*.

(2) Centuries and Loosely Defined Historical Periods

Do not capitalize the names of centuries or of general historical periods.

seventeenth-century poetry   the automobile age

Do, however, capitalize names of specific historical, anthropological, and
geological periods.

the Renaissance   Iron Age   Paleozoic Era

CHAPTER 39

ITALICS

39a Setting Off Titles and Names

Use italics for the titles and names listed in the box below. All other titles are set off with **quotation marks**.

See
35c

?

TITLES AND NAMES SET IN ITALICS

BOOKS: *David Copperfield, The Bluest Eye*

NEWSPAPERS: the *Washington Post,* the *Philadelphia Inquirer*

(Articles and names of cities are italicized only when they are part
of a title.)

MAGAZINES: *Rolling Stone, Scientific American*

PAMPHLETS: *Common Sense*

FILMS: *Casablanca, Schindler's List*

TELEVISION PROGRAMS: *60 Minutes, The X-Files*

RADIO PROGRAMS: *All Things Considered, A Prairie Home Companion*

LONG POEMS: *John Brown's Body, The Faerie Queen*

PLAYS: *Macbeth, A Raisin in the Sun*

LONG MUSICAL WORKS: *Rigoletto, Eroica*

SOFTWARE PROGRAMS: *Word, PowerPoint*

PAINTINGS AND SCULPTURE: *Guernica, Pietá*

SHIPS: *Lusitania,* U.S.S. *Saratoga*

(S.S. and U.S.S. are not italicized.)

continued on the following page

Italics
  http://www.rpi.edu/dept/11c/writecenter/web/text/prose2.html#9

continued from the previous page

TRAINS: *City of New Orleans, The Orient Express*

AIRCRAFT: *The Hindenburg, Enola Gay*

(Only particular aircraft, not makes or types such as Piper Cub or Boeing 757, are italicized.)

SPACECRAFT: *Challenger, Enterprise*

SACRED BOOKS AND WELL-KNOWN DOCUMENTS

Names of sacred books, such as the Bible, and well-known documents, such as the Constitution and the Declaration of Independence, are neither italicized nor placed within quotation marks.

39b Setting Off Foreign Words and Phrases

Italics are often used to set off foreign words and phrases that have not become part of the English language.

"C'est la vie," Madeleine said when she noticed the new, lower price.

Spirochaeta plicatilis is a corkscrew-like bacterium.

If you are not sure whether a foreign word has been assimilated into English, consult a dictionary.

39c Setting Off Elements Spoken of as Themselves and Terms Being Defined

Italics are used to set off letters, numerals, and words that refer to the letters, numerals, and words themselves.

Is that a *p* or a *g?*

I forget the exact address, but I know it has a *3* in it.

Does *through* rhyme with *cough?*

Italics also set off words and phrases that you go on to define.

A *closet drama* is a play meant to be read, not performed.

39d   Using Italics for Emphasis   ❓

Italics can occasionally be used for emphasis.

Initially, poetry might be defined as a kind of language that says *more* and says it *more intensely* than does ordinary language.

(Lawrence Perrine, *Sound and Sense*)

However, overuse of italics is distracting. Instead of italicizing, try to indicate emphasis with word choice and sentence structure.

CLOSE UP   USING ITALICS

MLA style recommends that you underline to indicate italics. However, you may italicize if your instructor prefers.

CHAPTER 40

HYPHENS

Hyphens have two conventional uses: to break a word at the end of a line and to link words in certain compounds.

40a   Breaking a Word at the End of a Line

A computer never breaks a word at the end of a line unless you command it to. Sometimes you will want to hyphenate—for example, to fill in space at the end of a line. When you break a word at the end of a line, divide it only between syllables, consulting a dictionary if necessary. Never divide a word at the end of a page, and never hyphenate one-syllable words. In addition, never leave a single letter at the end of a line or carry only one or two letters to the next line.

See 40b

If you must divide a **compound word** at the end of a line, put the hyphen between the elements of the compound (*snow-mobile,* not *snowmo-bile*).

?

DIVIDING ELECTRONIC ADDRESSES (URLs)

Do not use a hyphen to divide an electronic address (URL) at the end of a line. (Readers might think the hyphen is part of the address.) MLA style requires that you break the URL at a slash. If this is not possible, break it in a logical place—after a period, for example—or avoid the problem entirely by moving the entire URL to the next line.

Using Hyphens
    http://owl.english.purdue.edu/Files/18.html

40b   Dividing Compound Words

A **compound word** is composed of two or more words. Some famil- ❓
iar compound words are always hyphenated: *no-hitter, helter-skelter.*
Other compounds are always written as one word: *fireplace, peacetime.*
Finally, some compounds are always written as two separate words: *labor
relations, bunk bed.* Your dictionary can tell you whether a particular
compound requires a hyphen.

Hyphens are generally used in the following compounds:

(1) In Compound Adjectives

When a **compound adjective** *precedes* the noun it modifies, its elements are joined by hyphens.

The research team tried to use <u>nineteenth-century</u> technology to design
a <u>space-age</u> project.

When a compound adjective *follows* the noun it modifies, it does not
include hyphens.

The three <u>government-operated</u> programs were run smoothly, but
the one that was not <u>government operated</u> was short of funds.

⊗ USING HYPHENS

A compound adjective formed with an adverb ending in *-ly* is
not hyphenated, even when it precedes the noun.

Many <u>upwardly mobile</u> families are on tight budgets.

Use **suspended hyphens**—hyphens followed by a space or by appropriate punctuation and a space—in a series of compounds that have the
same principal elements.

The <u>three-</u>, <u>four-</u>, and <u>five-year-old</u> children sang songs.

(2) With Certain Prefixes or Suffixes

Use a hyphen between a prefix and a proper noun or proper adjective.

mid-July   pre-Columbian

Use a hyphen to connect the prefixes *all-, ex-, half-, quarter-, quasi-,* and *self-* and the suffix *-elect* to a noun.

ex-senator   self-centered
quarter-moon   president-elect

NOTE: The words *selfhood, selfish,* and *selfless* do not include hyphens. In these cases, *self* is the root, not a prefix.

(3) In Compound Numerals and Fractions

Hyphenate compounds that represent numbers below one hundred, even if they are part of a larger number.

the <u>twenty-first</u> century   three hundred <u>sixty-five</u> days

Also hyphenate the written form of a fraction when it modifies a noun.

a <u>two-thirds</u> share of the business

(4) For Clarity

Hyphenate to prevent readers from misreading one word for another.

In order to <u>reform</u> criminals, we must <u>re-form</u> our ideas about prisons.

Hyphenate to avoid certain hard-to-read combinations, such as two *i*'s (*semi-illiterate*) or more than two of the same consonant (*shell-less*).
Hyphenate in most cases between a capital initial and a word when the two combine to form a compound: *A-frame, T-shirt.*

(5) In Coined Compounds

A **coined compound,** one that uses a new combination of words as a unit, requires hyphens.

He looked up with a <u>who-do-you-think-you-are</u> expression.

CHAPTER 41

ABBREVIATIONS

Abbreviations are not always appropriate in college writing. Some are acceptable in scientific, technical, or business writing, or only in a particular discipline. If you have questions about the appropriateness of a particular abbreviation, check a style manual in your field.

41a Abbreviating Titles

Titles before and after proper names are usually abbreviated.

Mr. Homer Simpson   Rep. Chaka Fattah

Henry Kissinger, PhD   Dr. Martin Luther King, Jr.

Do not, however, use an abbreviated title without a name.

                 doctor
The ~~Dr.~~ diagnosed hepatitis.

41b Abbreviating Organization Names and Technical Terms

You may refer to well-known businesses and government, social, and civic organizations by capitalized initials. These **abbreviations** fall into two categories: those in which the initials are pronounced as separate units (MTV) and **acronyms,** in which the initials form new words (NATO).

See 31a2

You may also use accepted abbreviations for complex technical terms that are not well known, but be sure to spell out the full term the first time you mention it, followed by the abbreviation in parentheses.

Grammar Girl's Guide to Abbreviations and Acronyms
    http://webwitch.dreamhost.com/grammar.girl/grammar1.html#abbrev
Abbreviations and Acronyms (U. Colorado)
    http://www.colorado.edu/Publications/styleguide/abbrev.html

Citrus farmers have been using ethylene dibromide (EDB), a chemical pesticide, for more than twenty years. Now, however, EDB has contaminated water supplies.

41c   Abbreviating Dates, Times of Day, Temperatures, and Numbers

Dates, times of day, temperatures, and numbers are often abbreviated.

50 BC (BC follows the date)   AD 432 (AD precedes the date)

3:03 p.m.   180° F (Fahrenheit)

Always capitalize BC and AD. (The alternatives BCE, for "before the Common Era," and CE, for "Common Era," are also capitalized.) The abbreviations a.m. and p.m. are used only when they are accompanied by numbers.

I'll see you in the ~~a.m.~~ morning.

Avoid the abbreviation *no.* except in technical writing, and then use it only before a specific number: *The unidentified substance was labeled no. 52.*

41d   Editing Misused Abbreviations

In college writing, abbreviations are not used in the following cases.

(1) Names of Days, Months, or Holidays

On ~~Sat., Dec.~~ Saturday, December 23, I started my ~~Xmas~~ Christmas shopping.

(2) Names of Places, Streets, and the Like

He lives on Riverside ~~Dr.~~ Drive in ~~NYC~~ New York City.

Exceptions: The abbreviation *US* is often acceptable (*US Coast Guard*), as is *DC* in *Washington, DC*. Also permissible are *Mt.* before the name of a mountain (*Mt. Etna*) and *St.* in a place name (*St. Albans*).

(3) Names of People and Academic Subjects

Robert   William
Mr. Harris's boys were named ~~Robt.~~ and ~~Wm.~~

Psychology   literature
~~Psych.~~ and English ~~lit.~~ are required courses.

(4) Names of Businesses

Write company names exactly as the firms themselves write them, including the distinction between the ampersand (&) and the word *and: Western Union Telegraph Company, Charles Schwab & Co., Inc.* Abbreviations for *company, corporation,* and the like are used only along with a company name.

corporation   company
The ~~corp.~~ merged with a ~~co.~~ in Ohio.

Exception: MLA style requires abbreviations of publishers' company names.

See 9a2

(5) Latin Expressions

Abbreviations of the common Latin phrases *i.e.* ("that is"), *e.g.* ("for example"), and *etc.* ("and so forth") are sometimes appropriate in informal writing. In college writing, however, write out an equivalent phrase.

for example,
Other musicians (~~e.g.~~ Bruce Springsteen) have been influenced by Dylan.

and other poems.
Poe wrote "The Raven," "Annabel Lee," ~~etc.~~

(6) Units of Measurement

In technical writing, some units of measurement are abbreviated when preceded by a numeral.

The hurricane had winds of 35 mph.

One new Honda gets over 50 mpg.

In most situations, write out units of measurement, and spell out words such as *inches, feet, years, miles, pints, quarts,* and *gallons.*

(7) Symbols

The symbols %, =, +, #, and ¢ are acceptable in technical and scientific writing but not in nontechnical college writing. The symbol $ is acceptable before specific numbers ($15,000), but not as a substitute for the words *money* or *dollars.*

(8) Parts of Books

Although abbreviations that designate parts of written works *(ch. 3, sec. 7)* may be used in the Works Cited list and in parenthetical documentation, they should not be used elsewhere in a paper.

CHAPTER 42

NUMBERS

Convention determines when to use a **numeral** (22) and when to spell out a number (twenty-two). Numerals are commonly used in scientific and technical writing and in journalism, but less often in academic or literary writing.

NOTE: The guidelines in this chapter are based on the *MLA Handbook for Writers of Research Papers*. APA style requires that all numbers below ten be spelled out if they do not represent specific measurements and that numbers ten and above be expressed in numerals.

42a Spelled-Out Numbers versus Numerals

❓

Unless a number falls into one of the categories listed in **42b,** spell it out if you can do so *in one or two words.*

The Hawaiian alphabet has only <u>twelve</u> letters.

Class size stabilized at <u>twenty-eight</u> students.

The subsidies are expected to total about <u>two million</u> dollars.

Numbers *more than two words* long are expressed in figures.

The dietitian prepared <u>125</u> sample menus.

The developer of the community purchased <u>300,000</u> doorknobs, <u>153,000</u> faucets, and <u>4,000</u> manhole covers.

Numbers
  http://www.edunet.com/english/grammar/sect-2.html#numbers
Steve Tripp's "Number's in Formal English"
  http://www.u-aizu.ac.jp/~tripp/numbers.html

NOTE: Numerals and spelled-out numbers should generally not be mixed in the same passage. For consistency, then, the number 4,000 in the preceding example is expressed in figures even though it could be written in just two words.

Never begin a sentence with a numeral. If necessary, reword the sentence.

FAULTY: 250 students are currently enrolled in World History 106.

REVISED: Current enrollment in World History 106 is 250 students.

42b   Conventional Uses of Numerals

(1) Addresses

111 Fifth Avenue, New York, NY 10003

(2) Dates

January 15, 1929   1914–1919

(3) Exact Times

9:16   10 a.m. (or 10:00 a.m.)

Exceptions: Spell out times of day when they are used with *o'clock: eleven o'clock,* not *11 o'clock.* Also spell out times expressed as round numbers: *They were in bed by ten.*

(4)   Exact Sums of Money

$25.11 $6,752.00

NOTE: You may write out a round sum of money if the number can be expressed in one or two words.

five dollars   two thousand dollars

(5) Divisions of Written Works

Use arabic (not roman) numerals for chapter and volume numbers; acts, scenes, and lines of plays; chapters and verses of the Bible; and line numbers of long poems.

(6) Measurements before an Abbreviation or Symbol

12″   55 mph

32°   15 cc

(7) Percentages, Decimals, and Fractions

80 percent (or 80%)   3.14   6¾

(8) Ratios, Scores, and Statistics

Children preferred Fun Flakes over Graino by a ratio of 20 to 1.

The Orioles defeated the Phillies 6 to 0.

The median age of the voters was 42; the mean age was 40.

(9) Identification Numbers

Route 66   Track 8   Channel 12

Appendices

APPENDIX A

PARTS OF SPEECH

The eight basic **parts of speech**—the building blocks for all English sentences—are *nouns, pronouns, verbs, adjectives, adverbs, prepositions, conjunctions,* and *interjections.* How a word is classified depends on its function in a sentence.

A1   Nouns

Nouns name people, places, things, ideas, actions, or qualities.

A **common noun** names any of a class of people, places, or things: *artist, judge, building, event, city.*

A **proper noun,** always capitalized, refers to a particular person, place, or thing: *Mary Cassatt, World Trade Center, Crimean War.*

A **count noun** names something that can be counted: *five dogs, two dozen grapes.*

A **noncount noun** names a quantity that is not countable: *time, dust, work, gold.* Noncount nouns generally have only a singular form.

A **collective noun** designates a group thought of as a unit: *committee, class, family.* Collective nouns are generally singular unless the members of the group are referred to as individuals.

An **abstract noun** refers to an intangible idea or quality: *love, hate, justice, anger, fear, prejudice.*

Glossary of Grammatical Terms (Rhodes College)
   http://www.rhodes.edu/kamhi/center/glossary.html
Ask a Grammar Expert (e-mailed responses to grammar questions)
   http://www.grammarnow.com/
University of Illinois' "Grammar Safari"
   http://deil.lang.uiuc.edu/web.pages/grammarsafari/html
Nouns Defined (Illinois)
   http://www.english.uiuc.edu/cws/wworkshop/nounsdefined.htm
Common and Proper Nouns (Illinois)
   http://www.english.uiuc.edu/cws/wworkshop/commonproper.htm

A2   Pronouns

Pronouns are words used in place of nouns or other pronouns. The word for which a pronoun stands is called its **antecedent.**

If you use a <u>quotation</u> in your paper, you must document <u>it</u>.

NOTE: Although different types of pronouns may have exactly the same form, they are distinguished from one another by their functions in a sentence.

A **personal pronoun** stands for a person or thing: *I, me, we, us, my, mine, our, ours, you, your, yours, he, she, it, its, him, his, her, hers, they, them, their, theirs.*

<u>They</u> made <u>her</u> an offer <u>she</u> couldn't refuse.

An **indefinite pronoun** does not refer to any particular person or thing, and so it does not require an antecedent. Indefinite pronouns include *another, any, each, few, many, some, nothing, one, anyone, everyone, everybody, everything, someone, something, either,* and *neither.*

<u>Many</u> are called, but <u>few</u> are chosen.

A **reflexive pronoun** ends with *-self* and refers to a recipient of the action that is the same as the actor: *myself, yourself, himself, herself, itself, oneself, themselves, ourselves, yourselves.*

They found <u>themselves</u> in downtown Pittsburgh.

An **intensive pronoun** emphasizes a preceding noun or pronoun. (Intensive pronouns have the same form as reflexive pronouns.)

Darrow <u>himself</u> was sure his client was innocent.

A **relative pronoun** introduces an adjective or noun clause in a sentence: *which, who, whom, that, what, whose, whatever, whoever, whomever, whichever.*

Pronouns Defined (Illinois)
  http://www.english.uiuc.edu/cws/wworkshop/pronoundef.htm
Jack Lynch's Guide to Grammar and Style (much on mechanics)
  http://andromeda.rutgers.edu/~jlynch/Writing/contents.html

People <u>who</u> drink should not drive. (introduces adjective clause)

<u>Whatever</u> happens will be a surprise. (introduces noun clause)

An **interrogative pronoun** introduces a question: *who, which, what, whom, whose, whoever, whatever, whichever.*

<u>Who</u> was that masked man?

A **demonstrative pronoun** points to a particular thing or group of things: *this, that, these, those.*

<u>This</u> is one of Shakespeare's early plays.

A **reciprocal pronoun** denotes a mutual relationship: *each other, one another. Each other* indicates a relationship between two individuals; *one another* denotes a relationship among more than two.

Cathy and I respect <u>each other</u> for our differences; all people should respect <u>one another's</u> differences as we do.

A3 Verbs

A verb may express either action or a state of being.

He <u>ran</u> for the train. (action)

Jen <u>became</u> ill after dinner. (state of being)

Verbs can be classified into two groups: *main verbs* and *auxiliary verbs.*

Main Verbs   **Main verbs** carry most of the meaning in a sentence or clause.

Some main verbs are action verbs.

Emily Dickinson's work <u>anticipated</u> much of twentieth-century poetry.

Other main verbs function as linking verbs. A **linking verb** does not show any physical or mental action. It links the subject to a **subject complement,** a word or phrase that renames or describes the subject.

Linking verbs include *be, become,* and *seem* and verbs that describe sensations—*look, appear, feel, taste, smell,* and so on.

Carbon disulfide <u>smells</u> bad.

Auxiliary Verbs **Auxiliary verbs,** such as *be* and *have,* combine with main verbs to form **verb phrases.** The auxiliary verbs, also known as *helping verbs,* indicate tense, voice, or mood.

[auxiliary] [main verb] [auxiliary] [main verb]

The train <u>has started</u>. We <u>are leaving</u> soon.

[verb phrase]   [verb phrase]

Certain auxiliary verbs, known as **modal auxiliaries,** indicate necessity, possibility, willingness, obligation, or ability.

MODAL AUXILIARIES

must	shall	might	need [to]
will	should	can	ought [to]
would	may	could	

Verbals **Verbals,** such as *known* or *running* or *to go,* are verb forms that act as adjectives, adverbs, or nouns. A verbal cannot serve as a sentence's main verb unless it is used with one or more auxiliary verbs (*is going*). Verbals include *participles, infinitives,* and *gerunds.*

Participles Virtually every verb has a **present participle**, which ends in -*ing* (*loving, learning*) and a **past participle**, which either ends in -*d* or -*ed* (*agreed, learned*) or is formed irregularly (*gone, begun, written*). Participles may function in a sentence as adjectives or as nouns.

Twenty brands of <u>running</u> shoes were on display. (Present participle serves as adjective modifying *shoes.*)

The <u>wounded</u> were given emergency first aid. (Past participle serves as subject.)

Infinitives An **infinitive**—the base form of the verb preceded by *to*—may serve as an adjective, an adverb, or a noun.

Ann Arbor was clearly the place <u>to be.</u> (Infinitive serves as adjective modifying *place.*)

Carla went outside <u>to think.</u> (Infinitive serves as adverb modifying *went.*)

<u>To win</u> was everything. (Infinitive serves as subject.)

Gerunds   **Gerunds,** which like present participles end in *-ing,* are always used as nouns.

<u>Seeing</u> is <u>believing.</u> (Gerunds serve as subject and subject complement.)

Andrew loves <u>skiing.</u> (Gerund is direct object of verb *loves.*)

A4   Adjectives

Adjectives describe, limit, qualify, or in some other way modify nouns or pronouns.
Descriptive adjectives name a quality of the noun or pronoun they modify.

After the game, they were <u>exhausted.</u>

They ordered a <u>chocolate</u> soda and a <u>butterscotch</u> sundae.

When articles, pronouns, numbers, and the like function as adjectives, limiting or qualifying nouns or pronouns, they are referred to as **<u>determiners</u>**.

See
C1.3

A5   Adverbs

Adverbs describe the action of verbs or modify adjectives; other adverbs; or complete phrases, clauses, or sentences. They answer the questions "How?" "Why?" "Where?" "When?" "Under what conditions?" and "To what extent?"

He walked <u>rather hesitantly</u> toward the front of the room. (walked *how?*)

Let's meet <u>tomorrow</u> for coffee. (meet *when?*)

Adverbs that modify adjectives or other adverbs limit or qualify the words they modify.

He pitched an <u>almost perfect</u> game yesterday.

Interrogative Adverbs   The **interrogative adverbs** (*how, when, why,* and *where*) introduce questions.

<u>Why</u> did the compound darken?

Conjunctive Adverbs   **Conjunctive adverbs** act as **transitional words**, joining and relating independent clauses.

FREQUENTLY USED CONJUNCTIVE ADVERBS

accordingly	furthermore	meanwhile	similarly
also	hence	moreover	still
anyway	however	nevertheless	then
besides	incidentally	next	thereafter
certainly	indeed	nonetheless	therefore
consequently	instead	now	thus
finally	likewise	otherwise	undoubtedly

A6   Prepositions

A **preposition** introduces a noun or pronoun or a phrase or clause functioning in the sentence as a noun. The word or word group that the preposition introduces is its **object.**

They received a postcard <u>from</u> Bobby telling <u>about</u> his trip
prep obj

<u>to</u> Canada.

FREQUENTLY USED PREPOSITIONS

about	beneath	inside	since
above	beside	into	through
across	between	like	throughout
after	beyond	near	to
against	by	of	toward
along	concerning	off	under
among	despite	on	underneath
around	down	onto	until
as	during	out	up
at	except	outside	upon
before	for	over	with
behind	from	past	within
below	in	regarding	without

A7 Conjunctions

Conjunctions connect words, phrases, clauses, or sentences.

Coordinating Conjunctions **Coordinating conjunctions** (*and, or, but, nor, for, so, yet*) connect words, phrases, or clauses of equal weight.

The choice was difficult: pheasant <u>or</u> venison. (*Or* links two nouns.)

Thoreau wrote *Walden* in 1854, <u>and</u> he died in 1862. (*And* links two independent clauses.)

Correlative Conjunctions Always used in pairs, **correlative conjunctions** also link items of equal weight.

<u>Both</u> Hancock <u>and</u> Jefferson signed the Declaration of Independence. (Correlative conjunctions link nouns.)

<u>Either</u> I will renew my lease, <u>or</u> I will move. (Correlative conjunctions link independent clauses.)

FREQUENTLY USED CORRELATIVE CONJUNCTIONS

both . . . and	neither . . . nor
either . . . or	not only . . . but also
just as . . . so	whether . . . or

Subordinating Conjunctions Words such as *since, because,* and *although* are <u>**subordinating conjunctions**</u>. They introduce adverb clauses and thus connect the sentence's independent (main) clause to a dependent (subordinate) clause to form a **complex sentence.**

See
24a2

<u>Although</u> people may feel healthy, they can still have medical problems.

It is best to diagram your garden <u>before</u> you start to plant.

A8 Interjections

Interjections **Interjections** are words used as exclamations to express emotion: *Oh! Ouch! Wow! Alas! Hey!* They may be set off by commas or, for greater emphasis, by an exclamation point.

APPENDIX B

SENTENCE REVIEW

B1   Basic Sentence Elements

A **sentence** is an independent grammatical unit that contains a subject and a predicate and expresses a complete thought.

The quick brown fox jumped over the lazy dog.

It came from outer space.

A **simple subject** is a noun or noun substitute (*fox, it*) that tells who or what the sentence is about. A **simple predicate** is a verb or verb phrase (*jumped, came*) that tells or asks something about the subject. The **complete subject** of a sentence includes the simple subject plus all its modifiers (*the quick brown fox*). The **complete predicate** includes the verb or verb phrase and all the words associated with it—such as modifiers, objects, and complements (*jumped over the lazy dog, came from outer space*).

B2   Basic Sentence Patterns

A **simple sentence** consists of at least one subject and one predicate. Simple sentences conform to one of five patterns.

Glossary of Grammatical Terms (Rhodes College)
   http://www.rhodes.edu/kamhi/center/glossary.html
Ask a Grammar Expert (e-mailed responses to grammar questions)
   http://www.grammarnow.com/
University of Illinois' "Grammar Safari"
   http://deil.lang.uiuc.edu/web.pages/grammarsafari/html
Sentences (Purdue)
   http://owl.english.purdue.edu/files/Sentences.html

Subject + Intransitive verb (s + v)

$$\underline{\text{The price of gold}}^{\text{s}}\ \underline{\text{rose}}^{\text{v}}.$$

$$\underline{\text{Stock prices}}^{\text{s}}\ \underline{\text{may fall}}^{\text{v}}.$$

Here, the verbs *rose* and *may fall* are **intransitive**—that is, they do not need an object to complete their meaning.

Subject + Transitive Verb + Direct Object (s + v + do)

$$\underline{\text{Van Gogh}}^{\text{s}}\ \underline{\text{created}}^{\text{v}}\ \overset{\text{do}}{\textit{The Starry Night}}.$$

$$\underline{\text{Caroline}}^{\text{s}}\ \underline{\text{saved}}^{\text{v}}\ \overset{\text{do}}{\text{Jake}}.$$

Here, the verbs *created* and *saved* are **transitive**—they require an object to complete their meaning. In each case, a **direct object** indicates where the verb's action is directed and who or what is affected by it.

Subject + Transitive Verb + Direct Object + Object Complement
(s + v + do + oc)

This pattern includes an object complement that describes or renames the direct object.

$$\underline{\text{I}}^{\text{s}}\ \underline{\text{found}}^{\text{v}}\ \overset{\text{do}}{\text{the exam}}\ \overset{\text{oc}}{\textit{easy}}.\ (\text{Object complement }\textit{easy}\text{ describes direct object }\textit{exam}.)$$

$$\underline{\text{The class}}^{\text{s}}\ \underline{\text{elected}}^{\text{v}}\ \overset{\text{do}}{\text{Bridget}}\ \overset{\text{oc}}{\text{treasurer}}.\ (\text{Object complement }\textit{treasurer}\text{ renames direct object }\textit{Bridget}.)$$

Elementary Rules of Composition from Strunk's *Elements of Style*
  http://www.bartleby.com/141/strunk.html#III
Sentence Craft (L. Behrens, UCSB)
  http://www.writing.ucsb.edu/faculty/behrens/cid/index
Sentence Craft Exercises (at bottom)
  http://www.writing.ucsb.edu/faculty/behrens/tc.htm

Subject + Linking Verb + Subject Complement (s + v + sc)

$\quad\quad$ s $\quad\quad$ v $\quad$ sc
The injection was painless.

$\quad\quad$ s $\quad\quad$ v $\quad\quad$ sc
Tony Blair became prime minister.

**See
A3**

Here, a **linking verb** (*was, became*) connects a subject to a **subject complement** (*painless, prime minister*), a word or phrase that describes or renames the subject. In the first sentence, the complement is a **predicate
adjective** that describes the subject; in the second, the complement is a
predicate nominative that renames the subject. The linking verb is like
an equal sign, equating the subject with its complement (*Tony Blair =
prime minister.*)

*Subject + Transitive Verb + Indirect Object + Direct Object
(s + v + io + do)*

$\quad$ The **indirect object** tells to whom or for whom the verb's action
was done.

$\quad\quad$ s $\quad\quad$ v $\quad\quad$ io $\quad\quad$ do
Cyrano wrote Roxanne a poem. (Cyrano wrote a poem for Roxanne.)

$\quad\quad$ s $\quad\quad$ v $\quad$ io $\quad$ do
Hester gave Pearl a kiss. (Hester gave a kiss to Pearl.)

B3 Phrases and Clauses

(1) Phrases

$\quad$ A **phrase** is a group of related words that lacks a subject or predicate
or both and functions as a single part of speech. It cannot stand alone as
a sentence.

$\quad$ A **verb phrase** consists of a **main verb** and all its auxiliary verbs.
(Time *is flying.*) A **noun phrase** includes a noun or pronoun plus all related modifiers. (I'll climb *the highest mountain.*)

Sentence Combining Basics (Bowling Green)
$\quad$ http://www.bgsu.edu/departments/writing-lab/sentence_combining_b.html

A **prepositional phrase** consists of a <u>**preposition**</u>, its object, and any modifiers of that object.

They discussed the ethical implications <u>of the animal studies.</u>

He was last seen heading <u>into the sunset.</u>

A **verbal phrase** consists of a <u>**verbal**</u> and its related objects, modifiers, or complements. A verbal phrase may be a **participial phrase,** a **gerund phrase,** or an **infinitive phrase.**

<u>Encouraged by the voter turnout,</u> the candidate predicted a victory. (participial phrase)

<u>Taking it easy</u> always makes sense. (gerund phrase)

The jury recessed <u>to evaluate the evidence.</u> (infinitive phrase)

An **absolute phrase** usually consists of a noun and a participle, accompanied by modifiers. It modifies an entire independent clause rather than a particular word or phrase.

<u>Their toes tapping,</u> they watched the auditions.

(2) Clauses

A **clause** is a group of related words that includes a subject and a predicate. An **independent** (main) **clause** may stand alone as a sentence, but a **dependent** (subordinate) **clause** cannot. It must always be combined with an independent clause to form a <u>**complex sentence**</u>.

[Lucretia Mott was an abolitionist]. [She was also a pioneer for women's rights.] (two independent clauses)

[Lucretia Mott was an abolitionist] [who was also a pioneer for women's rights]. (independent clause, dependent clause)

[Although Lucretia Mott was known for her support of women's rights], [she was also a prominent abolitionist]. (dependent clause, independent clause)

Phrases:
   http://webster.commnet.edu/hp/pages/darling/grammar/phrases.htm
Clauses:
   http://webster.commnet.edu/hp/pages/darling/grammar/clauses.htm

Dependent clauses may be adjective, adverb, or noun clauses.

Adjective clauses, sometimes called **relative clauses,** modify nouns or pronouns and always follow the nouns or pronouns they modify. They are introduced by relative pronouns—*that, what, which, who,* and so forth—or by the adverbs *where* and *when.*

Celeste's grandparents, <u>who were born in Romania</u>, speak little English. (Adjective clause modifies the noun *grandparents.*)

The Pulitzer Prizes are prestigious awards <u>that are presented for excellence in journalism</u>. (Adjective clause modifies the noun *awards.*)

Sophie's Choice is a novel set in Brooklyn, <u>where the narrator lives in a pink house</u>. (Adjective clause modifies the noun *Brooklyn.*)

Adverb clauses modify verbs, adjectives, adverbs, entire phrases, or independent clauses. They are always introduced by subordinating conjunctions.

Mark will go <u>wherever there's a party</u>. (Adverb clause modifies *will go,* telling *where* Mark will go.)

<u>Because 75 percent of its exports are fish products</u>, Iceland's economy is heavily dependent on the fishing industry. (Adverb clause modifies independent clause, telling *why* the fishing industry is so important.)

Noun clauses function as subjects, objects, or complements. A noun clause may be introduced by a relative pronoun or by *whether, when, where, why,* or *how.*

<u>What you see</u> is <u>what you get</u>. (Noun clauses are subject and subject complement.)

They wondered <u>why it was so quiet.</u> (Noun clause is direct object.)

To <u>whom it may concern:</u> (Noun clause is object of preposition.)

B4   Types of Sentences

(1) Simple, Compound, Complex, and Compound-Complex Sentences

A **simple sentence** is a single independent clause. A simple sentence can consist of just a subject and a predicate.

<u>Jessica</u> <u>fell</u>.

Or, a simple sentence can be quite elaborate, including a variety of different kinds of modifying words and phrases.

Jessica and her younger sister Victoria almost immediately fell hopelessly in love with the very mysterious Henry Goodyear.

A <u>**compound sentence**</u> consists of two or more simple sentences (independent clauses) linked by a comma and a coordinating conjunction, by a semicolon (alone or with a transitional word or phrase), or by a colon.

                Independent clause   Independent clause
[The moon rose in the sky], <u>and</u> [the stars shone brightly].

                        Independent clause
[José wanted to spend a quiet afternoon fishing and reading]; <u>however,</u>
                        Independent clause
[his friends surprised him with a new set of plans].

A <u>**complex sentence**</u> consists of an independent clause along with one or more dependent clauses.

        Independent clause   Dependent clause
[It was hard for us to believe] [that anyone could be so cruel].

                        Dependent clause
[Because the program had been so poorly attended in the past],
        Independent clause   Dependent clause
[the committee wondered] [whether it should be funded this year].

A <u>**compound-complex sentence**</u> is a compound sentence—made up of at least two independent clauses—that also includes at least one dependent clause.

Dependent clause Independent

[Because driving a cab can be so dangerous], [my mother always

clause Dependent clause Independent

worried] [when my father had to work late], and [she could rarely

clause

sleep more than a few minutes at a time].

(2) Declarative, Interrogative, Imperative, and Exclamatory Sentences

Sentences can also be classified according to their function.

Declarative sentences, the most common type, make statements: *World War II ended in 1945.*

Interrogative sentences pose questions, usually by inverting standard subject-verb order (often with an interrogative word) or adding a form of *do: Is Maggie at home? Where is Maggie? Does Maggie live here?*

Imperative sentences express commands or requests, using the second-person singular of the verb and generally omitting the pronoun subject *you: Go to your room. Please believe me. Stop that.*

Exclamatory sentences express strong emotion and end with an exclamation point: *The killing must stop now!*

APPENDIX C

ENGLISH FOR SPEAKERS OF OTHER LANGUAGES

✔ CHECKLIST: ENGLISH LANGUAGE BASICS

✔ **Words in English sentences may change their form according to their function.** In some languages, words do not change form, or they change form according to rules different from those of English. For example, in English, verbs change form to communicate whether an action is taking place in the past, present, or future; in Chinese, however, other words may be added to the sentence to indicate when the action took place (yesterday, last month, ten years ago), but the verb itself does not change form to indicate past tense action.

✔ **In English, context is extremely important to understanding function.** Sometimes it is impossible to identify the function of an English word without noting its context. In the following sentences, for instance, the very same words can perform different functions according to their relationships to other words:

Juan and I are taking a <u>walk</u>. (*Walk* is a noun, a direct object of the verb *taking*, with an article, *a*, attached to it.)

If you <u>walk</u> whenever you can instead of driving, you will help conserve the earth's resources. (*Walk* is a verb, the predicate of the subject *you*.)

continued on the following page

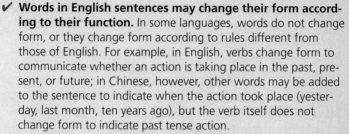

The ESL Study Hall (George Washington U.)
   http://gwis2.circ.gwu.edu/~gwvcusas/
Dave Sperling's ESL (Eng. as a Second Language) Cafe
   http://www.eslcafe.com/
Self-study Quizzes for ESL Students (TESL)
   http://www.aitech.ac.jp/~iteslj/quizzes/
Activities for ESL Students (TESL)
   http://www.aitech.ac.jp/~iteslj/s/

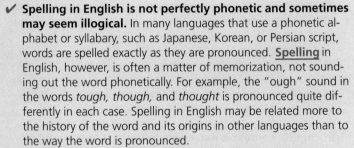

See
Ch. 37

continued from the previous page

Jie was <u>walking</u> across campus when she met her chemistry professor. (*Walking* is part of the verb, predicate of the subject *Jie.*)

<u>Walking</u> a few miles a day will make you healthier. (*Walking* is a noun, the subject of the verb *will make.*)

Next summer we'll take a <u>walking</u> tour of southern Italy. (*Walking* is an adjective describing *tour.*)

✔ **Spelling in English is not perfectly phonetic and sometimes may seem illogical.** In many languages that use a phonetic alphabet or syllabary, such as Japanese, Korean, or Persian script, words are spelled exactly as they are pronounced. <u>Spelling</u> in English, however, is often a matter of memorization, not sounding out the word phonetically. For example, the "ough" sound in the words *tough, though,* and *thought* is pronounced quite differently in each case. Spelling in English may be related more to the history of the word and its origins in other languages than to the way the word is pronounced.

✔ **Word order is extremely important in English sentences.** For example, word order may indicate which word is the subject of the sentence and which is the object, or whether the sentence is a question or a statement.

C1   Nouns

See
A1

A **<u>noun</u>** *names* things: people, objects, places, feelings, ideas.

Nouns can be quite different in different languages. In some languages, nouns have gender; that is, they may be **masculine** or **feminine.** In Spanish, for example, the word for *moon* (*la luna*) is feminine, whereas the word for *sun* (*el sol*) is masculine. In other languages, there is no difference between the singular and plural forms of nouns. In Japanese, for instance, one person is *hito,* and many people are still *hito.* In some languages (including English), nouns may be used as adjectives: "She ate a <u>cheese</u> sandwich."

(1)   Singular, Plural, and Noncount Nouns

In English, nouns may have **number;** that is, they may change in form according to whether they name one thing or more than one thing. If a

noun names one thing, it is a **singular** noun; if a noun names many
things, it is a **plural** noun.

Some English nouns do not have a plural form. These are called **noncount nouns** because what they name cannot be counted. (**Count
nouns** name items that can be counted, such as *woman* or *desk.*)

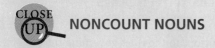

NONCOUNT NOUNS

The following commonly used nouns are noncount nouns.
These words have no plural forms. Therefore, you should never
add *s* to them.

advice	homework
clothing	information
education	knowledge
equipment	luggage
evidence	merchandise
furniture	revenge

(2) Using Articles with Nouns

English has two **articles:** *a* and *the. A* is called the **indefinite** article;
the is the **definite** article. *A* is replaced by *an* if the word that follows begins with a *vowel (a, e, i, o,* or *u*)—or with a *vowel sound: a* book, *an*
apple, *an* honor. If the vowel is pronounced like a consonant, use *a: a
onetime offer.*

Use an **indefinite article** with a noun when readers have no reason to
be familiar with the noun you are naming—when you are introducing
the noun for the first time, for example. To say, "Jatin entered *a* building,"
signals to the audience that you are introducing the idea of the building
into your speech or writing for the first time. The building is indefinite,
or not specific, until it has been identified.

Use the **definite article** when the noun you are naming has already
been introduced. The definite article indicates that the noun introduced
may already be familiar to readers. To say, "Jatin entered *the* building,"

Articles, Determiners, and Qualifiers
   http://webster.commnet.edu/HP/pages/darling/grammar/determiners/
   determiners.htm

signals to readers that you are referring to the same building you mentioned earlier. The building now has become specific and may be referred to by the definite article.

CLOSE UP   USING ARTICLES WITH NOUNS

There are two main exceptions to the rules governing the use of articles with nouns.

- **Plural nouns** do not require **indefinite articles:** "I love horses, not "I love <u>a</u> horses." (Plural nouns do, however, require definite articles: "I love <u>the</u> horses in the national park near my house.")
- **Noncount nouns** may not require articles: "Love conquers all," not "<u>A</u> love conquers all" or "<u>The</u> love conquers all."

---

(3) Using Other Determiners with Nouns

See
A4

Determiners are words that function as <u>adjectives</u> to limit or qualify the meaning of nouns. In addition to articles, nouns may be identified by other determiners that function in ways similar to articles, such as **demonstrative pronouns, possessive nouns and pronouns, numbers** (both **cardinal** and **ordinal**), and other words indicating number and order.

1. **Demonstrative pronouns** (*this, that, these, those*) communicate

   - the relative nearness or farness of the noun from the speaker's position (*this* and *these* for things that are *near, that* and *those* for things that are *far*): *this* book on my desk, *that* book on your desk; *these* shoes on my feet, *those* shoes in my closet.
   - the *number* of things indicated (*this* and *that* for singular nouns, *these* and *those* for *plural* nouns): *this* (or *that*) flower in the vase, *those* flowers in the garden.

2. **Possessive nouns** and **possessive pronouns** (*Ashraf's, his, their*) show who or what the noun belongs to: *Maria's* courage, *everybody's* fears, the *country's* natural resources, *my* personality, *our* groceries.

3. **Cardinal** numbers (*three, fifty, a thousand*) and **ordinal** numbers (*first, tenth, thirtieth*) indicate how many of the noun you mean and in what order the noun appears among other items: *seven* continents, *third* planet.

4. Words other than numbers may indicate **amount** (*many, few*) and **order** (*next, last*) and function in the same ways as cardinal and ordinal numbers: *few* opportunities, *last* chance.

For information on the order of adjectives in a series, see **C42.**

C2   Pronouns

Any English noun may be replaced by a **pronoun**. For example, *doctor* may be replaced by *he* or *she, books* by *them,* and *computer* by *it.* The English language uses more pronouns than most other languages. Whereas in Japanese, for example, it is common to repeat the noun again and again without using a pronoun replacement, such repetition would sound odd to a native speaker of English.

C3   Verbs

Though **verbs** in all languages perform similar functions, they differ in form and usage from language to language perhaps more than any other part of speech or grammatical unit.

Although all languages use verbs to express *states of being,* many languages use two different verbs to describe permanent and impermanent states of being—for example, *ser* and *estar* in Spanish. Other languages use two different verbs to describe animate and inanimate objects—for instance, *aru* and *iru* in Japanese. With its single verb *to be,* English is in this respect simpler than many other languages.

Languages may also differ in the ways they use verbs to communicate *action.* In Arabic, verbs change form to communicate whether the action they describe is complete or not. In Japanese, verbs can be conjugated to communicate the speaker's feelings about the action of the verb—for example, whether the action was overdone. Again, because English communicates such concepts in other ways, the forms of its action verbs are simpler in these contexts than those in other languages.

(1) Person and Number

Person refers to *who* or *what* is performing the action of the verb (for example, *myself, you,* or someone else), and **number** refers to *how many* people or things are performing the action (one or more than one). Unless you use the correct person and number in the verbs in your sentences, you will confuse your English-speaking audience by communicating meanings you do not intend.

(2) Tense

See
21b

See
21a2

Tense refers to *when* the action of the verb takes place. For example, adding *ed* to many English verbs creates a past tense and places the action of the verb in the past. One problem that many nonnative speakers of English have with English verb tenses results from the large number of **irregular verbs** in English: for example, the first-person singular present tense of *to be* is not "I be" but "I am," and the past tense is not "I beed" but "I was."

(3) Auxiliary Verbs

See
A3

Meaning is also communicated in English through the use of **auxiliary verbs** (also known as **helping verbs**), such as forms of the verbs *to be* and *to have* ("Julio *is taking* a vacation," "I *have been* tired lately") and also verbs such as *would, should,* and *can* ("We *should conserve* more of our resources," "You *can succeed* if you try"). Such auxiliary verbs are necessary because English verbs do not change their form, as verbs in other languages do, to express ideas such as the probability, desirability, or necessity of the action described by the verb.

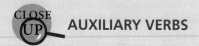

AUXILIARY VERBS

The important thing to remember about auxiliary verbs is that *they,* and not the verbs they "help," change form to indicate person, number, and tense.

> had   go
> We ~~have~~ to ~~went~~ downtown yesterday. (Only the auxiliary verb
>
> *had* should be in the past tense.)

(4) Verb Tense

See
21b

Some non-native speakers of English use tenses that are more complicated than they need to be. Such speakers may do this because their native language uses more complicated tenses where English does not, or because they are nervous about using simple tenses and "overcorrect" their verbs into complicated tenses.

Specifically, non-native speakers tend to use **progressive** (present and past) verb forms instead of **simple** (present and past) verb forms and **perfect** (present and past) verb forms instead of **simple** (present and past) verb forms. To communicate your ideas clearly to an English-speaking audience, choose the simplest possible verb tense.

(5) Double Negatives

The meaning of a verb may be made negative in English in a variety of ways, chiefly by adding the words *not* or *does not* to the verb (is, *is not;* can ski, *can't* ski; drives a car, *does not* drive a car).

Non-native speakers (and some native speakers of English) sometimes use **double negatives.** A double negative occurs when the meaning of a verb is negated not just once but twice in a single sentence. In some languages, a double structure is actually required in order to negate a verb; for example, the French phrase "Je ne sais pas" ("I don't know") uses the double structure *ne + pas* around the verb *sais.* However, a double negative is incorrect in English.

CLOSE UP **CORRECTING DOUBLE NEGATIVES**

Henry doesn't have ~~no~~ friends at all. (*or* Henry ~~doesn't have~~ no
friends at all.)

I looked for articles in the library, but there weren't none. (*or* I
looked for articles in the library, but there weren't ~~none~~.)

---

(6) Using Verbs as Nouns and Adjectives

When English verbs are used as **nouns** or **adjectives,** speakers of other languages may be confused, particularly if in their native language words do not change their function according to their position in a sentence. Two verb forms may be used as nouns: **infinitives** (which always begin with *to*, as in *to work, to sleep, to eat*) and **gerunds** (which always end in *-ing*, as in *working, sleeping, eating*). **Present participles** (which also end in *-ing*) and **past participles** (which usually end in *-ed, -t,* or *-en*, as in *worked, slept,* and *eaten*) are frequently used as adjectives.

> To bite into this steak requires better teeth than mine. (infinitive used as a noun)

> Cooking is one of my favorite hobbies. (gerund used as a noun)

> Some people think raw fish is healthier than cooked fish. (past participle used as an adjective)

> According to the Bible, God spoke to Moses from a burning bush. (present participle used as an adjective)

C4   Adjectives and Adverbs

    Adjectives generally describe the qualities of nouns. A book might be *large* or *small, red* or *blue, difficult* or *easy, expensive* or *cheap*. Unlike adjectives in other languages, English adjectives change their form only to indicate degree (*fast, faster, fastest*). In English, adjectives do not have to agree in number or gender with the nouns they describe, as they must in French and German, for example.

    Adverbs in English are easily identified; nearly all end in *-ly* (*calmly, loudly, rapidly*), except for a small number of "intensifiers" such as *very, rather,* and *quite*. Adverbs generally describe the qualities of verbs. A person may walk slowly or quickly, shyly or confidently, elegantly or clumsily. Adverbs may also modify adjectives (*very blue eyes, truly religious man*) or other adverbs (answer *rather stupidly*, investigate *extremely thoroughly*).

(1) Position of Adjectives and Adverbs

    In Arabic and in Romance languages such as Spanish, French, and Italian, **adjectives** generally *follow* the nouns they describe. In English, however, adjectives usually appear *before* the nouns they describe. A native speaker of English would not say, "*Cars red and black* are involved in more accidents than *cars blue, green, or white*," but would say instead, "*Red and black cars* are involved in more accidents than *blue, green, or white cars*."

Adverbs may appear *before or after* the verbs they describe, but they should be placed as close to the verb as possible: not "I *told* John that I couldn't meet him for lunch *politely*," but "I *politely told* John that I couldn't meet him for lunch" or "I *told* John *politely* that I couldn't meet him for lunch." When an adverb describes an **adjective** or **another adverb,** it usually comes *before* that adjective or adverb: "The essay has *basically sound* logic"; "You must express yourself *absolutely clearly.*"

(2) Order of Adjectives

A single noun may be described by more than one adjective, perhaps even by a whole list of adjectives in a row. Given a list of three or four adjectives, most native speakers would arrange them in a sentence in the same order. If shoes are to be described as *green* and *big,* numbering *two,* and of the type worn for playing *tennis,* a native speaker would say "two big green tennis shoes." Generally, the adjectives most important in completing the meaning of the noun are placed closest to the noun.

 ORDER OF ADJECTIVES

1. articles (*a, the*), demonstratives (*this, those*), and possessives (*his, our, Maria's, everybody's*)
2. amounts (*one, five, many, few*), order (*first, next, last*)
3. personal opinions (*nice, ugly, crowded, pitiful*)
4. sizes and shapes (*small, tall, straight, crooked*)
5. ages (*young, old, modern, ancient*)
6. colors (*black, white, red, blue, dark, light*)
7. nouns functioning as adjectives to form a unit with the noun (*soccer* ball, *cardboard* box, *history* class)

C5   Prepositions

In English, **prepositions** (such as *to, from, at, with, among, between*) give meaning to nouns by linking them with other words and other parts of the sentence. Prepositions convey several different kinds of information:

Prepositions
 http://webster.commnet.edu/HP/PAGES/darling/grammar/
 prepositions.htm

- relations to **time** (*at* nine o'clock, *in* five minutes, *for* a month)
- relations of **place** (*in* the classroom, *at* the library, *beside* the chair) and **direction** (*to* the market, *onto* the stage, *toward* the freeway)
- relations of **association** (go *with* someone, the tip *of* the iceberg)
- relations of **purpose** (working *for* money, dieting *to* lose weight)

In some languages, prepositions may be used in quite different ways, may exist in forms quite different from English, or may not exist at all. Therefore, speakers of those languages may have a lot of difficulty with English prepositions. Speakers of languages with prepositions very similar to those in English—especially Romance languages such as Spanish, French, and Italian—have a different problem. They may be tempted to translate prepositional phrases directly into English, although idiomatic use of prepositions varies widely among languages.

CLOSE UP **PREPOSITIONS IN IDIOMATIC EXPRESSIONS**

Common non-native speaker usage	*Native speaker usage*
according *with*	according *to*
apologize *at*	apologize *to*
appeal *at*	appeal *to*
believe *at*	believe *in*
different *to*	different *from*
for least, *for* most	*at* least, *at* most
refer *at*	refer *to*
relevant *with*	relevant *to*
similar *with*	similar *to*
subscribe *with*	subscribe *to*

C6   Word Order

The importance of word order varies from language to language. In English, word order is extremely important, contributing a good deal to the meaning of a sentence.

(1) Standard Word Order

Like Chinese, English is an "SVO" language, or one in which the most typical sentence pattern is "subject-verb-object." (Arabic, by contrast, is an example of a "VSO" language.) If you deviate from the SVO pattern, you may not communicate your ideas clearly.

(2) Word Order in Questions

Word order in questions can be particularly troublesome for speakers of languages other than English, partly because there are so many different ways to form questions in English.

CLOSE UP   WORD ORDER IN QUESTIONS

1. To create a yes/no question from a statement using the verb *to be*, simply invert the order of the subject and the verb:

   <u>Rasheem is</u> researching the depletion of the ozone layer.

   <u>Is Rasheem</u> researching the depletion of the ozone layer?

2. To create a yes/no question from a statement using a verb other than *to be*, use a form of the auxiliary verb *do* before the sentence without inverting the subject and verb:

   <u>Does</u> Rasheem want to research the depletion of the ozone layer?

   <u>Do</u> Rasheem's friends want to help him with his research?

   <u>Did</u> Rasheem's professors approve his research proposal?

3. A question can also be formed by adding a **tag question** (such as *won't he?* or *didn't I?*) to the end of a statement. If the verb of the main statement is *positive*, then the verb of the tag question is *negative*; if the verb of the main statement is *negative*, then the verb of the tag question is *positive*:

   Rasheem <u>is</u> researching the depletion of the ozone layer, <u>isn't</u> he?

continued on the following page

continued from the previous page

Rasheem <u>doesn't</u> intend to write his dissertation about the depletion of the ozone layer, <u>does</u> he?

4. To create a question asking for information, use **interrogative** words (*who, what, where, when, why, how*), and invert the order of the subject and verb (note that *who* functions as the subject of the question in which it appears):

<u>Who is</u> researching the depletion of the ozone layer?

<u>What is Rasheem</u> researching?

<u>Where is Rasheem</u> researching the depletion of the ozone layer?

Index and FAQs

INDEX & FAQs

CREDITS

Netscape Netcenter website (c) 2000 Netscape Communications Corporation. Screenshot used with permission.

Excerpt from "How the Middle Class Has Helped Ruin the Public Schools" by Joseph Nocera from *The Washington Monthly* September/October 1989 is reprinted with permission of The Washington Monthly Company, 1611 Connecticut Avenue NW, Washington, DC 20009. (202) 462-0128.

Excerpt from *The American Heritage Dictionary,* copyright © 1996 by Houghton Mifflin Company, is reproduced with permission from the *American Heritage Dictionary of the English Language,* Third College Edition.

Excerpt of Netscape home page. Netscape Netcenter website © 2000 Netscape Communications Corporation. Screenshot used with permission.

Yahoo! home page. Copyright © 2000 Yahoo! Inc. All rights reserved. Screenshot used with permission.

INDEX

INDEX

INDEX

INDEX

Parallelism, 42, 337–339
  for emphasis, 328–329
  in headings, 238
  in list design, 239
  repeating signals of, 339
  revising faulty, 338–339
  in sentence structure, 230
  use of, 337–338
  using parallel elements, 339
Paraphrase, 86, 90–91
  with identifying tag, 136
  integrating into writing, 137–138
  syntax, phrasing, and, 141
Parentheses
  within parentheses, 402
  using, 401
Parenthetical documentation, in
  writing about literature, 235
Parenthetical references, 147
  APA style, 185–188
  CBE style, 215–216
  MLA style, 147–151
Part-of-speech labels, in dictionary,
  352
Participial phrase, 445
Participle(s), 293, 301, 438, 456
  past, 293, 438, 456
  present, 293, 438, 456
Parts of speech. *See also* specific
  parts of speech
  adjectives, 309–310
  pronoun, 304–308
  verb, 293–301
Passed, past, 361
Passive voice, 303
  dangling modifiers and, 289
  eliminating, 335
  for emphasis, 329–330
Past participle, 293, 301, 438, 456
  as principal part of verb, 293
Past perfect, 299
Past perfect progressive tense, 300
Past progressive tense, 299–300
Past subjunctive, 302
Past tense, 298
Past tense form, of verb, 293
Pattern of development, 16
People, abbreviating names of, 427
Percent, percentage, 361

Percentages, numerals in, 431
Perfect infinitive, 301
Perfect tenses, 297, 299, 455
Period(s)
  with acronyms, 370
  with clipped forms, 370
  in dramatic, poetic, and biblical
    references, 370
  in electronic addresses, 371
  quotation marks with, 396
  run-on sentence, 271
  use of, 369–371
Periodic sentence, 327–328
Periodical, 106
Periodical indexes, 106–107
  online, 102–103
Perrine, Lawrence, 421
Person, 282, 453
  agreement, 274
  unwarranted shifts in, 282
Person (people), capitalizing names
  of, 415
Personal communication, APA style
  for, 187
Personal pronouns, 436
  apostrophes with, 388
Personification, 348
Persuade, writing to, 4–5
Petrunkevitch, Alexander, 4
Phenomenon, phenomena, 361
Photographs, 242
Phrase(s), 444–445. *See also*
  Transitional expressions
  absolute, 379, 445
  contradictory, 379
  gerund phrase, 445
  infinitive phrase, 445
  intervening between subject and
    verb, 275
  key, 43
  misplaced, 287
  misused semicolon with, 385
  noun, 336
  participial, 445
  prepositional, 267, 335, 375–376,
    377, 445
  restrictive and nonrestrictive
    modifiers, 376–377
  sentence fragment and, 267

INDEX

INDEX

managing for research paper, 86
paraphrasing of, 90–91
quoting, 90
summary of, 88–89, 90
synthesizing, 138
in writing about literature,
235–236
Spacing, of paper, 237
Spatial order, 39
Speak, principal parts, 296
Special library collections, 109. *See
also* Libraries
Specialized indexes, 107
Specialized reference works. *See*
References
Specialized search engines, 124–125
Specific words, 346
Speed, principal parts, 296
Spell checkers, 30, 409–410
Spelling, 407–413
-*able,* -*ible,* 411
American and British, 408
doubling final consonants,
410–411
in English compared with other
languages, 450
foreign plurals, 412
homophones, 408–409
ie/ei combinations, 410
one word or two, 409
plurals, 411–412
pronunciation and, 407–410
rules of, 410–412
seed endings, 411
silent *e* before suffix, 411
silent letters, 408
of unfamiliar words, 413
vowels in unstressed positions,
407
words pronounced carelessly, 408
y before suffix, 411
"Spider and the Wasp, The"
(Petrunkevitch), 4
Spin, principal parts, 296
Spock, Benjamin, 48
Spring, principal parts, 296
Squinting modifier, 287
-*ss,* plurals of words ending in, 412
Staging, in drama, 234

Stand, principal parts, 296
Stationary, stationery, 363
Statistics
crediting, 141–142
numerals in, 431
Steal, principal parts, 296
Steiner, Elaine B., 385
Straw man, 67
Streets, abbreviating names of,
426–427
Strike, principal parts, 296
Style, in literature, 233
Style manuals. *See also* References;
Works Cited lists; specific styles
guide to, 222
Subheadings, 238
Subject
complete, 442
creating new, 289
joined by *and,* 275
joined by *or,* 275–276
sentence fragment and, 266
separating from verb, 324
simple, 442
singular with plural form, 277
Subject-by-subject comparison,
48–49
Subject complement, 309, 437,
444
Subject guides, 121, 122
Subject search, 97, 98
Subject-verb agreement. *See*
Agreement, subject-verb
Subjective case, 304–305
Subjective mood, 302
Subjunctive mood, 302–303
Subordinate clause. *See* Dependent
(subordinate) clauses
Subordinating conjunctions, 318,
441
revising with, 272–273
sentence fragment and, 265, 269
Subordination, 320
Sudo, Phil, 89
Sufficient evidence, 58
Suffixes
hyphens with, 424
silent *e* before, 411
y before, 411

INDEX

FREQUENTLY ASKED QUESTIONS

FAQ

FAQ

WEB SITE RESOURCES

WRITING
Elements of Style: http://www.bartleby.com/141/index.html
Sentence Craft: http://writing.ucsb.edu/faculty/behrens/index
Online Writing Lab: http://owl.english.purdue.edu
Getting Started: http://webware.princeton.edu/Writing/wc4a.htm
Critical Thinking: http://www.umsl.edu/~klein/Critical_Thinking.html
The Reading Comprehension Page: http://muskingum.edu/~cal/database/
    reading/html#Strategies
Logic in Argumentation: http://owl.english.purdue.edu/Files/123.html
Writing Argumentative Papers: http://www2.rscc.cc.tn.us/~jordan_jj/OWL/
    Argumentation.html
English Verb Tenses: http://deil.lang.uiuc.edu/class.pages/structure1/tenses.htm
Paragraphs: http://www.fas.harvard.edu/~wricntr/para.html
Plagiarism: http://www.indiana.edu/~wts/wts/plagiarism.html
Tips on Essay Exams (UNC): http://www.unc.edu/depts/wcweb/handouts/
    essay-exams.html

RESEARCH
Research paper.com: http://www.researchpaper.com/
MLA Homepage: http://www.mla.org/
APA: http://www.beadsland.com/weapas
Web Resources by Paper Topic: http://www.sau.edu/bestinfo/
    Hot/hotindex.htm
Guide to Internet Research and Resources: http://www.miracosta.cc.ca.us/
    home/gfloren/INTNET.HTM

GRAMMAR/PUNCTUATION
Grammarland: http://www.guilford.edu/ASC/grammarland
Dictionary.com's List of Online Dictionaries: http://www.dictionary.com/

OTHER RESOURCES
Roget's Thesaurus: http://www.thesarus.com
Guide to Literary Resources on the Net: http://andromeda.rutgers.edu/
    ~jlynch/Lit/
Business Letters: Accentuating the Positives: http://owl.english.purdue.edu/
    Files/92.html